D1171812

MESSIAH IN CONTEXT

THE FOUNDATIONS OF JUDAISM:
Method, Teleology, Doctrine
PART TWO: *Teleology*

MESSIAH

IN CONTEXT

Israel's History and Destiny
in Formative Judaism

JACOB NEUSNER

FORTRESS PRESS   PHILADELPHIA

BM601
N48
1983
pt. 2

COPYRIGHT © 1984 BY FORTRESS PRESS

All rights reserved. No part of this publication may be reproduced, stored in a retrieval system, or transmitted in any form or by any means, electronic, mechanical, photocopying, recording, or otherwise, without the prior permission of the copyright owner.

Library of Congress Cataloging in Publication Data

Neusner, Jacob, 1932–
   Messiah in context.

   (The Foundations of Judaism : method, teleology, doctrine ; pt. 2, teleology)
   Includes index.
   1. Messiah — History of doctrines.   2. Rabbinical literature — History and criticism.   I. Title
II. Series: Neusner, Jacob, 1932–   . Foundations of Judaism ; pt. 2.
BM601.N48   1983 pt. 2   296s [296.3'3]   83-20542
[BM615]
ISBN 0-8006-0716-3

K477I83   Printed in the United States of America   1–716

For
Peter Brown

An inspiration to us all

MAR 27 1985

Contents

Preface

This book asks whether Judaism as we know it constitutes a messianic religion, a religious tradition in which hope for a Messiah at the end of time frames the faith's worldview and way of life. The question is critical because the heritage upon which Judaism in its rabbinic or talmudic form draws has nourished profoundly messianic offshoots (both Christianity and the Essene community at Qumran, for example). The kind of Judaism at hand, becoming normative later on, yielded one messianic movement after another. Given the character of the prophetic and apocalyptic literature of the Old Testament, we may hardly be surprised. So we wonder whether the formative canon of the kind of Judaism under study here both falls into the category of a messianic religion and also contains a systematic and well-formed doctrine worthy of an -ism, that is, a messianism. Does Judaism present a messianism, and may we therefore speak of the messianic idea or doctrine of Judaism?

The answer, spelled out in what follows, is a qualified negative, yielding a flat no. Judaism as we know it contains numerous allusions to a Messiah and references to what he will do. But so far as we examine the original canon of the ancient rabbis, framed over the second through seventh centuries, we find these inherited facts either reformed and reshaped for use in an essentially nonmessianic and ahistorical system, or left like rubble after a building has been completed: stones that might have been used, but were not. So Judaism as we know it presents no well-crafted doctrine of the Messiah, and thus its eschatology is framed within the methods of an essentially ahistorical teleology. Let me now spell out this thesis.

The Mishnah, which was the first document in the canon of formative Judaism, ca. A.D. 200, presented a system of Judaism aimed at the sanctification of Israel and bore a teleology lacking an eschatological dimension. From 400 to 600 the several successive documents of exegesis—the Talmud of the Land of Israel, the exegeses of scriptural books, and the Talmud of Babylonia—supplied the larger system of formative Judaism and rested upon the constitution of the Mishnah, with the well-established, eschatologically oriented teleology of the Messiah and his salvation that the Mishnah's framers had rejected. The Judaism that emerged was, and now remains, profoundly devoted to questions of history and its meaning and promised salvation through holy deeds of eschatological and salvific value. So the Mishnah, a system aimed at sanctification and built upon the main beams of nature and supernature, drew nearer to the orbit of the everyday life of Israel. (Instead of being the basis for Judaism's sanctification, the document became the foundation of its historical salvation.) The Talmuds and (in lesser measure) the collections of scriptural exegeses presented a system of Judaism focused upon salvation and which promised to carry Israel to the age that was to bring the Messiah and the end of history. Yet, as we shall see, the Messiah in the talmudic sector of the formative canon emerged as a figure meant to encourage and foster a view of life above time and beyond history, a life lived in full acceptance of God's rule in eternity, a life which rejected man's rule in history. The Mishnah had originally made that life the foundation of its system. Accordingly, when the canon of Judaism reached the end of its formative period, it presented a version of the Messiah myth entirely congruent with the character of the foundation document, the Mishnah. The Judaism emerging from late antiquity would then deliver to Israel an enduring message of timeless sanctification, in the guise of historical, and hence eschatological, salvation.

Here we trace two reciprocal processes: first, the "remessianization" of the canon of formative Judaism, and second, a re-formation of the Messiah myth to fit into the larger system expressed in that canon. In the end we shall be helped to grasp what is happening if we compare the Messiah in the canon of formative Judaism with the Messiah-myth development in the Christian understanding of Jesus as the Christ. Early on, Christ the Messiah marked the end of history, the expectation of the imminent resurrection of the dead. Later on, the eschatological Messiah would become Jesus the rabbi, teacher, preacher, wonder-worker, God-man, perfect priest, and oblation. In other words the continuing life of the church turned Christ, the Messiah-Savior at the eschaton, into whatever Christians needed the Christ to be through the eternity of time. So the Messiah myth, originally defined in terms of antecedent Israelite conventions, entered the grid of Christian being, to be reframed and reformed within that experience of the enduring "life in Christ." So too, in the formation of Judaism, was the eschatological Messiah (so critical to Paul's Christ) initially rejected as a category useful to the Mishnah's place in the canon. The Messiah myth would then regain pride of place within the Talmud's sector of the canon, but only in terms natural to the system inaugurated and defined by the Mishnah. Established conventions, whatever they were, would give way. The Messiah would serve Israel precisely as Israel's rabbis directed and would serve the Christian church just as the Christians wished.

In framing the issues in this way, I have used conventional understandings and categories. That is to say, I have worded matters as if there were such a thing as "the Messiah myth" which was connected with the resurrection of the dead, the rebuilding of the Temple, the last judgment, and various other familiar matters. These details derive from a well-known composite of information, "the Messiah idea" in "Judaism." But just as there was no single "Judaism," so, I shall argue, shall we look in vain for "the Messiah myth." First, "myth" promises a story, but there is no story. Second, as I shall show in this book, "the Messiah" is an all but blank screen onto which a given community would project its concerns. The words "Messiah myth" bear little meaning other than the established and conventional one, which is wrong. I frame my argument not against but for, not to tear down what I believe to be unrefined and dull conceptions but to construct nuanced ones. In seeking to differentiate what has heretofore been treated as whole and coherent, I aim to do for the history of rabbinic ideas what I have already done for the history of rabbinic literature of late antiquity.

In these few paragraphs I have expressed the entire thesis of this book. Now let me unpack the material more systematically.

First, let me define the basic terms. By "formative Judaism" I mean the formative stage in the history of the Judaism known for close to twenty centuries. Labeled "rabbinic," after the title of its principal authority (the rabbi), or "talmudic" on account of one of its authoritative books (the Babylonian Talmud), or "classical"—or "normative"—because of its authoritative status in later times, the kind of Judaism studied here succeeded all others of antiquity and defined all to come. Its myth and rite governed the religion of Judaism from late antiquity to modern times. All modernized forms of Judaism refer (in diverse ways, to be sure) to the sort of Judaism that took shape in late antiquity and reigned paramount and definitive from then until the twentieth century. Today, moreover, the larger portion of the Jewish people who regard themselves as religious, and not merely ethnically Jewish, consider this type of Judaism to be authentic.

Accordingly, I propose to describe a principal belief of Judaism (the coming of the Messiah at the end of Israel's history to save and redeem Israel) and to ask about its place in the larger system of Judaism. Since the myth of the Messiah takes up, in secular terms, the doctrine of history and, consequently, the destiny of the nation, the larger issue at hand is clear. Through what is said about the Messiah we actually investigate the doctrine of Israel's history and destiny.

So, as is now clear, Judaism as we know it, which took shape in the first six centuries of the Common Era, was defined through its central symbol in the Torah, by its holy man the rabbi, and through the sanctification and salvation of the people Israel. Its principal literary evidence comes to us through the Mishnah, the two Talmuds, the earliest collections of biblical exegeses (generally called *midrashim*), and the oldest parts of the Jewish prayer books (the *Siddur*, for ordinary days, and the *Mahzor*, for the New Year and Day of Atonement). There are two other important literary sources of this period, the religious poetry called *piyyutim* (first in evidence in the fifth and sixth centuries) and the *Targumim* (translations of the Hebrew Scriptures from Hebrew into Aramaic, of undetermined date). In neither instance can we demonstrate that we are dealing with distinctively rabbinic compositions, so we are not certain just how these writings testify to the history of Judaism in its formative age. We shall briefly reckon with that imponderable in the appendix.

Taken together and at the end of its formation, the literary record of the formative centuries presents us with a profoundly messianic kind of Judaism, structurally not much different from the former kinds of Judaism which bore a teleology conceived through a messianic figure and doctrine. Yet upon closer examination, the documents, examined one by one in the sequence of their completion, do not present a uniform picture. On the contrary, the figure of the Messiah makes its appearance in a rather particular literary context, hence under quite distinctive circumstances. The problem of this book is to discover the context in which the canonical documents of Judaism as we know it became "messianized." That is to say, when did the canon of rabbinic Judaism receive and set at its head and heart the person of the Messiah and the hope of redemption, as framed through a messianic myth? What were its consequences for the unfolding system of Judaism? These are the questions I shall answer here.

As I suggested at the outset, when we speak of the Messiah we address the deeper issues which confront any system of Judaism, not only the rabbinic. The figure of the Messiah bears within itself the shared view of a society that bonds family to family, village to village, and the whole into "Israel." In the nature of things, one critical aspect of Israel's self-conception—as that self-conception reaches expression in the rabbinic, or any, canon—comes to the surface in its messianic idea. Israel's understanding of what happens as history and what happens as destiny reaches full expression in the mythic construction assembled around the person of the Messiah. When Jews in ancient times reflected on the meaning of their lives as a group, these reflections commonly (though not always) took the form of stories about the Messiah. He was depicted as whatever people most wanted—king, savior, wonder-worker, perfect priest, invincible general, or teacher—but also as the figure of the end and conclusion of history. Accordingly, when we consider the issue at hand, we deal with what the rabbis, who were represented by the books under study, wished to say about the social group, Israel. The tales reflect their understanding of the things that happened to them seen as history, cast as destiny.

Before proceeding, we have to take account of yet another fundamental datum in this book, that diverse documents took shape and emerged from distinct settings and contexts. Any account of rabbinic sources speaks of only one life situation, the school. We base all of our understanding upon the simple fact that the rabbinic canon comes to us from late antiquity's circles of masters and disciples. We know the opinions of that group, as well as their worldview and way of life, since they approved and handed on the books as authoritative. Other documents come out of antiquity, those that clearly frame the worldview of Jews in synagogues and at worship but not in study. The canonical prayerbook is one such document; the liturgical poetry beginning in the period under study constitutes another; the translations of Scripture into Aramaic, the vernacular, a third. True, rabbis who were represented in the canonical literature of the Mishnah, Tosefta, the two Talmuds, and several compilations of biblical exegeses (midrashim), may well have approved these synagogue writings. But they still have to be treated as a distinct corpus of evidence. That body of writings is to be described on its own and compared and contrasted with that other distinct corpus composed of the authoritative writings of the rabbinical session and bureaucracy: the school, the court, the master-disciple circle, the estate of clerks with tasks and concerns quite distinctive to itself. Contextual distinctions are important because in this book I treat mainly the school and its perspective, not the synagogues and theirs.

In sum, I propose to examine the Messiah evidence in the documents produced in the formation of the Judaism which are now called talmudic, rabbinic, and classical. In so doing, I am seeking the underpinnings of formative Judaism which will point out the rabbis' consciousness of Israel as a society and nation and their consciousness of the meaning and end of its history as a sanctified people. Accordingly, my purpose is to trace the unfolding of the messianic myth in the canon of formative Judaism—and there alone.

The reader will have noticed that instead of repeated reference to the history of formative Judaism as a whole I have referred only to the history of one idea in the canonical writings of that Judaism. It therefore is clear that my claim is framed in exceedingly conservative terms. I here trace the history of an idea as it is attested in a sequence of documents—that alone, nothing more. I do not claim that the documents represent the state of popular or synagogue opinion. I do not know whether the history of the idea in the unfolding official texts corresponds to the history of the idea among the people who stand behind those documents. Even less do I claim to speak about the history of the Messiah myth outside of rabbinical circles, among the Jewish nation at large. All of those larger dimensions of the matter lie wholly beyond the perspective of this book. The reason is that the evidence at hand is of a particular sort and hence permits us to investigate one category of questions and not another. That category is defined by established and universally held conventions about the order in which the canonical writings reached completion.

Therefore we trace the way in which the Messiah myth and associated matters emerge in the sequence of writings followed here. First came the Mishnah, then the exegesis of the Mishnah written down in the Talmud of the Land of Israel, then, more or less in the same period, the exegesis of Scripture. This last was generated by the exegesis of the Mishnah, shaped in the model of that exegesis, and written down in the earliest collections of scriptural exegeses called midrashim, alongside exegesis of the Mishnah as written down in the Talmud of Babylonia. At the end, very briefly, we take note of the same matters as they occur in documents from another life situation, not of the rabbis and their circles of masters and disciples, but of the synagogue. I refer in particular to the liturgy and Aramaic versions of Scripture.

Accordingly, the canon of rabbinical writings in late antiquity consists of documents that reached completion in the order of the chapters of this book, first the Mishnah, then the Talmud of the Land of Israel, and finally the earliest compilations of scriptural exegeses, a few somewhat prior to and a few in tandem with the Talmud of Babylonia. We trace the way in which the idea of the Messiah was taken up and spelled out in these successive stages in the formation of the canon. Let the purpose of the exercise be emphasized: *When we follow this procedure, we discover how, within the formation of the rabbinical canon of writings, the idea of the Messiah, with its associated conceptions of history and destiny, came to literary expression and how it was then shaped to serve the larger purposes of the nascent canonical system as a whole.*

By knowing the place and uses of the Messiah within the literary evidences of the rabbinical system, we gain a better understanding of the formative history of that system. What we do not learn is much different: neither the condition of the people at large nor the full power of the rabbinical thinkers' imagination comes to the fore. About these other, larger historical and intellectual matters we have no direct knowledge at all. Consequently I claim to report only what we learn about the canonical literature of a system evidenced by a limited factual base—if not also about how the system works. No one who wants to know the history of the messianic idea in all of Judaism in late antiquity, or the role of that idea in the history of all the Jews in all parts of the world in the first seven centuries of the Common Era, will find it here.

In order to understand the method of this book, we must recognize the character of the evidence presented. The sources constitute a collective, and therefore official, literature, and I claim to expound the collective and official account of a principal idea contained in that literature. All of the documents took shape and attained a place in the canon of the rabbinical movement as a whole. None was written by an individual in such a way as to testify to personal choice or decision. Accordingly, we cannot provide an account of the theory of a given individual at a particular time. We have numerous references to what a given individual said about the topic at hand. But these references do not reach us in the authorship of that person, or even in his or her language. They come to us only in the setting of a *collection* of sayings and statements, some associated with names, others unattributed and anonymous. The collections by definition were composed under the auspices of rabbinical authority—a school or a circle. They tell us what a group of people wished to preserve and hand on as authoritative doctrine about the meaning of the Mishnah and Scripture. The compositions reach us because the larger rabbinical estate chose to copy and hand them on. Accordingly, we know the state of doctrine at the stages marked by the formation and closure of the several documents.

The alternative method is to assume that, if a given document ascribes an opinion to a named authority, the opinion actually was stated in that language by that sage. On this assumption, the history of an idea, and not merely of the literary evidences of that idea, may be worked out. Whatever is assigned to an authority assumed to have lived earlier, without regard to the date of the document at hand, is earlier than what is assigned to someone believed to have lived later. Within this theory of evidence, we have the history of what individuals thought on a common topic. It is obvious why I cannot proceed to outline the sequence of ideas solely on the basis of the sequence of sages to whom ideas are attributed. I simply cannot demonstrate that a given authority really said what a document assigns to him. On the other hand, as I said above, I follow the established pattern in assuming, as is generally held, that the Mishnah comes first, before the Tosefta, and that the Talmud of the Land of

Israel follows; the earliest compilations of scriptural exegeses come somewhat after the closure of the Talmud of the Land of Israel, and the Babylonian Talmud still later. The two imponderables, as I said, are the Siddur (the prayer book of Judaism) and the Targumim (the synagogue corpus). We do not have, however, a firm date for the text of the present Siddur or for any of the Targumim.

My purpose in this book is not to prove a point but to examine a number of possibilities. Let me list the range of uncertainty that necessitates this approach.

First, if the order of the documents were fully sound and the contents representative of rabbinical opinion, then the result would be a history of the advent of the messianic idea and the development and articulation of that idea in formative Judaism. We should then have a fairly reliable picture of the idea of history and the explanation of Israel's destiny, as these unfolded in orderly sequence. But we do not know that the canonical history corresponds to the actual history of ideas. Furthermore, we cannot even be sure that the order of documents presently assumed in scholarly convention is correct.

Second, if a rabbi really spoke the words attributed to him, then a given idea would have reached expression within Judaism prior to the redaction of the document. Dividing things up by documents will tend to give a later date, thus a different context for interpretation, to opinions held earlier than we can presently demonstrate.

Third, as I emphasize, we have no firm dates for the prayerbooks or the Targumim. Nor do we know, except for Onqelos's Targum, whether the translations were originally produced by rabbis, that is, by the same sort of people who stood behind the Mishnah and its documents of exegesis and expansion (the Talmuds) as well as by the compilations of scriptural exegeses (midrash collections). If, as I suspect, the other Targumim neither emerged from the rabbinic movement nor expressed viewpoints distinctive to it, we also do not know when, whether, or how they found a legitimate place within Judaism as rabbis shaped it.

Fourth, as I have said although we are focusing upon the literature produced by a particular group, we have no clear notion of what people were thinking outside that group. We therefore do not know how opinions held by other groups or by the Jewish people in general came to shape the vision of rabbis. When, for example, we note that there also existed poetic literature characteristic of the synagogue worship at the end of the period at hand, we cannot determine whether the poetry spoke for rabbis or for some quite different group.

For these reasons I have chosen to address the contextual question of the Messiah within the very narrow limits of the canon. Obviously, if I could, in a given formulation, relate the appearance of the Messiah myth to events affecting rabbis in particular or to the life of Israel in general, the results would be exceedingly suggestive. But since we do not know for whom the documents speak, how broadly representative they are, or even how comprehensive is their evidence about rabbis' views, we must carefully define what we do and do not know. Accordingly, we cannot at this time speak about what people in general were thinking, let alone the circumstances in which they were thinking. So, for this early stage in research, the context in which the Messiah myth is described, analyzed, and interpreted is the canon. This first step alone carries us to new territory. I hope that, in due course, others will move beyond the limits that, at the moment, seem to me to mark the earliest possible advance.

It remains to stress that, when I speak of the "Messiah myth," I mean the story Jews told about the Messiah, his role, person, tasks, and powers. By myth I do not mean "untruth." I do not suggest that the ancient hope of Israel, the hope for the coming Messiah, bears false witness. Recognizing two disparate uses of the word "myth," I make it clear that I use the word consistently in one way only— "myth" as equivalent to, but more appropriate than, the word "idea." Much that is said about the Messiah falls into other categories than abstract ideas or narrow philosophical allegations. Rather, discourse about the Messiah is concrete, often narrative. Hence, in the context of the religious and supernatural life, we deal with a "myth" in exactly the sense in which the entire biblical history imposes transcendental, supernatural, and mythic dimensions and meanings upon ancient Israel.

Citations of biblical books employ the standard abbreviations. Biblical verses are marked in the conventional way.

Mishnah passages are signified by chapter and paragraph, thus: M. [Mishnah] [tractate name] 9:9 [chapter 9, paragraph 9].

Passages in the Talmud of the Land of Israel are marked in two further ways, with a Roman numeral, indicating the unit of discourse in which a passage appears, and with a letter, indicating the clause of that unit; hence 1:1 XII Q stands for the chapter of a Mishnah tractate, the paragraph of the chapter, the unit of discourse of the larger construction serving that paragraph, and the clause of that unit. The chapter and paragraph references are standard; the unit of discourse and clause indications derive from my *Talmud of the Land of Israel: A Preliminary Translation and Explanation* (Chicago: The University of Chicago Press, 1982) i–xxxv.

The references to compilations of biblical exegeses (midrashim) follow the systems of the respective translations, indicated ad loc.

Passages in the Babylonian Talmud follow the standard reference to tractate, folio number, with "a" for the obverse, "b" for the reverse side of the folio, hence B. Sot. 9a: Babylonian Talmud, tractate Sotah, folio 9, the obverse side of the folio. I hope to provide a still more specific reference system for the English language in my forthcoming translation of the Talmud of Babylonia.

I have used italics in two ways. First, all verses of Scripture are cited in italics. This allows the way in which verses serve as proof-texts to be immediately visible. Second, in chapter two, I have also presented in italics citations of a Mishnah pericope, in the context of abstracts from the Palestinian Talmud. The purpose is the same, namely, to allow the reference to a proof text, outside of the frame of discourse, to stand out from the discourse itself. When in chapter one the Tosefta cites the Mishnah, that too is in italics. I do not think the resort to italics for two distinct purposes will cause much confusion. Finally, when the Talmud of the Land of Israel cites a passage also found in the Tosefta, I present that passage in boldface type. Here too the purpose is to distinguish the several sources by a unit of discourse from the discussion of those sources, or the use made of them, by the unit's own framers.

As to bibliography, translations of the Mishnah, Tosefta, and Talmud of the Land of Israel are all my own, unless otherwise indicated. Translations used in chapter three of various Midrash compositions are by those signified; where, as for Sifra and Sifré, no translator is noted, it is my own work.

All translations of the Babylonian Talmud derive from the complete English translation published by Soncino Press. The names of the individual translators and the pages on which the passages occur are specified in context.

The bibliography (see p. 249) includes only those items referred to in an abbreviation. Other books consulted are cited in context; these are few. In chapter four and in the appendix, I have provided brief ad hoc bibliographies serving topics of those units in particular.

Other abbreviations, used only in a single section, are signified just prior to their first use.

A bibliography on messianism in general would fill a book larger than this one, and a bibliography on messianism in Judaism (and Christianity) would do the same. Yet while studies on the Messiah in various specific settings, e.g., communities or documents, take up the topic, I cannot point to a single article or book that asks the question at hand: what do various documents in the rabbinic canon, viewed one by one as autonomous statements, have to say about the Messiah? What facts do they repeat, and how do the authors of various compilations use those facts to make the larger points the documents' framers wish to make? One example of the sort of article that is, happily, quite commonplace and exemplary is "The Concept of the Messiah in IV Ezra," Michael Stone, *Religions in Antiquity: Essays in Memory of Erwin R. Goodenough* (Leiden, 1968), pp. 295–312. There Stone treats a single document, a single problem. By contrast, whenever the rabbinic canon comes into view, it forms an undifferentiated whole, a statement of "Judaism," hence, "the messianic idea in Judaism."

Now, as I point out in the concluding chapter, once we have differentiated among the documents and systematically asked each one to speak for itself on our topic, we can no longer find intelligible the results of any other approach but this one. It follows that the bibliography for the present work is not going to be very long, so far as writings specifically relevant to our problem as I have framed it require specification. In fact, there is none. To compose a long bibliography relevant to the topic, but *not* to this book, seems to me to do what already has been done. I refer the reader to the anthology, *Messianism in the Talmudic Era*, ed. Leo Landman (New York: KTAV, 1979), and 27 items he reprints as well as to the four-page bibliography he has assembled.

At the same time, I should be remiss if I were to leave matters as they stand at the end of this account of the messianic ideas utilized in successive documents of the rabbinic canon in its formative period. If my approach is sound, then it should produce useful results elsewhere, and those results should, furthermore, illuminate mine. Accordingly, as this book goes to press, I am in process of organizing a sequence of meetings on the subject, *Judaisms and Their Messiahs*. The book that will emerge from these meetings, under the auspices of the American Academy of Religion section on the History of Judaism, which I chair, will appear in due course. So we shall see how things look when we know what particular groups had to say about the Messiah and how their convictions on that topic fit into their larger worldview and way of life—their Judaism—in its whole and systematic expression.

In the end we shall see whether we may conceive of a systematic doctrine, an "-ism," involving the Messiah, in a single and encompassing "-ism," a whole and harmonious Judaism. My own impression is that to claim there was a ("the") messianic idea in Judaism is to produce a picture we cannot replicate in any single and distinctive group and its definitive system of thought and life. It is a construct of (a philosophy made up in) the scholar's study, not of the disorderly world in which diverse groups think diverse things. But let us see how things emerge. For now, as I said, the question framed in this book is now asked, for the sources under examination here, for the first time.

This book stands in the middle of a trilogy; it follows *Midrash in Context: Exegesis in Formative Judaism* and precedes *Torah: From Scroll to Symbol in Formative Judaism*. The first book explains the method of collecting exegesis of Scripture and how that method contributes to an understanding of the formation of Judaism. This one, as is clear, spells out what I conceive to be the teleology of that same system of Judaism. The final volume describes the literary stages in the formation of the definitive symbol of Judaism, the Torah, as it emerges at the end of late antiquity. When the results of these three books have flowed together, I hope to offer in a single statement my picture of when and why Judaism as we know it took shape, with a thesis, as well, on why that particular Judaic system persisted as long and successfully as it did. But even now I should like to provide a picture of how the three books fit together and present a consistent and integrated result. Briefly stated, my conception of Judaism's historical formation rests on a basic view: I see two distinct stages. First came the question, second, the answer.

The question confronted by "our sages of blessed memory" emerged from the Mishnah (ca. A.D. 200) and the documents most closely associated with it: the Abot (ca. A.D. 250), the Tosefta (ca. A.D. 300–350), and the so-called tannaitic midrashim (ca. A.D. 300–350). (We do not know whether these collections actually derive from the time of the authorities named in them. We only know for sure that those compilations fall precisely within those doctrinal taxa in which the Mishnah, Abot, and Tosefta find their place; in that sense, they may be called "tannaitic," that is, closely associated with the viewpoints of the authorities, Tannas, of the Mishnah itself.) The questions that emerge from this aggregate of rabbinical writings focus upon the Mishnah itself: What is this document? Where does it come from? What is its authority?

The answer to these questions appears then in the pages of the two Talmuds, the Talmud of the Land of Israel (ca. A.D. 400) and the Talmud of Babylonia (ca. A.D. 600), and in certain collections of scriptural exegesis which were composed between the formation of the first and that of the second Talmud, ca. A.D. 400–600. The answers provided by this second and distinct aggregate of writings, mainly within the two Talmuds, tell us that the Mishnah is part of the Torah. This group, which comes from Sinai, enjoys the authority of God's instruction to Moses. In the course of giving those answers, the talmudic (as distinct from the mishnaic) circle of writings created the doctrine of Judaism as received and believed from the fifth and sixth centuries to the twentieth.

The advent of the Mishnah thus provoked the laying down of the foundations of Judaism as outlined by the sages. The result is in three basic dimensions.

First, the question of the Mishnah's status generated distinctive modes of exegesis and the classification and organization of exegesis, systematically applied first to Mishnah, then to Scripture. That is the result of volume one, *Midrash in Context: Exegesis in Formative Judaism*.

Second, questions about the purpose of Israel's life, answered by the Mishnah's framers through an ahistorical teleology that differed from the established eschatology, provoked the Mishnah's heirs and successors to rethink the entire question of teleology. This they did by reframing the inherited eschatology and reshaping, in accord with the ontological emphasis of the Mishnah itself, the symbol of the Messiah and the mass of diverse doctrines about his coming and his role. Not only was there a message of salvation at the end of time grafted onto a central doctrine of sanctification in an ahistorical ontology of unchanging natural-supernatural eternity in the here and now. The available salvific doctrines were also remade to serve a system of sanctification. That is the result of *Messiah in Context: Israel's History and Destiny in Formative Judaism*.

Third, the inherited doctrine of the Torah as a canon of Scripture, as attested in diverse Israelite writings of the fifth century B.C. to the second century A.D., underwent radical revision. In particular the word "Torah" ceased to refer to a scroll and its contents. The advent of the Mishnah, which demanded entry into the canon, carried with it the need to reframe the meaning of the word "Torah." Once the narrow literary limits of the word had given way, "Torah" came to encompass an entire way of life. The word "Torah" then served to differentiate not merely one book from another, but one ontic status from another. So "Torah" not only encompassed a broader range of existence than formerly, it also drew within itself the entire doctrinal heritage of the movement set in motion by the closure of the Mishnah. True, "Torah" continued to denote what it had for so very long, but it also began to connote, concretely and abstractly, more than anyone had earlier implied. Like "Wisdom" in the Wisdom tradition of ancient Israel, the word "Torah" now served to symbolize whatever sages wished to say about the salvation and sanctification of Israel. That is the result of the third book, *Torah: From Scroll to Symbol in Formative Judaism*.

With these three results, my theory of the formation of Judaism has found as full expression as I can presently provide. In the beginning was the Mishnah, but in the end the Talmud, in particular the Talmud of Babylonia, would impart to the Mishnah that full and final meaning—exegetical, teleological, doctrinal—that the Mishnah, as an integral component of the one whole Torah of Moses our rabbi, ever was to have. Thus the formative history of Judaism yields precisely the result that the traditional history of Judaism has always narrated, with only a few minor modifications.

Acknowledgments

My student, Mrs. Judith Romney Wegner, carefully edited the second draft of this book and made many contributions to improve the style. I appreciate her painstaking and astute criticism. Mr. Roger Brooks served as research assistant; he took responsibility for many matters and so made the work easy. Mrs. Marie Louise Murray of Riverside, Rhode Island, typed the first draft, and Miss Winnifred Bell of Providence, Rhode Island, the second.

I enjoyed the benefit of the critical reading and detailed comments of my dear friends and colleagues Professors Jonathan Z. Smith of the University of Chicago and William Scott Green of the University of Rochester.

My student, Paul Flesher, reworked parts of chapter four and surveyed important recent studies of the Targumim, to which I might otherwise not have enjoyed expert access. I am grateful not only to him, but also to his earlier teacher, Dr. Geza Vermes at Oxford University, for this valued contribution of learning in a field adjacent to mine.

Abbreviations

Ar.	Arakhin	Naz.	Nazir
A.Z.	Abodah Zarah	Ned.	Nedarim
B.	*Babli* Babylonian Talmud	Neg.	Negaim
B.B.	Baba Batra	Nid.	Niddah
Bek.	Bekhorot	Oh.	Ohalot
Ber.	Berakhot	Or.	Orlah
Bes.	Besah	Par.	Parah
Bik.	Bikkurim	Pe.	Peah
B.M.	Baba Mesia	Pes.	Pesahim
Dem.	Demai	Qid.	Qiddushin
Ed.	Eduyyot	Qin.	Qinnim
Er.	Erubin	R.	Rabbi
Git.	Gittin	R.H.	Rosh Hashanah
Hag.	Hagigah	San.	Sanhedrin
Hal.	Hallah	Shab.	Shabbat
Hor.	Horayot	Shebu.	Shebuot
Hul.	Hullin	Sheq.	Sheqalim
Kel.	Kelim	Sot.	Sotah
Ker.	Keritot	Suk.	Sukkah
Ket.	Ketubot	T.	Tosefta
Kil.	Kilayim	Ta.	Taanit
M.	Mishnah	Tam.	Tamid
Ma.	Maaserot	Tem.	Temurah
Mak.	Makkot	Ter.	Terumot
Makh.	Makhshirin	Toh.	Tohorot
Me.	Meilah	T.Y.	Tebul Yom
Meg.	Megillah	Uqs.	Uqsin
Men.	Menahot	Yeb.	Yebamot
Mid.	Middot	Yom.	Yoma
Miq.	Miqvaot	Y.T.	Yom Tob
M.Q.	Moed Qatan	Zab.	Zabim
M.S.	Maaser Sheni	Zeb.	Zebahim

Messiah in Context

The form of Judaism we know today reaches back to the origins of ancient Israel. But its lines of definition and distinctive structure flow more immediately out of a brief period in the long history of Israel, the history of the Jewish people. Specifically, Judaism as we know it took shape from A.D. 70, somewhat before the destruction of the Temple of Jerusalem, to 600, over a period of half a millennium. By about 600, it had been fully worked out and reached definitive articulation. The first document of the canon, the Mishnah, reached closure in ca. A.D. 200. The last pre-Islamic document, the Babylonian Talmud, was concluded in A.D. 500–600.

Why do I claim that Judaism took shape in late antiquity, and not long before? The reason is simple. Surveying the landscape of ancient Judaism from the perspective of the Maccabean times (ca. 150 B.C.) we search in vain for the definitive traits of Judaism as we know it. That is to say, we do not find the rabbi as model and authority, nor Torah as the principal and organizing symbol, nor study of Torah as the capital religious deed, nor a holy life of religious discipline as the prime expression of what it means to be Israel, the Jewish people. These distinctive and definitive characteristics of Judaism as the world has known it from late antiquity simply do not appear. In particular, we find no evidence whatsoever of the rabbi as Torah incarnate, as the human being who embodies what it means to be "like God," "in our image and likeness." These twin notions—oral Torah and rabbinical authority—define Judaism as it has flourished for nearly twenty centuries, and, as I said, we find no evidence whatsoever that anyone held them much before the first century, if even then.

True, we may find in writers of books of Wisdom, both canonical and otherwise, values congenial to the system of Torah study that later became paramount. The Judaism framed by rabbis drew freely from antecedent documents and beliefs, reshaping more than inventing. But the canon of Judaism as the rabbis define it jumps from the Hebrew Scriptures to the Mishnah. Rabbinic or talmudic Judaism pretends that nothing happened between the time of the prophets after the return to Zion and the time of the composition of the Mishnah, that is, from the sixth century B.C. to the early third century A.D. The seven intervening centuries, however, fed the Judaism of the kind that took shape in late antiquity as much as it did Christianity, defining for each the range of critical issues and points of universal insistence. Stress on the holy way of life, as was characteristic of all Israelites, for example, and familiar in Judaism through nearly twenty centuries, proves congruent to the conception of the good life—life as a cultic act—which was expressed by priestly writers. But the priests thought of themselves. Their caste in particular lived by divinely ordained rules; the ideal of all Israel as a kingdom of priests and a holy nation for the priests was fully realized, for the priests, in their caste. Others attained holiness through finding a position in relationship to the consecrated caste. Judaism would insist that all Israel become holy. But emphasis on sanctification comes from the priests; stress on learning ("Torah") speaks for scribes.

Accordingly, the principal traits of Judaism—defined as a worldview based on studying Torah and practicing its religious precepts so as to attain a holy way of life and give social expression to the distinctive ethos and ethic of Torah, with the whole design pointing toward the coming Messiah—coalesce in a single system only in the Judaism of the rabbinic type. As I just said, writers of the Wisdom books represent the first component; priests, the second; apocalyptic writers, as I shall suggest, the third, the messianic constituent. In the Essene community at Qumran we find the three components joined in a priestly commune, based on Torah study, and preparing for a messianic war. The Essenes also show us a model of Judaism as we have known it, because in their view they represented Israel.

Once again we note what is defining in Judaism once it took shape: its insistence upon speaking for all Israel, the entire Jewish people. Without that critical catalyst, the social aspiration, the components joined in the Judaism of which we speak—Wisdom's stress on learning in ancient Scripture and traditions, and the priesthood's focus upon living in accordance with God's rules of sanctity and sanctification—never would have formed a single system. The formative Judaism that emerged from late antiquity would unite the ethics of Wisdom, the ethos of the priesthood, and the social focus of messianism into the peoplehood of Israel. The catalyst, above all, would be the entry of a messianic hope. That is why an account of the formative history of Judaism begins with the end time, the myth of the Messiah, and the doctrine of Israel's history and destiny expressed within that myth.

This is a book about the formation of the messianic hope within the framework of the Judaism of late antiquity known to us from writings attributed to sages or rabbis of that period: the Mishnah, the two Talmuds, collections of exegeses of Scripture called midrash(im), and some related documents. We want to know two things. The first is the context in which the messianic idea became important, particularly in these writings. The second is the content of the messianic idea as a mode of dealing with a range of critical questions of social and national consciousness that we define as issues of history and destiny, of the meaning, end, and goal of the system as a whole. Once we have framed a theory of the matter, I hope in another, separate study, to return to the larger question of how other systems of Judaism of the same period dealt with the same issues of national life. What answers did they find to that question by resorting, in particular, to the teleology framed as an eschatological Messiah myth? How did this formulation of a theory of the end explain the system as a whole and tell why people should participate in it?

Let me now define precisely what I mean by the *place* of the Messiah in the kind of Judaism at hand, that is, in the formative stages of the Judaism defined by the Talmuds and rabbis' scriptural exegeses.

When people came to believe that by studying the Torah and keeping the commandments they would play a critical role in the coming of the Messiah, Judaism, as we have known it for nearly two millennia, was born. Further, when Jews reached the conviction that the figure of the rabbi encompassed all three—the learning, the doing, the hope—Judaism had come to full and enduring expression. The rabbi—as Torah incarnate, avatar of hope, and model of the son of David—embodied Judaism. Indeed, he gave it his honorific, "rabbi," a mere commonplace title of respect when it first appeared.

Judaism thus became *rabbinic*. In due course, the entirety of Judaic existence, from remote past to yearned-for future, sustained a process of rabbinization. That process entailed the rereading of everything in terms of the rabbinic system, now portrayed as successor and heir of the priests, scribes, and messiahs of old. The rabbis' kind of Judaism quite naturally rewrote in its own image the entire pre-rabbinical history of Israel. Accordingly, the doctrine of the dual Torah (written and oral), as well as the concept that the Mishnah forms an integral part of the revelation at Sinai and the conviction that the rabbi's way of life typifies the Israelite kings, priests, and prophets of old, would find their way into conventional accounts of the formation and history of Judaism.

Now if in our imagination we stand in the time and place of the Maccabees and look out at the world of Judaism, we scarcely discern even an adumbration of the revolution in Israelite existence represented by the figure and fantasy of the rabbi. The world we should see knows an Israel governed by a king and centered on the Temple, a king who commanded the priesthood as high priest (much like the wonderful fantasy portrayed in ca. A.D. 200 by Mishnah tractate Sanhedrin). But no rabbi is found here. If we leap forward to search for even incipient "rabbinism" in the portrayals of the life and teachings of Jesus, we find a picture of a community fairly continuous with that of the Maccabees. There is a Temple, with a high priest in charge, along with Jewish kings, who ruled by the grace of a distant empire—but still no rabbi as later known. The constant point of reference remains Scripture, the revelation of God to Moses at Sinai; the task of the holy man remains the interpretation and application of that revelation, that is, *torah*, to the life of the people, on the one side, and to its destiny on the other. But the definitive claims and forms of rabbinic authority remain absent.

So, well into the first century, the principal institutions of Israel remained priesthood and monarchy, Scripture and its way of life, holy Temple, land, and people. Various groups—Essenes and Pharisees—claimed to possess traditions that supplemented Scripture. But that does not add up to the dual Torah, with the rabbi as its embodiment. Later scholarship would read into this claim of extrascriptural traditions the much later doctrine of the dual Torah, one in writing, the other oral, the latter culminating in the Mishnah.* They then would imagine that the oral Torah emerged out of a systematic exegesis of the written one, with the further conviction that, when the results were restated as generalizations, they reached the form in which the Mishnah preserves them. But while it is sound doctrine, this view is unlikely to represent historical truth. It hardly tells us what was actually happening in the long centuries between the formation of the Torah book in ca. 500 B.C. and the composition of the Mishnah in ca. A.D. 200. In sources produced in the period (as opposed to those referring to it but produced much later), we find no references to an additional, oral Torah, revealed to Moses at Sinai along with the written one. Nor do we find portraits of rabbis as holy men. In the Gospels, "rabbi" is an honorific, as I said, not a title specific to a particular group, just as, for a long time, "rabbi" or "rabban" served as a title for holy men in Syriac Christianity as much as in Rabbinic Judaism.

If now we take the long step forward by yet another two hundred years, to the third century, the world has begun to change. Israel's life in the Land of Israel has come under the domination of not priests or kings, but rabbis. No longer paramount in splendid isolation, Scripture shares the proscenium of Israel's mind and imagination. Also on stage is the Mishnah, soon to be declared the other, the oral, Torah from Sinai. The Temple is no more. People no longer worship God by bringing animals, killing them, sprinkling the blood on the stones of an altar, and burning up the entrails on a fire, the smoke to please God's nose. (In Roman terms Judaism thus was no religion.) Everything has changed, yet all of the critical constituents of the Israelite system of earlier days remain; all have been rearranged and, more important, everything has been reworked. In the rabbis' transvaluation, a priest no longer was what he had long

*In the third volume of this trilogy, Torah: From Scroll to Symbol in Formative Judaism, I trace the appearance of the doctrines of, first, a revelation at Sinai in addition to, and in a form other than, the written Torah, and second, of the Mishnah and successive documents as this other, oral Torah. It is in the talmudic, not the (earlier) mishnaic, sector of the rabbinic canon that these ideas reach full exposure. If we did not know that the Mishnah was the oral Torah, we should not be able to find a clear statement in the Mishnah or its associated documents, Abot and the Tosefta, or even in the (later) exegetical compilations in the name of mishnaic authorities, Sifra, Sifré Numbers, Sifré Deuteronomy, that such is the case. (I locate only two passages in the so-called tannaitic midrashim that speak of the myth of the dual Torah.) For the talmudic sector of the rabbinic canon, by contrast, these ideas prove critical and reach rich and full expression. They play a major role in the formed Judaism of the end of the period at hand.

been; "Torah" too had come to stand for something more. Accordingly, between the time of the composition of the Gospels, in the late first century, and the formation of the Mishnah, in the late second, Israel with all its heritage was turning in a direction never before taken; it was taking a path from which—we now know—there would be no return.

The long-term task at hand, of which this book stands only at the threshold, is to sort out the main lines of movement in a confused age. Recognizing the diversity of the antecedent structures—the types of Judaism—and the symbols that embodied them, we want to know how these coalesced into Judaism of the rabbinic type and canon. Since we are seeking to describe and interpret modes of piety within Israel of late antiquity, we ourselves seek to imagine how things appeared to people whom we now know only at a considerable distance. From what people said and did we attempt to figure out what they thought and how they felt. And this we do by treating the complex as simple, the mixed as pure. To begin with, we have to sort out the strands of faith and to characterize each one. Only in that way will the definition of one particular strand, the messianic one, begin to emerge in the context of choices and principles of selection. Only then shall we see the Messiah myth in its larger heuristic setting. If we confuse things that in reality require separate description, we lose all possibility of tracing the combination of several things into something new.

The principal strands I discern comprise the distinct types of holy men we know as priests, scribes, and messiahs, and the definitive activities of cult, school and government offices and (ordinarily) battlefield. Ancient Israel's heritage yielded the cult with its priests, the Torah with its scribes and teachers, and the prophetic and apocalyptic hope for meaning in history and an eschaton embodied in messiahs. The choices then derive from these three: Temple, school, and (in the apocalyptic expectation) battlefield on earth and in heaven. Each system of Judaism—worldview, way of life, mode of bonding people into the social group, "Israel"—worked out its Judaism in its own way.

When we approach the use of one of the three components of ancient Judaism to define the formative and (later) normative Judaism of the rabbis, we realize that in its time the Messiah myth represented a sole and exclusive choice. To seek the Messiah and follow him was to declare that what happened to Israel constituted history, expressed God's wish and will, and would lead, in but a little while, to the fulfillment of Israel's destiny in the messianic triumph. While one might know Torah, learning was not central; while one would continue to revere the sacrificial cult in the name of the Messiah's war, one would still risk the holy Temple itself. That was then. What became of that expectation in the formation of a system not defined around the messianic issue is the tale I tell here.

In positing three ideal types of Israelite piety—priest, scribe, Messiah—we must suspend for the moment our disbelief that things can have ever been so simple. As I just said, we recognize the contrary. The troops of a messianic army also observed Scripture's sacred calendar. Their goal was not only to enthrone the King-Messiah, their general, but also to rebuild the Temple, reestablish the priesthood, and restore the sacrificial cult. That the Messiah's army valued the scribal heritage, moreover, is readily apparent in the writings Bar Kokhba's troops preserved. These include women's carefully wrapped up documents covering divorces and marriage settlements, land titles and other deeds. The Essene community at Qumran, as already noted, joined together the themes we treat as separate: priesthood, Messiah, Torah study. Among earliest writers in the Israelite sector of Christianity, Jesus finds ample representation not only as King-Messiah, but also as prophet and king, perfect priest and sacrifice, and always as sage and rabbi (which accounts for the fact that most of the sublime ethical sayings given to him are commonplaces in the other versions of Judaism). Accordingly, none of the symbolic systems at hand, with their associated modes of piety, faith, and religious imagination, ever existed as we treat them here: pure and unalloyed, ideal types awaiting description and interpretation.

To seek a typology of the modes of Israelite piety, we must look for the generative symbol of each mode: an altar, for the priestly ideal; a scroll of Scripture, for the ideal of wisdom; a coin marked "Israel's freedom: year one," for the messianic modality. In each of these visual symbols we perceive things we cannot touch, hearts and minds we can only hope to evoke. We enter into the imagination of someone else, long ago and far away, by our effort to understand the way in which that other person framed the world, captured everything in some one thing: the sheep for the sacrifice, the memorized aphorism for the disciple, the stout heart for the soldier of light. Priest, sage, soldier—all of these figures stand for Israel, or part of the nation. When all would meld into one, that one would stand for a fresh and unprecedented Judaism.

Jesus represented as perfect priest, rabbi, Messiah was one such protean figure. The talmudic rabbi as Torah incarnate, priest manqué, and model of the son of (Rabbi) David, was another. In both cases we find a fresh reading of an old symbol, and, more important, an unprecedented rereading of established symbols in new and striking ways. The history of Judaism is the story of successive arrangements and revisions of available symbols. From ancient Israelite times onward, there would be no classification beyond the three established taxa. But no category would long be left intact. When Jesus asked people what they thought he was, the enigmatic answer proved less interesting than the question. For the task he set before them was to reframe everything they knew in the encounter with what they did not know: a taxonomic enterprise. When the rabbis of late antiquity rewrote in their own image and likeness the entire Scripture and history of Israel, dropping whole eras as though they had never been, ignoring vast bodies of old Jewish writing, inventing whole new books for the canon of Judaism, they did the same thing. They reworked what they had received in light of what they proposed to give. No mode of piety could be left untouched, for all proved promising. But every mode of piety would be reworked in light of the vast public events represented by the religious revolutionaries at hand, rabbi-clerk, rabbi-priest, rabbi-messiah.

The issues of the symbols under discussion, Temple altar, sacred scroll, victory wreath for the head of the King-Messiah, comprehended Jewish society at large. We need not reduce them to their social dimensions to recognize that, at the foundations, we deal with the organization of the people of Israel's society and the selection and interpretation of its history. Let us rapidly review the social groups envisaged and addressed by framers of these symbols.

The priest, as we know, viewed society as organized through lines of structure emanating from the Temple. His caste stood at the top of a social scale in which all things were properly organized, each with its correct name and proper place. The inherent sanctity of Israel, the people, came through genealogy to its richest embodiment in him, the priest. Food set aside for his rations at God's command possessed that same sanctity; so too did the table at which he ate his food. To the priest the sacred society of Israel produced history as an account of what happened in, and (alas) on occasion to, the Temple.

To the sage, the life of society demanded wise regulation. Relationships among people required guidance by the laws embodied in the Torah and best interpreted by the sage. Accordingly, the task of Israel was to construct a way of life in accordance with the revealed rules of the Torah. The sage, master of the rules, stood at the head.

As for prophecy's insistence that the fate of the nation depended upon the faith and moral condition of society, history testified to the external context and inner condition of Israel, viewed as a whole. Both sage and priest saw Israel from the aspect of eternity. But the nation lived out its life in this world, among other peoples coveting the very same land, within the politics of empires. The Messiah's kingship would resolve the issues of Israel's subordinated relationship to other nations and empires, establishing once for all time the correct context for priest and sage alike.

Implicit in the messianic framework was a perspective on the world out there beyond Israel for which priest and sage cared not at all. The priest perceived the receding distances of the world beyond the Temple, as first less holy, then unholy, then unclean. All lands outside of the Land of Israel were chronically unclean with corpse uncleanness; all other peoples were inherently unclean just as corpses were unclean. Accordingly, life abided within Israel, and, in Israel, within the Temple. Outside, in the far distance, were vacant lands and dead peoples, comprising an undifferentiated wilderness of death. From such a perspective on the world, no doctrine of Israel among the nations, no interest in the history of Israel and its meaning, was apt to emerge.

The sagacity of the sage, in general, pertained to the streets, marketplaces, and domestic establishments (the household units) of Israel. What the sage said was wise, indeed, as much for Gentiles as for Israel. Wisdom in the nature of things proved international, moving easily across the boundaries of culture and language, from eastern to southern to western Asia. It focused, by definition, upon universal human experience, undifferentiated by nation, essentially unaffected by the large movements of history. Wisdom spoke about fathers and sons, masters and disciples, families and villages, not about nations, armies, and destiny.

Because of their very diversity, the three principal motifs of Israelite existence might readily cohere. Each focused on a distinct and particular aspect of the national life, so none essentially contradicted any other. One could worship at the Temple, study the Torah, and fight in the army of the Messiah—and some did all three. Yet we must see these modes of being, and their consequent motifs of piety, as separate, each with its own potentiality of full realization without reference to the others.

The three modes of human existence expressed in the symbolic systems of cult, Torah, and Messiah demand choices. If one thing is more important, then the others must be less important. History matters, or it happens "out there" without significance. The proper conduct of the cult determines the course of the seasons and the prosperity of the land, or it is mere ritual. The Messiah will save Israel, or he will ruin everything. Accordingly, while we take for granted that people could live within the multiple visions of priest, sage, and Messiah, we also recognize that it was vertiginous, a blurred perception. Narratives of the war of 66–73 emphasize that priests warned messianists not to endanger the Temple. Later sages—talmudic rabbis—paid slight regard to the messianic struggle led by Bar Kokhba and after 70 claimed the right to tell priests what to do. It must follow that the way in which symbols are arranged and rearranged settles everything. Symbol change is social change. A mere amalgam of all three symbols by itself hardly serves as a mirror for the mind of Israel. The particular way the three are bonded in a given system reflects an underlying human and social reality.

That is how it should be, since the three symbols with their associated myths, the worldviews they project, and the ways of life they define, stand for different views of what really matters. In investigating the existential foundations of the several symbolic systems available to Jews of antiquity, we seek to penetrate to the bedrock of Israel's reality, to the basis of the life of the nation and of each Israelite, to the ground of being—even to the existential core that we the living share with them.

Let us unpack the two foci of existence, public history and private establishment: home, hearth, guild and village. We may call one "time"; its interest is in the events, what happens day by day in the here and now of continuing history. The other we may call "eternity"; its focus of interest is on the recurrent patterns of life, birth and death, planting and harvest, the regular movement of the sun, moon, and stars in heaven, night and day, Sabbaths, and festivals, and regular seasons on earth. The shared existential issue is this: How do we respond to the ups and downs of life? Every group that survives experiences those noteworthy events we call "history." The events of individual life, birth, maturing, marriage, and death do not make, or add up to, history, except for individuals. But the events of group life—the formation of groups, development of social norms and patterns, depression and prosperity, war and peace—do make history. When a small people coalesces and begins its course through history in the face of adversity, two things can happen. Either the group disintegrates in the face of disaster and loses its hold on its individual members, or the group fuses, being strengthened by trial, and turns adversity into renewal.

The points around which human and national existence were interpreted—those of priests, sages, and messianists (including prophets and apocalyptists)—emerge, we must remember, from the national and social consciousness of ancient Israel. The heritage of the written Torah (*Tanakh*, the Hebrew Scriptures or "Old Testament") was carried forward in all three approaches to Judaism. The Jewish people knows the mystery of how to endure through history, for it is among the oldest peoples still surviving on the face of the earth. Even in ancient Israel, adversity elicited self-conscious response. Things did not merely *happen* to Israelites. Events were shaped, reformed, and interpreted, being treated as raw material for renewing the life of the group. Israelites regarded their history as important, as teaching significant lessons. History was not merely "one damn thing after another." It had a purpose and was moving somewhere. The writers of Leviticus and Deuteronomy, of the hisorical books from Joshua through Kings, and of the prophetic literature, agreed that, when Israel does God's will, it enjoys times of peace, security, and prosperity; and when it does not, it is punished at the hands of mighty kingdoms raised up as instruments of God's wrath. This conception of the meaning of Israel's life produced another question: How long? When do the great events of time come to their climax and conclusion? And as one answer to that question, there arose the hope for the Messiah, the anointed of God who would redeem the people and set them on the right path forever, thus ending the vicissitudes of history.

Now, when we reach the first century A.D., we come to a turning point in the messianic hope. No one who knows the Gospels will be surprised to learn of the intense, vivid, prevailing expectation that the Messiah was coming soon. And that anticipation is hardly astonishing. People who fix their attention on contemporary events of world-shaking dimensions naturally look to a better future. That represents one context for the Messiah myth.

More surprising is the development of a second, quite different response to history. It is the response of people prepared once and for all to transcend historical events and to take their leave of wars and rumors of wars, of politics and public life. These people undertook to construct a new reality beyond history, one that focused on the meaning of humdrum everyday life. After 70 there was no mere craven or exhausted passivity in the face of world-shaking events. We witness the beginnings, among the Mishnah's sagas in particular, of an active construction of a new mode of being. The decision was to exercise freedom, autonomous of history, to reconstruct the meaning and ultimate significance of events. It is a seeking of a world not outside this one, but different from, and better than, the one formed by ordinary history. This second approach is a quest for eternity in the here and now, an effort to form a society capable of abiding amid change and storm. Indeed, it is a fresh reading of the meaning of history: the nations of the world *make* "history" and think that their actions matter. But Israel knows that it is God who makes history, and it is the reality formed in response to God's will that counts as history: God is the King of kings of kings.

That reality, that conception of time and change, forms the focus and the vision of the priestly tradition, continued later in the Judaism called rabbinic or talmudic. This sort of Judaism is essentially a meta-historical approach to life. It lives above history and its problems. It expresses an intense inwardness. The Judaism attested in the rabbis' canon of writings stresses the ultimate meaning contained within small and humble affairs. Rabbinic Judaism in the time to come would set itself up as the alternative to all the forms of messianic Judaism—whether in the form of Christianity or militaristic zealotry and nationalism—that claimed to know the secret of history, the time of salvation and way to redemption. But the canonical writings of rabbis also disclosed the answers to these questions. The Messiah myth was absorbed into the rabbis' system and made to strengthen it. So the context created by the rabbinical canon defined in a new way the uses and purposes of all else that had gone before.

This approach to the life of Israel, stressing continuity and pattern and promising change only at the end, when all was in order at the last, represents the union of two trends. The one was symbolized by the altar, the other by the Torah scroll—the priest and the sage. In actual fact, the union was effected by a special *kind* of priest manqué, and a special *kind* of sage. The former was the Pharisee, the latter the scribe. The former was a particular sect of people who pretended, in their homes, that they were priests in the Temple. The scribe, on the other hand, was not a member of a sect but of a profession. The scribes knew and taught Torah. They took their interpretation of Torah very seriously, and the act of study had for them special importance. The Pharisees had developed, for their part, a peculiar perception of how to live and interpret life, which we may call an "as if" perception. In very specific ways the Pharisees had claimed to live as if they were priests, as if they must obey at home the laws that applied to the Temple. When the actual Temple was destroyed, the Pharisees were prepared for that tremendous change in the sacred economy. They continued to live *as if*—as if the Temple stood, as if there were a new Temple composed of the Jewish people. Joined to their mode of looking at life was the substance of the scribal ideal, the stress on learning Torah and carrying out its teachings.

These, then, represent the alternatives whereby great events were experienced and understood. One was the historical-messianic way, stressing the intrinsic importance of events and concentrating upon their weight and meaning. The other was the meta-historical, scribal-priestly-rabbinic way, which emphasized Israel's power of transcendence and the construction of an eternal, changeless mode of being, capable of riding out the waves of history.

Accordingly, once we have identified the principal strands of Judaic consciousness, we must deal with two questions. First, what made one particular focus—the priestly and the sagacious, or the messianic, trend—appear more compelling and consequential than the other? The answer becomes obvious when we realize that each kind of piety addresses its own point of concern and speaks about different things to different people. We may sort them out from one another if we return to our earlier observations. Priests and sages turn inward, toward the concrete everyday life of the community. They address the sanctification of Israel. Messianists and their prophetic and apocalyptic teachers turn outward, toward the affairs of states and nations. They speak of the salvation of Israel. Priests see the world of life in Israel, and death beyond. They know what happens to Israel without requiring a theory about the place of Israel among the nations. The nations, for priests, form an undifferentiated realm of death. Sages, all the more, speak of home and hearth, fathers and sons, husbands and wives, the village and enduring patterns of life within it. What place in this domestic scheme for the realities of history—wars and threats of war, the rise and fall of empires—encompasses the consciousness of a singular society amidst other societies? At issue for the priest is "being," for the prophet and Messiah, "becoming."

What draws the three foci together and makes them one? The answer is an event in which all were equally involved. We speak of a moment equally important to the messianists, to whom great events of history appear momentous, and to the priests and sages, who affected to ignore the events of history. The occurrence that proved definitive was the destruction of the Temple in A.D. 70. That event, by its nature, provided the catalyst that joined priest, sage, and messianist. That fusion created an amalgam that was the Judaism revealed in the rabbinical canon of writings, the Judaism framed by the rabbis of the Mishnah, the collectors of Midrash and the compilers of two Talmuds. The three definitive components were then bonded.

The characteristic view of Judaism as a way of life aimed at sanctification was contributed by the priestly trend. The definitive notion that Judaism demanded a life of study of Torah and the application of Torah to the community derived from the scribes. The distinctive conception that the community of Israel stood apart from the nations, living out a destiny of its own, was the legacy of the prophetic, apocalyptic, messianic trend. Events, then, added up to history. The history of Israel was shaped by God's response to Israel's study of Torah and life of sanctification. When the whole came together, forming the perfect creation as at the beginning of time, then would come the end of time, the enduring Sabbath, counterpart to the Sabbath of creation: the Messiah and his age.

So a single critical event of the age, the destruction of the Temple, presented a turning point for the priestly caste, the sages' profession, and the political and messianic sectors of the nation alike. What was important was not that the Temple was then destroyed. That had happened before. It was that the Temple was not rebuilt, as previously it had been. In 586 the Jerusalem Temple had fallen, but a scant three generations passed before it was restored. From that time onward, whatever happened to the Temple building, the cult had always endured. So the entire history of Israel testified to the Temple's prominence in the world of Israel. If it should again be destroyed, people had every reason to expect it would be rebuilt. Accordingly, the destruction in A.D. 70, while bearing profound consequences, by itself merely raised a question. The calamity was that, three generations later, Bar Kokhba's armies, intent on retaking the city and rebuilding the Temple, suffered total defeat, turning the earlier destruction, in retrospect, into a crisis. But in what direction would matters go? And, more important, with what meaning for the whole of Israel's past? The answer, simply stated, was that in the aftermath of the cultic, political, military disaster of 70 and 135, everything would be reworked, the entire heritage would be revised and redefined.

Accordingly, within the rabbinic Judaism born in the centuries after 70, the three elements, the distinct traditions of priest, sage, and messianist, were joined in a new way. In the person of the rabbi, holy man, Torah incarnate, avatar and model of the son of David, rabbinic Judaism found its sole overarching system. So the diverse varieties of Judaic piety present in Israel before 70 came to be bonded over the next several centuries in a wholly unprecedented way, with each party to the union imposing its logic upon the other constituents of the whole. The ancient categories remained. But they were so profoundly revised and transformed that nothing was preserved intact. Judaism as we know it, the Judaism of Scripture and Mishnah, Midrash and Talmud, thereby effected the ultimate transvaluation of all the values, of all the kinds of Judaism that had come before, from ancient Israel onward. Through the person and figure of the rabbi, the whole burden of Israel's heritage was taken up, renewed, and handed on from late antiquity to the present day.

Only when the union of time and eternity, of messianic hope and holy way of life, broke apart with the modern shaking of the iron consensus of the ages, did Judaism in its classic form unravel. Then its ancient strands were separately revealed to view once more. History, the events of wars and nations, the life of the citizen, once again opened up to receive Israel as the individual Jew. The remnant that believed in the holy way of life which would lead toward an as-yet-unrealized salvation in the Messiah went its solitary way. The result would be a renewed immediacy to the messianic expectation, just now, indeed, perceived and expressed most vividly by the generality of participants in the holy way of life. With rebirth of the near-term expectation that what we do here and now serves the Messiah's cause, the Judaic world came to replicate, once more, the conditions in which, to begin with, the Temple earlier had been destroyed and rabbinic Judaism born. With that observation, we leave ancient times and regain the hour at hand. But in stating this, we have moved far beyond the problem of this book. What we shall here investigate is only the Messiah in the successive documents of the rabbinical canon and the unfolding theory of Israel's history and destiny within a system of Judaism focused upon issues of eternity.

1

The Messiah in
the Foundation Document

THE MISHNAH

When the Temple of Jerusalem fell to the Babylonians in 586 B.C., Israelite thinkers turned to the writing of history to explain what had happened. From that time onward, with the composition of the Pentateuch and the historical books, Joshua, Judges, Samuel, and Kings, to teach the lessons of history, and of the prophetic and apocalyptic books to interpret and project those lessons into the future, Israel explained the purpose of its being by focusing upon the meaning of events. The critical issue then was salvation—from what? for what? by whom? In that context, the belief in a supernatural man, an anointed savior or Messiah, formed a natural complement to a system in which teleology took the form of eschatology. Israelites do their duty because of what is happening and of where events will lead. All things point to a foreordained end, presenting the task of interpreting the signs of the times. No wonder, then, that when the Temple of Jerusalem fell to the Romans in A.D. 70, established patterns of thinking guided writers of Judaic apocalypse to pay attention to the meaning of history. In that setting, Jesus, whom Paul had earlier grasped in an essentially ahistoric framework, now turned out, in the hands of the writers of the Gospels, to be Israel's Messiah. He was *the* Messiah at the end of time, savior and redeemer of Israel from its historical calamity, thus a historical-political figure, the king of the Jews.

The character of the Israelite Scriptures, with their emphasis upon historical narrative as a mode of theological explanation, leads us to expect Judaism to evolve as a deeply messianic religion. With all prescribed actions pointed toward the coming of the Messiah at the end of time, and all interest focused upon answering the historical-salvific questions ("how long?"), Judaism from late antiquity to the present day presents no surprises. Its liturgy evokes historical events to prefigure salvation; prayers of petition repeatedly turn to the speedy coming of the Messiah; and the experience of worship invariably leaves the devotee expectant and hopeful. Just as rabbinic (now normative) Judaism is a deeply messianic religion, secular extensions of Judaism have commonly proposed secularized versions of the focus upon history and have shown interest in the purpose and denouement of events. Teleology again appears as an eschatology embodied in messianic symbols.

Yet, for a brief moment, a vast and influential document presented a kind of Judaism in which history did not define the main framework by which the issue of teleology took a form other than the familiar eschatological one and in which historical events were absorbed, through their trivialization in taxonomic structures, into an ahistorical system. In the kind of Judaism in this document, messiahs played a part. But these "anointed men" had no historical role. They undertook a task quite different from that assigned to Jesus by the framers of the Gospels. They were merely a species of priest, falling into one classification rather than another.

That document is the Mishnah, from about A.D. 200; it is a strange corpus of normative statements which we may, though with some difficulty, classify as a law code or a school book for philosophical jurists. The difficulty of classification derives from the document's contents, which deal with topics to which we are reluctant to assign the title "law." Composed in an age in which people (the Romans included) were making law codes, the Mishnah presents a systematic account of the life of Israel, the Jewish people in the Land of Israel. The Mishnah comprises sixty-three tractates covering six categories of activity. These begin, first, with rules for the conduct of the economy (that is, agriculture) with special attention given to the farmers' provision of priestly rations. In the second are rules for various special holy days and seasons, especially for conducting the sacrificial service and life of the Temple cult on such occasions, and for the corresponding life in the home. Third are rules governing the status of women, with particular interest in the transfer of a woman from the domain of one man to that of another. Fourth is a code of civil laws, covering all aspects of commercial, civil, and criminal law, and offering a blueprint for an Israelite government based on the

Temple in Jerusalem and headed by a king and a high priest. Fifth, we find rules for the Temple's sacrificial service and for the upkeep of the Temple buildings and establishment, with emphasis upon the life of the cult on ordinary days. Finally, in the sixth category the Mishnah details taboos affecting the cultic life in the form of unclean things and gives rules on how to remove their effects.

This brief account of the document points toward its principal point of interest: sanctification. At issue is holiness in the life of Israel as it is lived out in relationship to the Temple and under the governance of the priesthood. What has been said indicates also what the document neglects to treat: salvation, that is, the historical life of the Jewish nation, where it is heading, and how it will get there. The Mishnah omits all reference to its own point of origin, and thus lacks a historical account or a mythic base. The framers of the code likewise barely refer to Scripture, rarely produce proof texts for their own propositions, and never imitate ancient Hebraic modes of speech, as do the writers of the Dead Sea Scrolls at Qumran. They hardly even explain the relationship between their book and the established holy Scriptures of Israel. As we shall see, the absence of sustained attention to events or to a doctrine of history serves also to explain why the Messiah as an eschatological figure makes no appearance in the system of the Mishnah.

Accordingly, the later decades of the second century, after the defeat of Bar Kokhba, witnessed the composition of a vast book, the Mishnah, which was later received as authoritative and turned into the foundations of the two Talmuds—one composed in Babylonia, the other in the Land of Israel—which define Judaism as we know it. If, then, we ask about the original context of this foundation document of the rabbinic canon, we find ourselves in an age that had witnessed yet another messianic war, this one fought by Israel against Rome under Bar Kokhba's leadership from 132 to 135. That war, coming three generations after the destruction of the Temple, aimed to regain Jerusalem in order to rebuild the Temple. It seems probable that Bar Kokhba in his own day was perceived as a messianic general and that the war was seen as coming at the expected end of time, the eschatological climax to the drama begun in 70. If so, the character of the Mishnah, the work of the war's survivors, proves truly astonishing. Here, as I said, we have an immense, systematic, and encompassing picture of the life of Israel, in which events scarcely play a role. History never intervenes. The goal and purpose of it all find full and ample expression with scarcely a word about either the end of time or the coming of the Messiah. In a word, the Mishnah presents us with a kind of Judaism that has an eschatology without the Messiah, a teleology beyond time. When, in the Mishnah, the point of insistence is sanctification and not salvation, we see the outcome.

In what follows, I provide an account of how history is absorbed and reframed into an ontological structure. Here, specifically, is how history figures in the fantasy of a world beyond time, a world constructed in the minds of the Mishnah's sages. Survivors of the messianic cataclysm and catastrophe begun in the war of 66–73 and concluded in that of 132–35, they confronted in a fresh way the issues of Israelite existence as worked out by others through messianism. With the Temple site plowed over and Jerusalem closed to Jews, these sages created an imaginary city to replace the forbidden one; it was a detailed prescription for a cult to be taken in mind and studied in fantasy—a world contrived in the intellect.

So this great document, created by survivors and their disciples, contains a rich stash of question marks. Its authors tell us nothing about a theological context: the character and authority of the document, why they have made it, or what they want people to do with it. They ignore the entire antecedent literary heritage of Israel, referring only occasionally to Scripture but never to any other writing. The generative issues persistently addressed throughout the Mishnah's discourse concern sorting out matters of doubt, plotting the way in which conflicts between valid principles are resolved, and, in all, examining the way in which things reach their proper classification. These deeply philosophical questions take up problems of potentiality and actuality, intention and deed, the genus and the species, mixtures of various kinds, and similar perennial issues of thought. Inquiry comes to full exposure in discussions of arcane topics, most of them rarely, if ever, addressed in previous Israelite writings, except, in varying measure, in Scripture itself.

Accordingly, for all Judaism prior to its day, the document in context was unique. It adopted a position of splendid isolation from nearly all that had intervened from the closure of the scriptural writings to the formation of the Mishnah itself. The authors of the Mishnah obviously drew upon facts available from their context, both contemporary and historical. But even here they pretended that Scripture was the sole source of facts. Where they assumed matters of fact that were not found in Scripture and sometimes even contradictory to Scripture, they silently passed over the issue of how they knew what they knew. They never squared what Scripture said, or did not say, with what they knew.

It was Judah the Patriarch (ca. 180–230), recognized by the Roman government as head of the Jewish community of the Land of Israel, who defined the standing of the Mishnah. Apparently he sponsored the document as the law code of the Jewish administration. Consequently, whatever the original intent of the framers—which we may guess only by induction from the things they did and did not do—the Mishnah, together with Scripture, rapidly became the constitution and bylaws of the Jewish nation in its Land. The clerks of Judah's government, who served also as judges in the petty claims courts governing the Jewish sector of the Land's mixed population, took over the Mishnah. They studied its laws, applied those that were relevant to their immediate task, and over a period of two hundred years developed a rather substantial corpus of mishnaic exegesis. That corpus, organized around specific clauses or paragraphs of the vast Mishnah, reaches us as the Talmud of the Land of Israel, brought to closure in the late fourth and early fifth centuries. The second Talmud, produced in Babylonia by the exilarch's clerks (counterparts of the patriarch's bureaucrats), reached closure probably a century and a half later. When, therefore, we approach the Mishnah, we take a path laid out for us by people who read the Mishnah with a particular purpose in mind. They transformed it into a document serviceable in courts and government bureaus. It became the original document, after Scripture, in the canon of formative Judaism.

If, for the moment, we turn back to the Mishnah of the beginning, as it stood before it took its large and commanding position over the life of Israel, the Jewish people, we survey the world as perceived by the Mishnah's framers, philosophical lawyers of the late second century. To be sure, as I said, they made ample use of whatever they chose to utilize out of the antecedent heritage of Israel. But it is their vision of how things should be framed and phrased that testifies to the original perspective. They laid the foundations. They selected the topics and arranged them. They determined the mode of thought (polythetic taxonomy) and the paramount method of discourse (list-making). They defined the logic and decided the system's distinctive structure and definitive traits.

To be sure, as I have explained, their successors in the Talmuds almost immediately rejected the system constructed by the sages of the second century. The heirs took whatever they found necessary, using the parts to make a different whole. The Talmuds' reading of the Mishnah consequently produced something quite different from what the framers of the Mishnah had anticipated. The talmudic system rested on foundations in the Mishnah, but proved to be radically asymmetrical to the Mishnah's own foundation. To state matters simply, by ca. A.D. 600 a system of Judaism emerged in which the Mishnah as foundation document would be asked to support a structure at best continuous with, but in no way fully defined by the outlines of, the Mishnah itself. The rabbi at the end was not the rabbi at the outset, and neither was his Torah, that is, his Judaism. The rabbi at the end saw himself as bearer and authority of the Mishnah, now legitimated as one half of the entire Torah of Moses, whom they called "our rabbi" and to whom they attributed the origin and foundation of the whole. So from whatever it was—perhaps a kind of remarkably arcane way of doing philosophy—the Mishnah became *torah* (revelation) and thus formed part of *the* Torah, the "one, whole" Torah revealed by God to Moses ("our rabbi") at Sinai. Hence, after Scripture itself, the Mishnah was the beginning of it all.

That is why, coming at the system from the endpoint, we ask the Mishnah to answer the questions at hand. What of the Messiah? When will he come? To whom, in Israel, will he come? And what must, or can, we do while we wait to hasten his coming? If we now reframe these questions and divest them of their mythic cloak, we ask about the Mishnah's theory of the history and destiny of Israel and the purpose of the Mishnah's own system in relationship to Israel's present and end: the implicit teleology of the philosophical law at hand.

Answering these questions out of the resources of the Mishnah is not possible. The Mishnah presents no large view of history. It contains no reflection whatever on the nature and meaning of the destruction of the Temple in A.D. 70, an event which surfaces only in connection with some changes in the law explained as resulting from the end of the cult. The Mishnah pays no attention to the matter of the end time. The word "salvation" is rare, "sanctification" commonplace. More strikingly, the framers of the Mishnah are virtually silent on the teleology of the system; they never tell us why we should do what the Mishnah tells us, let alone explain what will happen if we do. Incidents in the Mishnah are preserved either as narrative settings for the statement of the law, or, occasionally, as precedents. Historical events are classified and turned into entries on lists. But incidents in any case come few and far between. True, events do make an impact. But it always is for the Mishnah's own purpose and within its own taxonomic system and rule-seeking mode of thought. To be sure, the framers of the Mishnah may also have had a theory of the Messiah and of the meaning of Israel's history and destiny. But they kept it hidden, and their document manages to provide an immense account of Israel's life without explicitly telling us about such matters. To what may be implicit I confess myself blind and deaf: I see and hear only thin echoes of a timeless eternity governed by orderly rules.

Let me digress to provide an important qualification to the argument that is to come. Since the Mishnah constitutes the foundation document of Judaism, our interest is in that document as such, and not in other ideas that may or may not also have been held by its framers. Of these the Mishnah tells us nothing. What is assigned or attributed to them in later documents testifies only to what the framers of those documents thought their predecessors had stated long ago. Whether or not the Mishnah's authorities had actually made such statements we do not know. In the Mishnah we have ample evidence concerning the statements they did make in the document for which, along with Scripture, they secured recognition as Israel's constitution. Accordingly, the Mishnah (and the Mishnah alone) defines the original boundaries of the canon of Judaism as the rabbinic system. Whatever else second-century thinkers may have believed surfaced only later on. It was not until the third or fourth or fifth centuries that these other opinions, allegedly held in the second century, proved important and made their impact upon the public and collective statement in literature coming forth from rabbinical institutions and defining rabbinic Judaism. So in the Mishnah we deal with what was official and definitive at the beginnings.

When we walk the frontiers laid out by the Mishnah, we turn inward to gaze upon a portrait of the world at rest, in which, as I said, events take place, but history does not. It is a world of things in the right place, each with its proper name, all in the appropriate classification. In the Mishnah's world, all things aim at stasis both in nature and in society, with emphasis upon proper order and correct form. As we saw, the world of the Mishnah in large part encompasses the cult, the priesthood, and protection of the cult from sources of danger and uncleanness. The Mishnah presents a priestly conception of the world and creates a system aimed at the sanctification of Israel under the rule of the priests as a holy people. The world subject to discussion encompasses a temple, whose rules are carefully studied; a high priest, whose actions are meticulously chronicled; and a realm of the clean and the holy, whose taboos are spelled out in exquisite detail.

But, since none of these things existed when the framers of the Mishnah wrote about them, the Mishnah turns out to be something other than what it appears. It purports to describe how things are. But it tells us much more about a fantasy than about the real, palpable world, the world concretely known to the people who wrote about it. So the Mishnah is a work of imagination—using bits and pieces of facts, to be sure—made up in the minds of the framers of the Mishnah. The Mishnah does not undertake a description of a real building out there, maintained by real flesh-and-blood people, burning up kidneys of real lambs whose smoke you can smell and see. It is all a realm of made-up memories, artificial dreams, hopes, and yearnings. When we turn from the inner perspective to the sheltering world beyond, we see how totally fantastic was the fantasy. For the Mishnah provides prescriptions for preserving a world of stable order. Living in the aftermath of Bar Kokhba's defeat, the framers of the Mishnah in fact carried on through chaos and crisis, paying the psychic, as much as the political, costs of catastrophic defeat.

Lacking a temple or credible hope for one for the first time in Israelite history in the millennium from the rule of David onward, the sages confronted an Israel without blood rites to atone for sin and win God's favor. Under such circumstances, their minds might well have turned back to the time of David, and therefore forward to the age in which David's heir and successor would come to restore the Temple and rule Israel as God's anointed. Perhaps they did. Maybe in writing the Mishnah, they meant to describe how David's son would do things just as David had done things long ago. But if that was their purpose, they did not say so. And the one thing any student of the Mishnah knows is that its framers are pitiless in giving detail, in saying everything they wish, and in holding back—so far as we can tell—nothing we might need to know to plumb their meaning.

Yet we do not have to argue from their silence to find out what was in their minds. True, they speak little of the Messiah and rarely refer to events perceived as history. But they do record the events of the day when it serves their purposes. They do hint at the Messiah's coming. So let us rapidly survey some facts, rather than harping on the absence of evidence. If, for example, they give us no doctrine of the Messiah, no stories about him, no account of where he will come from, or how we shall know him, and what he will do, still, they do use the word "Messiah." How do they use it?

THE MESSIAH IN THE MISHNAH

In a legal context, the Mishnah's framers know the anointing of a leader in connection with two officials: the high priest consecrated with oil, in contrast to the one consecrated merely by receiving the additional garments that indicate the office of high priest (M. Mak. 2:6; M. Meg. 1:9; M. Hor. 3:4), and the (high) priest anointed for the purpose of leading the army in war (M. Sot. 7:2; 8:1; M. Mak. 2:6). When the Mishnah uses the word Messiah in legal contexts the assumed meaning is always the anointed priest (M. Hor. 2:2, 3, 7; 3:4, 5).

Yet the Mishnah's framers know a quite separate referent for the same term. When they wish to distinguish between this age and the world to come, they speak (M. Ber. 1:5) of "this world and the days of the Messiah." That Messiah can only be the anointed savior of Israel. The reference is casual, the language routine, the purpose merely factual. Likewise, at M. Sot. 9:9–15 there is a reference to "the footsteps of the Messiah," again in the setting of the end of time and the age to come. That passage, a systematic eschatology, is critical for us in assessing whatever the Mishnah offers as a theory of Israel's history, so we shall review it in its entirety. (Biblical verses are cited in italics.)

M. SOTAH 9:9–15

9:9   I   A. When murderers became many, the rite of breaking the heifer's neck was canceled.

B. [This was] when Eleazar b. Dinai came along, and he was also called Tehinah b. Perishah. Then they went and called him, "Son of a murderer."

II   C. When adulterers became many, the ordeal of the bitter water was canceled.

D. And Rabban Yohanan b. Zakkai canceled it, since it is said, *I will not punish your daughters when they commit whoredom, nor your daughters-in-law when they commit adultery, for they themselves go aside with whores* [Hos. 4:14].

III   E. When Yose b. Yoezer of Seredah and Yose b. Yohanan of Jerusalem died, the grape clusters were canceled,

F. since it is said, *There is no cluster to eat, my soul desires the first ripe fig* [Mic. 7:1].

9:10   A. Yohanan, high priest, did away with the confession concerning tithe.

B. He also canceled the rite of the Awakeners and the Stunners.

C. Until his time a hammer did strike in Jerusalem.

D. And in his time no man had to ask concerning doubtfully tithed produce.

9:11   IV   A. When the Sanhedrin was canceled, singing at wedding feasts was canceled, since it is said, *They shall not drink wine with a song* [Isa. 24:9].

9:12   V   A. When the former prophets died out, the Urim and Tummim were canceled.

VI   B. When the sanctuary was destroyed, the Shamir worm ceased and [so did] the honey of *supim*.

C. And faithful men came to an end,

D. since it is written, *Help, O Lord, for the godly man ceases* [Ps. 12:2].

E. Rabban Simeon b. Gamaliel says in the name of R. Joshua, "From the day the Temple was destroyed, there is no day on which there is no curse, and dew has not come down as a blessing. The good taste of produce is gone."

F. R. Yose says, "Also: the fatness of produce is gone."

9:13   A. R. Simeon b. Eleazar says, "[When] purity [ceased], it took away the taste and scent; [when] tithes [ceased], they took away the fatness of corn."

B. And sages say, "Fornication and witchcraft made an end to everything."

9:14 I   A. In the war against Vespasian they decreed against the wearing of wreaths by bridegrooms and against the wedding drum.

II   B. In the war against Titus they decreed against the wearing of wreaths by brides.

C. And [they decreed] that a man should not teach Greek to his son.

III   D. In the last war [Bar Kokhba's] they decreed that a bride should not go out in a palanquin inside the town.

E. But our rabbis [thereafter] permitted the bride to go out in a palanquin inside the town.

9:15   A. When R. Meir died, makers of parables came to an end.

B. When Ben Azzai died, diligent students came to an end.

C. When Ben Zoma died, exegetes came to an end.

D. When R. Joshua died, goodness went away from the world.

E. When Rabban Simeon b. Gamaliel died, the locust came and troubles multiplied.

F. When R. Eleazar b. Azariah died, wealth went away from the sages.

G. When R. Aqiba died, the glory of the Torah came to an end.

H. When R. Hanina b. Dosa died, wonderworkers came to an end.

I. When R. Yose Qatnuta died, pietists went away.

J. (And why was he called "Qatnuta"? Because he was the least of the pietists.)

K. When Rabban Yohanan b. Zakkai died, the splendor of wisdom came to an end.

L. When Rabban Gamaliel the Elder died, the glory of

the Torah came to an end, and cleanness and separateness perished.

M. When R. Ishmael b. Phiabi died, the splendor of the priesthood came to an end.

N. When Rabbi died, modesty and fear of sin came to an end.

O. R. Pinhas b. Yair says, "When the Temple was destroyed, associates became ashamed and so did free men, and they covered their heads.

P. "And wonderworkers became feeble. And violent men and big talkers grew strong.

Q. "And none expounds and none seeks [learning] and none asks.

I R. "Upon whom shall we depend? Upon our Father in heaven."

S. R. Eliezer the Great says, "From the day on which the Temple was destroyed, sages began to be like scribes, and scribes like ministers, and ministers like ordinary folk.

T. "And the ordinary folk have become feeble.

U. "And none seeks.

II V. "Upon whom shall we depend? Upon our Father in heaven."

W. With the footprints of the Messiah: presumption increases, and dearth increases.

X. The vine gives its fruit and wine at great cost.

Y. And the government turns to heresy.

Z. And there is no reproof.

AA. The gathering place will be for prostitution.

BB. And Galilee will be laid waste.

CC. And the Gablan will be made desolate.

DD. And the men of the frontier will go about from town to town, and none will take pity on them.

EE. And the wisdom of scribes will putrefy.

FF. And those who fear sin will be rejected.

GG. And the truth will be locked away.

HH. Children will shame elders, and elders will stand up before children.

II. *For the son dishonors the father and the daughter rises up against her mother, the daughter-in-law against her mother-in-law; a man's enemies are the men of his own house* [Mic. 7:6].

JJ. The face of the generation in the face of a dog.
KK. A son is not ashamed before his father.
III   LL. Upon whom shall we depend? Upon our Father in heaven.
MM. Pinhas b. Yair says, "Heedfulness leads to [hygienic] cleanliness, [hygienic] cleanliness leads to [cultic] cleanness, [cultic] cleanness leads to abstinence, abstinence leads to holiness, holiness leads to modesty, modesty leads to the fear of sin, the fear of sin leads to piety, piety leads to the Holy Spirit, the Holy Spirit leads to the resurrection of the dead, and the resurrection of the dead comes through Elijah, blessed be his memory. Amen."

This is a long and rather complex construction. Concluding the tractate, it is located after a legal passage on the topic of murder. I see the following large, freestanding units: (1) M. Sot. 9:9–12, on the gradual cessation of various rites, with an insertion at M. Sot. 9:10 and an addition at M. Sot. 9:13; (2) M. Sot. 9:14, a triplet appropriately inserted; (3) the melancholy list about how the deaths of various great sages form a counterpart to the decline in the supernatural life of Israel, M. 9:15A–N, presenting a rabbinic counterpart to the cultic construction at the outset; (4) M. 9:15O–MM is diverse, but the main beam—the phrase, "Upon whom shall we depend? Upon our Father in heaven"—does appear. It appears to me that M. 9:15O–R form the bridge, since the theme of the foregoing, the decline of the age marked by the decay of the virtue associated with sages, is carried forward, while the key phrase in what is to follow is introduced. W–LL then go over the matter yet again.

The Messiah, we notice, occurs rather incidentally and tangentially at M. 9:15W. The important statement is at M. 9:15MM, where Pinhas b. Yair accounts for the steps toward the end of time. The important fact is that the Messiah does *not* mark off a rung. Instead Pinhas lays emphasis upon personal virtues, the very virtues anyone may master if he keeps the law of the Mishnah, with its interest in particular in cultic cleanness, on the one side, and holiness on the other. The virtue of each person governs the passage to the resurrection of the dead; everyone is supposed to be modest, fear sin, and attain piety. All then are candidates, as potential sages, to receive the Holy Spirit. If the Mishnah's pages contain a view of history and a statement of the teleology of the law, it is in this brief statement of Pinhas, and here alone.

Elijah's insertion as herald of the resurrection of the dead, of course, draws upon the well-known biblical allusion at Mal. 4:5, "Behold, I will send you Elijah the prophet before the great and terrible day of the Lord comes." The Mishnah's authors refer to Elijah as the forerunner of the end at M. Sheq. 2:5, M. B.M. 1:8, 2:8, 3:4–5. His task is to settle various disputed questions, in particular involving genealogy (M. Ed. 8:7). Allusion to Elijah here follows what again is a routine convention, established in Scripture, and in no way proposes a revision of it. For the philosophers of the Mishnah the Messiah figure presents no rich resource of myth or symbol. The Messiah forms part of the inherited, but essentially undifferentiated, background of factual materials. The figure is neither to be neglected nor to be exploited.

We therefore hardly find astonishing the failure of the Mishnah's lawyers to pay attention to the possibility of a false Messiah, nor do we even know what sort of Messiah would fall into that classification. The main concern expressed in the law on people who might mislead Israel focuses upon false prophets (M. San. 11:1B, 5) and blasphemers (M. San. 7:2). The principal concern is that people of this sort pose the danger of incitement to idolatry.

Accordingly, the figure of a Messiah at the end of time, coming to save Israel from whatever Israel needs to be saved, plays a negligible role in the Mishnah's discourse. It follows that fear of the wrong sort of Messiah likewise scarcely comes to the surface. Whether, at M. San. 7:2ff., idolatry or blasphemy in general served to encompass people who might falsely claim to inaugurate the end of time or to do the work of eschatological forgiveness of sins and the ultimate salvation of Israel, no one can say. It seems unlikely.

In all, the Messiah in the Mishnah does not stand at the forefront of the framers' consciousness. The issues encapsulated in the myth and person of the Messiah are scarcely addressed. The framers of the Mishnah do not resort to speculation about the Messiah as a historical-supernatural figure. So far as that kind of speculation provides the vehicle for reflection on salvific issues, or in mythic terms, narratives on the meaning of history and the destiny of Israel, we cannot say that the Mishnah's philosophers take up those encompassing categories of being: Where are we heading? What can we do about it? That does not mean questions found urgent in the aftermath of the destruction of the Temple and the disaster of Bar Kokhba failed to attract the attention of the Mishnah's sages. But they treated history in a different way, offering their own answers to its questions. To these we now turn.

THE USES AND MEANING OF HISTORY
IN THE MISHNAH

By "history" I mean not merely events, but how events serve to teach lessons, reveal patterns, tell us what we must do and what will happen to us tomorrow. In that context, some events contain richer lessons than others; the destruction of the Temple of Jerusalem teaches more than a crop failure, being kidnapped into slavery more than stubbing one's toe. Furthermore, lessons taught by events— "history" in the didactic sense—follow a progression from trivial and private to consequential and public. The framers of the Mishnah explicitly refer to very few events, treating those they do mention with a focus quite separate from the unfolding events themselves. They rarely create narratives; historical events do not supply organizing categories or taxonomic classifications. We find no tractate devoted to the destruction of the Temple, no complete chapter detailing the events of Bar Kokhba nor even a sustained celebration of the events of the sages' own historical lives. When things that have happened are mentioned, it is neither to narrate nor to interpret and draw lessons from the events. It is either to illustrate a point of law or to pose a problem of the law—always *en passant,* never in a pointed way.

So when sages refer to what has happened, this is casual and tangential to the main discourse. For example, the "men slain at Tel Arza" (by the Romans?) come under discussion only because we have to decide whether they are to be declared legally dead so their wives may remarry (M. Yeb. 16:7). The advent of Gentiles to Jerusalem (in 70?) raises the question whether we assume a priest's wife has been raped (M. Ket. 2:9). A war begins—not named, not important—only because of a queen's vow, taken when her son goes off "to war" (M. Naz. 4:1). Famous events, such as the return to Zion from Babylonia in the time of Ezra and Nehemiah, gain entry into the Mishnah's discourse only because of the genealogical divisions of Israelite society into castes among the immigrants (M. Qid. 4:1).

Where the Mishnah provides little tales or narratives, moreover, these more often treat how things in the cult are done in general than what, in particular, happened on some one day. For instance, there is the tale of the burning of the red cow (M. Par. chapter 3) or of the purification of the *meṣora* of Lev. 13:2ff. (M. Neg. chapter 14). The names of Temple officers are cataloged (M. Sheq. 51:1). But we learn no more about them than the jobs to which they were assigned. Allusions to famous events even within sages' own circles do not demand detailed narration (as at M. Kel. 5:10). It is sufficient to refer casually to well-known incidents. Narrative, in the Mishnah's limited rhetorical repertoire, is reserved for the narrow framework of what priests and others do on recurrent occasions and around the Temple. In all, that staple of history, stories about dramatic events and important deeds, provides little nourishment in the minds of the Mishnah's jurisprudents. Events, if they appear at all, are treated as trivial. They may be well known, but are consequential in some way other than is revealed in the detailed account of what actually happened.

The sages' treatment of events, as we shall now see in detail, determines what in the Mishnah is important *about* what happens. Since the greatest event in the century and a half (ca. A.D. 50 to ca. 200) in which the Mishnah's materials came into being was the destruction of the Temple in 70, we must expect the Mishnah's treatment of that incident to illustrate the document's larger theory of history. The treatment of the destruction occurs in two ways.

First, the destruction of the Temple constitutes a noteworthy fact in the history of the law. Why? Because various laws about rite and cult had to undergo revision on account of the destruction. The following provides a stunningly apt example of how the Mishnah's philosophers regard what actually happened as being simply changes in the law:

M. ROSH HASHANAH 4:1-4

4:1 A. On the festival day of the New Year which coincided with the Sabbath,

B. in the Temple they would sound the *shofar*.

C. But not in the provinces.

D. When the Temple was destroyed, Rabban Yohanan ben Zakkai made the rule that they should sound the *shofar* in every locale in which there was a court.

E. Said R. Eleazar, "Rabban Yohanan b. Zakkai made that rule in the case of Yabneh alone."

F. They said to him, "All the same are Yabneh and every locale in which there is a court."

4:2 A. And in this regard also was Jerusalem ahead of Yabneh:

B. in every town which is within sight and sound [of Jerusalem], and nearby and able to come to Jerusalem, they sound the *shofar*.

C. But as to Yabneh, they sound the *shofar* only in the court alone.

4:3 A. In olden times the *lulab* was taken up in the Temple for seven days, and in the provinces for one day.

B. When the Temple was destroyed, Rabban Yohanan ben Zakkai made the rule that in the provinces the *lulab* should be taken up for seven days, as a memorial to the Temple;

C. and that the day [the sixteenth of Nisan] on which the *omer* is waved should be wholly prohibited [in regard to the eating of new produce] [M. Suk. 3:12].

4:4 A. At first they would receive testimony about the new moon all day long.

B. One time the witnesses came late, and the Levites consequently were mixed up as to [what] song [they should sing].

C. They made the rule that they should receive testimony [about the new moon] only up to the afternoon offering.

D. Then, if witnesses came after the afternoon offering, they would treat that entire day as holy, and the next day as holy too.

E. When the Temple was destroyed, Rabban Yohanan b. Zakkai made the rule that they should [once more] receive testimony about the new moon all day long.

F. Said R. Joshua b. Qorha, "This rule too did Rabban Yohanan b. Zakkai make:

G. "Even if the head of the court is located somewhere else, the witnesses should come only to the location of the council [to give testimony, and not to the location of the head of the court]."

The passages before us leave no doubt about what sages thought was important about the destruction: it produced changes in synagogue rites.

Second, although the sages surely mourned for the destruction and the loss of Israel's principal mode of worship, and certainly recorded the event of the ninth of Ab in the year A.D. 70, they did so in their characteristic way. They listed the event as an item in a catalog of things that are like one another and so demand the same response. But then the destruction no longer appears as a unique event. It is absorbed into a pattern of like disasters, all exhibiting similar taxonomic traits, events to which the people, now well-schooled in tragedy, well know the appropriate response. So it is in demonstrating regularity that sages reveal their way of coping. Then the uniqueness of the event fades away; its mundane character is emphasized. The power of taxonomy in imposing order upon chaos once more does its healing work. The consequence was the reassurance that historical events obeyed discoverable laws. Israel's ongoing life would override disruptive, one-time happenings. So catalogs of events, as much as lists of species of melons, served a brilliant apologetic by providing reassurance that nothing lies beyond the range and power of an ordering system and stabilizing pattern.

M. TAANIT 4:6-7

4:6 A. Five events took place for our fathers on the seventeenth of Tammuz, and five on the ninth of Ab.

B. On the seventeenth of Tammuz the tablets [or the Torah] were broken, the daily whole offering was canceled, the city wall was breached, Apostemos burned the Torah, and he set up an idol in the Temple.

C. On the ninth of Ab the decree was made against our forefathers that they should not enter the land, the first Temple was destroyed, then also the second, Betar was taken, and the city was plowed up [after the war of Hadrian].

D. When Ab comes, rejoicing diminishes.

4:7 A. In the week in which the ninth of Ab occurs it is prohibited to get a haircut and to wash one's clothes.

B. But on Thursday of that week these are permitted,

C. because of the honor due the Sabbath.

D. On the eve of the ninth of Ab a person should not eat two prepared dishes, nor should one eat meat or drink wine.

E. Rabban Simeon b. Gamaliel says, "He should make some change from ordinary procedures."

F. R. Judah declares people obligated to turn over beds.

G. But sages did not concur with him.

I include M. Taanit 4:7 to show the context of M. 4:6. The stunning calamities catalogued at M. 4:6 form groups, reveal common traits, and so are subject to classification. Then the laws of M. 4:7 provide regular rules for responding to and coping with these untimely catastrophes, all in a single classification. So the raw material of history is absorbed into the ahistorical, supernatural system of the Mishnah. The process of absorption and regularization of the unique and one-time moment is illustrated in the passage at hand.

Along these same lines, the entire history of the cult, so critical in the larger system created by the Mishnah's lawyers, produced a patterned, and therefore sensible and intelligible, picture. As is clear, everything that happened turned out to be susceptible of classification once the taxonomic traits were specified. A monothetic exercise, sorting out periods and their characteristics, took the place of narrative, to explain things in its own way: first this, then that, and, in consequence, the other. So in the neutral turf of holy ground, as much as in the trembling earth of the Temple mount, everything was absorbed into one thing, all classified in its proper place and by its appropriate rule. Indeed, so far as the lawyers proposed to write history at all, they wrote it into their picture of the long tale of the way in which Israel served God: the places in which the sacrificial labor was carried on, the people who did it, the places in which the priests ate the meat left over for their portion after God's portion was set aside and burned up. This "historical" account forthwith generated precisely that problem of locating the regular and orderly, which the philosophers loved to investigate: the intersection of conflicting but equally correct taxonomic rules, as we see at M. Zeb. 14:9, below. The passage that follows therefore is history, so far as the Mishnah's creators proposed to write history, that is, to reduce events to rules forming compositions of regularity.

M. ZEBAHIM 14:4–9

14:4 I   A. Before the tabernacle was set up, the high places were permitted, and [the sacrificial] service [was done by] the first born [Num. 3:12–13, 8:16–18].

B. When the tabernacle was set up, the high places were prohibited, and the [sacrificial] service [was done by] priests.

C. Most Holy Things were eaten within the veils; Lesser Holy Things [were eaten] throughout the camp of Israel.

14:5 II A. They came to Gilgal.

B. The high places were permitted.

C. Most Holy Things were eaten within the veils, Lesser Holy Things, anywhere.

14:6 III A. They came to Shiloh.

B. The high places were prohibited.

C. There was no roof beam there, but below was a house of stone, and hangings above it, and it was *"the resting place"* [Deut. 12:9].

D. Most Holy Things were eaten within the veils, Lesser Holy Things and second tithe [were eaten] in any place within sight [of Shiloh].

14:7 IV A. They came to Nob and Gibeon.

B. The high places were permitted.

C. Most Holy Things were eaten within the veils, Lesser Holy Things, in all the towns of Israel.

14:8 V A. They came to Jerusalem.

B. The high places were prohibited.

C. And they never again were permitted.

D. And it was *"the inheritance"* [Deut. 12:9].

E. Most Holy Things were eaten within the veils, Lesser Holy Things and second tithe within the wall.

14:9 A. All the Holy Things which one sanctified at the time of the prohibition of the high places and offered at the time of the prohibition of high places outside—

B. lo, these are subject to the transgression of a positive commandment and a negative commandment, and they are liable on their account to extirpation [for sacrificing outside the designated place, Lev. 17:8–9, M. Zeb. 13:1A].

C. [If] one sanctified them at the time of the permission of high places and offered them up at the time of the prohibition of high places,

D. lo, these are subject to transgression of a positive commandment and to a negative commandment, but they are not liable on their account to extirpation [since if the offerings had been sacrificed when they were sanctified, there should have been no violation].

E. [If] one sanctified them at the time of the prohibition

of high places and offered them up at the time of the permission of high places,

    F. lo, these are subject to transgression of a positive commandment, but they are not subject to a negative commandment at all.

The inclusion of M. Zeb. 14:9, structurally matching M. Ta. 4:7, shows us the goal of the historical composition. It is to set forth rules that intersect and produce confusion, so that we may sort out confusion and make sense of all the data. To see M. Zeb. in context, we have to return to the passage of M. Sot. discussed above (pp. 26–31.

History as a composition of successive, internally symmetrical patterns provides one model for lawyers proposing to relate Israel's life in time. A second historical picture has already passed before us, in which sages propose a pattern of events, the one at M. Sot. 9:9–15. What is striking in that passage is that, when sages define the patterns of history, they scarcely speak about events— things that actually happen at some one time and bear deep meaning.

M. Sot. 9:15 expresses a view of history that we may represent as a V, a long downward progression followed by an upward ascent. The descent is marked, as we noticed, by the successive nullification of rites of the cult, by the disappearance of marks of supernatural favor to Israel. The destruction represents the climax, as well it should. At that point, the "faithful men" also come to an end. The cult's end then marks the beginning, also, of the loss of holy sages. These are not messiahs; their virtue is sagacity. The long path downward ends with the climactic assertion, three times, that Israel must depend upon the heavenly father. To this picture the Messiah is at best incidental. The upward side of the V is then traced in steps of priests' and sages' virtues, things people can do which at the end will lead to the Holy Spirit and the resurrection of the dead. To all of this, the Messiah is again incidental; the omission becomes striking when we learn that Elijah, not the Messiah, will restore the dead to life.

Now on the basis of this passage, we may posit the existence of a generally prevailing theory of the Messiah's coming. That theory was accepted by the framers of this passage. But they restated it in terms of what is particular and distinctive to their points of systemic insistence. Accordingly, we may surmise that Jews in general believed in the coming of a Messiah, and in the resurrection of the dead, which was somehow related to that advent. They further believed that the "footprints of the Messiah" would mark a path through deepening darkness and decay, a world so miserable that only supernatural intervention could save it. But in the Mishnah that conviction—a commonplace in Israel's life—is reworked in terms of the definitive values of the framers of the passage, the sages' group. In particular, in references to the wisdom of scribes and fear of sin, not to mention the absence of respect for elders and fathers so characteristic of this group, we see the marks of their distinctive set of values. To others it may have been a mere detail; to the framer of this passage it indicated the crux of the matter.

That Pinhas's saying at M. Sot. 9:15 also bespeaks a priestly conception is clear from the reference to cultic cleanness as a precondition of holiness. The mixture of virtues is confusing, since the insertion of abstinence, modesty, and fear of sin (which are surely this-worldly social virtues) ranks well above the surely supernatural stage of holiness. Perhaps the meaning is that the cultic values lead to social virtues, with holiness as a stage upward from cultic cleanness, leading onward to the still-higher levels of modesty, piety, and fear of sin. There can be no doubt that Pinhas's saying presents an upward aiming list, not merely a catalogue of things roughly equivalent to one another. But the saying bears no polemic against "ritual" as opposed to social virtues; the distinction between the two is intrinsic. Since the contrast is not drawn, it therefore probably was not perceived as invidious

If the Mishnah's theory of history omits all reference to things that happen only once and thus fall into no familiar pattern, then we should find a complementary trait when people compose prayers: equal disinterest in political events. If, for example, the destruction of the Temple and its rebuilding were to dominate in the construction of the Mishnah's system for the Israelite world, prayers for the restoration should appear (as they do in the Prayerbook). The yearnings of the people, as portrayed in prayers written for them in the Mishnah's pages, should turn to the ruins, speak of what had once happened there and of how, in time to come, God would once more be served where Israel had performed its sacred service. Now, there are a few passages in the Mishnah in which sages project onto the people at large the things for which they should pray, on the one side, or express a blessing in thanksgiving, on the other. In the first of the two passages that follow, we have a commentary and expansion of Deut. 26:13ff., the prayer prescribed for farmers upon delivering to the Temple the required agricultural produce. The prayer pertains wholly to the natural world of home and farm:

M. MAASER SHENI 5:13

A. *Look down from your holy dwelling place in heaven* [Deut. 26:15].
B. We did what you required of us, now do you what you promised us.
C. *Look down from your holy dwelling place in heaven and bless your people Israel*
D. with sons and daughters.
E. *And the earth which you gave us*
F. with dew and rain and with offspring of cattle.
G. *As you vowed to our fathers [to give them] a land flowing with milk and honey*
H. in order to give the fruit a [sweet] taste.

The Mishnah's exegesis of the passage makes no effort to place the farmer's prayer in a temporal context. The prevailing pretense that things are as they always were accounts for the passage at hand. The Mishnah encompasses vast constructions on the Temple, how it is built and maintained, how its personnel are fed, how its cult is carried on, both on special occasions and on ordinary days, and how the entire cultic world is protected from the dangers of levitical uncleanness. In that context the present prayer presents no surprises. But after 70, it is quite irrelevant to what people had on their minds.

Indeed, the whole is surprising, since, as we must always keep in mind, when the document was drawn up there was no Temple, nor any prospect of its restoration in the immediate future. True, through a supererogatory act of imagination, the intent may have been to overcome "history," that is, in this setting, the destruction of the Temple. The composition of the imaginary (and perhaps, in times past, real) rules may have served the purpose of doing, for the interim, all that could be done. In context, we may wish to read a messianic-eschatological teleology into the large-scale enterprise, and so regard the whole as a response, at the most profound level, to events, that is, to history. So it now appears. But the Mishnah's framers never breathed a word about this meaning that seems so obvious to us. Even when, as in the farmer's prayer, they have a ripe opportunity to refer to something that actually has happened, they refrain from doing so. The imaginary farmer brings his invisible crops to a Temple of the mind's eye, and is told to pray as if the world were as it should be. Surely this adds up not to history but also not to antihistory. We do not have a massive denial that anything that has happened matters much—or even has really happened. Rather, we have another kind of history, as I shall explain in a moment.

That fact is underlined in the Mishnah's prescriptions of special blessings for important occasions. As we shall now see, these pertain to patterns of life in the enduring realms of nature and supernature, but never to one-time events of history. So, we notice, no blessing is prescribed to say when people greet the face of the Messiah. All of the events detailed in these blessings derive from the natural world, on the one side, or from the supernatural on the other: natural occurrences such as lightning, thunder, and wind, and supernatural events such as the performance of an unspecified miracle, and the removal of idolatry from some locale in the Holy Land.

M. BERAKHOT 9:1–2

9:1 A. One who sees a place where miracles were performed for Israel says, "Blessed is he who performed miracles for our fathers in this place."
B. [One who sees] a place from which idolatry was removed says, "Blessed is he who removed idolatry from our land."

9:2 A. For meteors, earth tremors, lightning, thunder, and the winds, one says, "Blessed [is he] whose power [and might] fill the world."

The result may now be stated briefly. The Mishnah absorbs into its encompassing system all events, small and large. With them the sages accomplish what they accomplish in everything else: a vast labor of taxonomy, an immense construction of the order and rules governing the classification of everything on earth and in heaven. The disruptive character of history—one-time events of ineluctable significance—scarcely impresses the philosophers. They find no difficulty in showing that what appears unique and beyond classification has in fact happened before and so falls within the range of trustworthy rules and known procedures. Once history's components, one-time events, lose their distinctiveness, then history as a didactic intellectual construct, as a source of lessons and rules, also loses all pertinence.

So lessons and rules come from sorting things out and classifying them from the procedures and modes of thought of the philosopher seeking regularity. To this labor of taxonomy, the historian's way of selecting data and arranging them into patterns of meaning to teach lessons proves inconsequential. One-time events are not important. The world is composed of nature and supernature. The laws that count are those to be discovered in heaven and, in heaven's creation and counterpart, on earth. Keep those laws and things will work out. Break them, and the result is predictable: calamity of whatever sort will supervene in accordance with the rules. But just because it is predictable, a catastrophic happening testifies to what has always been and must always be, in accordance with reliable rules and within categories already discovered and well explained. That is why the lawyer-philosophers of the mid second century produced the Mishnah—to explain how things are. Within the framework of well-classified rules, there could be messiahs, but no single Messiah (in Christian theological terms: *Geschichte*, but no *Historie*).

Up to now I have contrasted "history" with "eternity," and framed matters in such a way that the Mishnah's system appears to have been ahistorical and anti-historical. Yet in fact the framers of the Mishnah recognized the past-ness of the past and hence, by definition, laid out a conception of the past that constitutes a historical doctrine. But it is a different conception from the familiar one. To express the difference, I point out that, for modern history-writing, what is important is to describe what is unique and individual, not what is ongoing and unremarkable. History is the story of change, development, movement, not of what does not change, develop, or move. For the thinkers of the Mishnah, historical patterning emerges through taxonomy, the classification of the unique and individual, the organization of change and movement within unchanging categories. That is why the dichotomy between history and eternity, change and permanence, signals an indefinite exegesis of what was, in fact, a subtle and reflective doctrine of history. That doctrine proves entirely consistent with the large perspectives of scribes, from the ones who made omen-series in ancient Babylonia to the ones who made the Mishnah. That is why the category of salvation does not serve, but the one of sanctification fits admirably.

DOCUMENTS OF SUCCESSION (I):
ABOT

If the end of time and the coming of the Messiah do not serve to explain, for the Mishnah's system, why people should do what the Mishnah says, then what alternative teleology does the Mishnah's first apologetic, Abot, provide? Only when we appreciate the clear answers given in that document, brought to closure at ca. 250, shall we grasp how remarkable is the shift, which took place in later documents of the rabbinic canon, to a messianic framing of the issues of the Torah's ultimate purpose and value. Let us see how the framers of Abot, in the aftermath of the creation of the Mishnah, explain the purpose and goal of the Mishnah: an ahistorical, non-messianic teleology.

The first document generated by the Mishnah's heirs took up the work of completing the Mishnah's system by answering questions of purpose and meaning. Whatever teleology the Mishnah *as such* would ever acquire would derive from Abot, a collection of sayings by authorities who flourished in the generation after Judah the Patriarch; in all likelihood the document is of the mid-third-century rabbinic estate of the Land of Israel. Abot presents statements to express the ethos and ethic of the Mishnah, and so provides a kind of theory. Abot's framers attained such remarkable success in their composition that it found its way into the Mishnah, though whether Abot formed part of the Mishnah in antiquity or attained that status only later is unclear. Abot bears no Tosefta or Talmud—that is, supplement, expansion, and systematic exposition—parallel to the Mishnah's Tosefta and its two Talmuds. So Abot's place and role in its own day remain mysterious to us.

But in our eyes the task of its redactors is blatant: to answer those questions of teleology ignored by Judah the Patriarch's generation in the Mishnah. These questions remained unanswered by the sixty-two tractates of the Mishnah that had emerged under Judah's auspices half a century before. Abot, the sixty-third and last tractate, would have to supply that omission. A large view of history, profound reflection on the meaning of the destruction of the Temple and its rebuilding, a definition of Israel's place in time and the end time, an explanation of why, with reference to the coming of the Messiah, people should now keep the law—so far as a teleology of the Mishnah based upon an essentially historical view of reality might emerge, it would have to come from Abot.

But Abot agreed with the other sixty-two tractates: history proved no more important here than it had been before. With scarcely a word about history and no account of events at all, Abot manages to provide an ample account of how the Torah—written and oral, thus in later eyes, Scripture and Mishnah—came down to its own day. Accordingly, the passage of time as such plays no role in the explanation of the origins of the document, nor is the Mishnah presented as eschatological. Occurrences of great weight ("history") are never invoked. How then does the tractate tell the story of Torah, narrate the history of God's revelation to Israel, encompassing both Scripture and Mishnah? The answer is that Abot's framers manage to do their work of explanation without telling a story or invoking history at all. They pursue a different way of answering the same question, by exploiting a non-historical mode of thought and method of legitimation. And that is the main point: teleology serves the purpose of legitimation, and hence is accomplished in ways other than explaining how things originated or assuming that historical fact explains anything.

We recall the enormous importance accorded by the priestly caste to the role of genealogy (another kind of history) in validating that caste's rights and authority. The genealogy of Torah (which sage begat which disciple), rather than the Torah's history (in any sense in which prophetic and apocalyptic writers would recognize history) forms the focus of the tractate's account and apologetic for the Mishnah. Since, we recall, the biblical storytellers always encapsulated the law in myths of events associated with revelation at Sinai, we cannot take for granted, or treat as predictable, this quite other approach to the same problem. That is to say, Abot contains no tales about how the Torah got going. The tractate tells only who received it and who handed it on. It thus gives us what I call the genealogy of Torah: how it was transmitted, like the holy seed of the priesthood, from one sage to the next. All of this is contained in the simple opening sentence of M. Abot 1:1A–B: "Moses received Torah at Sinai and handed it on to Joshua, Joshua to elders, elders to prophets, and prophets handed it on to the men of the great assembly."

Let us now take a closer look at this chain of transmission and see how, in form and substance, its authorities dispose of the possibility of historical explanation of the status and purpose of their document, this new Torah, this Mishnah. Specifically, what is it that the named sages in their sayings received and handed on? Whatever they received (let us assume it was the Torah), the sages are represented as actually having handed on sayings not found in the written Torah. Accordingly, the status and standing of these sayings are explained at the outset. What they received and handed on is in the status of Torah. The one before gave "Torah" (including the three sayings recorded for each sage). Then what the successor received, the Torah—including all the additions of those who came before, and what he handed on—is not quite the same. Why not? Because the newest sage adds his three sayings, too. Accordingly, what a sage in the Mishnah adds is joined to the Torah, and each link adds to the chain and becomes part of the chain as a whole. The point is that what masters or sages or teachers in the time of the Mishnah stated is asserted to form part of the Torah beginning at Sinai and extending onward through all time—a timeless world. The conclusion the writer wants to propose is that the Torah forms an unending chain of revelation, a seamless web of being, beyond time.

M. ABOT 1:1–18

1:1   A. Moses received Torah at Sinai and handed it on to Joshua, Joshua to elders, and elders to prophets.

I B. And prophets handed it on to the men of the great assembly.

C. They said three things:

(1) "Be prudent in judgment.

(2) "Raise up many disciples.

(3) "Make a fence for the Torah."

1:2 II A. Simeon the Righteous was one of the last survivors of the great assembly.

B. He would say: "On three things does the world stand:

(1) "On the Torah,

(2) "and on the Temple service,

(3) "and on deeds of loving kindness."

1:3   III   A. Antigonos of Sokho received [the Torah] from Simeon the Righteous.

            B. He would say,

                (1) "Do not be like servants who serve the master on condition of receiving a reward,

                (2) "but [be] like servants who serve the master not on condition of receiving a reward.

                (3) "And let the fear of Heaven be upon you."

1:4   I   A. Yose b. Yoezer of Seredah and Yose b. Yohanan of Jerusalem received [it] from them.

            B. Yose b. Yoezer says,

                (1) "Let your house be a gathering place for sages.

                (2) "And wallow in the dust of their feet.

                (3) "And drink in their words with gusto."

1:5   A. Yose b. Yohanan of Jerusalem says,

                (1) "Let your house be wide open.

                (2) "And seat the poor at your table ["make . . . members of your household"].

                (3) "And don't talk too much with women."

            B. (He spoke of a man's wife, all the more so is the rule to be applied to the wife of one's fellow. In this regard did sages say, "So long as a man talks too much with a woman, (1) he brings trouble on himself, (2) wastes time better spent on studying Torah, and (3) ends up an heir of Gehenna.")

1:6   II   A. Joshua b. Perahiah and Nittai the Arbelite received [it] from them.

            B. Joshua b. Perahiah says,

                (1) "Set up a master for yourself.

                (2) "And get yourself a fellow disciple.

                (3) "And give everybody the benefit of the doubt."

1:7   A. Nittai the Arbelite says,

                (1) "Keep away from a bad neighbor.

                (2) "And don't get involved with a bad man.

                (3) "And don't give up hope of retribution."

1:8   III   A. Judah b. Tabbai and Simeon b. Shatah received [it] from them.

            B. Judah b. Tabbai says,

                (1) "Don't make yourself like one of those who make advocacy before judges [while you yourself are judging a case].

                (2) "And when the litigants stand before you, regard them as guilty.

                (3) "And when they leave you, regard them as acquit-

ted (when they have accepted your judgment)."

1:9   A. Simeon b. Shatah says,

           (1) "Examine the witnesses with great care.

           (2) "and watch what you say,

           (3) "lest they learn from what you say how to lie."

1:10 IV A. Shemaiah and Abtalion received [it] from them.

       B. Shemaiah says,

           (1) "Love work.

           (2) "Hate authority.

           (3) "Don't get friendly with the government."

1:11   A. Abtalion says,

           (1) "Sages, watch what you say,

           "lest you become liable to the punishment of exile, and go into exile to a place of bad water, and disciples who follow you drink bad water and die, and the name of heaven be thereby profaned."

1:12 V   A. Hillel and Shammai received [it] from them.

       B. Hillel says,

           (1) "Be disciples of Aaron,

           (2) "loving peace and pursuing grace,

           (3) "loving people and drawing them near to the Torah."

1:13   A. He would say [in Aramaic],

           (1) "A name made great is a name destroyed.

           (2) "And one who does not add detracts.

           (3) "And who does not learn is liable to death.

           (4) "And the one who uses the crown passes away."

1:14   A. He would say,

           (1) "If I am not for myself, who is for me?

           (2) "And when I am for myself, what am I?

           (3) "And if not now, when?"

1:15   A. Shammai says,

           (1) "Make your learning of Torah a fixed obligation.

           (2) "Say little and do much.

           (3) "Greet everybody cheerfully."

1:16 I   A. Rabban Gamaliel says,

           (1) "Set up a master for yourself.

           (2) "Avoid doubt.

           (3) "Don't tithe by too much guesswork."

1:17 II A. Simeon his son says,

           (1) "All my life I grew up among the sages, and I found nothing better for a person [lit.: the body] than silence.

           (2) "And not the learning is the thing, but the doing.

(3) "And whoever talks too much causes sin."
1:18   III   A. Rabban Simeon b. Gamaliel says, "On three things does the world stand:
(1) "on justice,
(2) "on truth,
(3) "and on peace,
B. "as it is said, *Execute the judgment of truth and peace in your gates* [Zech. 8:16]."

There is one striking and recurrent pattern in the chapter as a whole: the use of the language "receive" and "hand on." Moses "received" and "handed on" Torah, and so did the prophets; Antigonos "received"; the several pairs "received." So the principal thing sages do is "*receive* Torah," on the one side, and *say* three things on the other. We are not told whether the things the sages say form part of the Torah they received, or whether these things constitute their contribution to the Torah. Accordingly, we cannot know the status of the three sayings assigned to each authority. But we do know the purpose of the chapter as a whole. It is to tell us how the Torah came from Sinai to the sages of the Mishnah. For the figures mentioned at the end, from Hillel onward, were well known. They were in fact the masters and teachers of the Mishnah authorities.

The real intent of the maker of this list, therefore, is to say that what the Mishnah's authorities learned from Hillel and Shammai, Gamaliel and Simeon ben Gamaliel, is part of the Torah received by Moses at Sinai and handed on from that time to their day. Since that is the fact, the conclusion to be drawn is that history is framed in taxonomic terms. How so? The chain of tradition recognizes no one-time events that differentiate one period from another except in the Torah. All sages therefore live within the same period. That period is not marked by what happens out there in the world of politics, wars, and upheavals. What matters is within the frame and web of Israel's true life, that is, beyond history. The authors do not merely ignore history. They establish an altogether different frame of reference from that indicated by successive events. Meaning emerges from another source (revelation), which was available equally to all sages through the genealogy of Torah transmission, a process unaffected by and unconcerned with the issue of events and the interpretation of their meaning. That then forms the foundation for the statements of purpose and ultimate goal assigned to "the Torah" and, in the present context, to the Mishnah's other sixty-two tractates. What is the substance of the matter?

To gain a glimpse at the proposed teleology for the Mishnah provided by this ahistorical system, we may rapidly classify the topics under discussion. What do the sages take as their center of interest? If we list the principal topics at hand, we find these:

1. teachings to sages and their disciples, to those who will be judges:

    Men of the great assembly (1:1C)
    Yose b. Yoezer (1:4)
    Joshua b. Perahiah (1:6)
    Judah b. Tabbai (1:8)
    Simeon b. Shatah (1:9)
    Abtalion (1:11)
    Shammai (1:15)
    Gamaliel (1:16)
    Simeon (1:17)

2. large and encompassing vision of the important things in the world:

    Simeon the Righteous (1:2)
    Simeon b. Gamaliel (1:18)

3. advice on how to serve God:

    Antigonos (1:3)

4. wise counsel on how to live the good life:

    Yose b. Yohanan (1:5)
    Nittai the Arbelite (1:7)
    Shemaiah (1:10)
    Hillel (1:12, 1:13, 1:14)

The chapter speaks to teachers, who are judges, and to their disciples. It tells them how to conduct their affairs. It also contains a fair amount of wisdom for other people. Only at the beginning and the end does it attend to matters we should call "religious." That is, we find only at those points a theory of what it means to be a human being created in the image of God, of how to see the world as the creation of God, and of how to love and serve God. Obviously, the people who composed this chapter did not make any distinction between the religious and the secular. Their assumption was that they spoke to a single, whole group. What we see, therefore, is a profession trying to frame a vision that would encompass the entire Jewish world.

In order to appreciate fully the contrast between what is to follow—the messianic mode of defining Israel's being and explaining things—and what is before us, let us dwell a little longer upon the substance of the matter. What in fact is this vision of being? To describe it, we turn to the sayings of the two Simeons. The sayings of the two Simeons coincide: (1) Torah, (2) Temple service, (3) deeds of loving kindness, against the triplet of (1) justice, (2) truth, (3) peace. The Torah in this context can only mean the entire revelation of God to Israel from Sinai, that is *torah*, including sayings of the sages. The Temple service in that age meant the worship of God through giving God the things God's holy land produced. This was done by casting into the flames of the altar the produce of the land: grain, meat, wine, and the like. That form of sharing, of giving part of God's gifts back to God, was obligatory. Simeon the Righteous therefore emphasizes that Israel builds the world through learning Torah, through doing duty to God, and through doing more than duty. The other Simeon, later on, phrases matters in more abstract language rather than referring to concrete things. The first Simeon speaks of the particular, the second, of the general; but they say the same thing.

The issue of teleology in the narrowest sense arises in the saying of Antigonos. It is in three clauses, but it says only two things which are really one. He sets up the contrast between doing things through hope of reward and doing things without hope for extrinsic compensation: to do something for its own sake, out of a sense of inner obligation, rather than for the sake of something else. In the one case we do our duty for the wrong reason; in the other, we do our duty for the right reason. One does one's duty out of awe and reverence for heaven. Service then must be for the right reason, which is, simply, recognition of who man is and who God is.

We observe, finally, that the system conveyed in the chain of tradition as a whole repeats in detail the main points of the triplet proposed by the two Simeons. At the center, we notice, are Hillel's sayings. A second glance at these will show us that Hillel, too, is assigned three sayings; but they are long and fully articulated, rather than just brief clauses or, at most, sentences assigned to others. He has a saying about the righteous priest and the right attitude toward people and Torah, then about Torah study, and finally about the true meaning of the moral and good life. What he has given, then, is a reworking of the themes of Simeon the Righteous, pertaining as they do to Temple service, Torah, and deeds of loving kindness. The same themes are before us, in somewhat revised order. Temple comes before Torah and leads to it, but the open-ended requirements of goodness remain as the climax of the whole.

Having dwelt on the way in which the Mishnah's first apologists explained the standing and authority of their document, hence how they expressed a teleology for its system, we now return to the main point. While the transmission of the Torah (including the Mishnah) took place in historical time, the main point is the Torah's genealogical pedigree: who handed the Torah to whom. The same chapter, inaugurating the mode of discourse of the document as a whole, further tells us sayings left behind in the names of cited authorities, extending from the men of the great assembly to the authors of the Mishnah itself. Accordingly, what the named sages did—their history-making deeds—plays no role; only their sayings do. Moreover, insofar as the sayings of Abot are constructed to correlate with the Mishnah, at the head of which Abot is supposed to stand, there is no effort to construct an explicit apologetic. The sayings in Abot in no way relate to other sayings of these same named authorities. The subject matter of Abot bears no resemblance to topics important in the other sixty-two tractates. There is, indeed, only a single point of contact between Abot and the rest of the Mishnah: the names of principal authorities, in particular those extending beyond the original chain of tradition (M. Abot 1:18). The chain of tradition ends with precisely those names the Mishnah knows in general as its earliest authorities: Hillel and Shammai, Gamaliel and his son Simeon.

How then is the Mishnah itself joined? The chain breaks off into a Y. One wing (M. Abot 2:8–14) is comprised of Yohanan ben Zakkai and his disciples late in the first century: the other (M. Abot 2:1) of Judah the Patriarch and his sons along with their third-century contemporaries. Now Yohanan's disciples included Eliezer and Joshua, the principal named authorities of the Mishnah period corresponding to the decades after the destruction of the Temple in A.D. 70. The relevance to the larger theory of the Mishnah in the naming of Judah the Patriarch and his sons and heirs hardly requires explanation. So, in all, the picture of the authority and standing imputed to the Mishnah by Abot is clear. The document's latest and most important authorities stand in a direct line to Sinai, to both patriarchs and sages alike.

What they say derives, therefore, from a chain of tradition equivalent in sanctity, strength, and solidity to the chain of genealogy of the priesthood. Just as the priests explain who they are and why people should listen to them, so the framers of the Mishnah explain who is in their book and why people should listen to those authorities. In both cases, what is omitted is clear: a hint or a trace of any claim to authority based upon things that have happened—the meaning and end of history.

When reference is made to history as presented by Scripture, it is abstracted from concrete events and, in fact, (predictably) turned into a list, e.g., "Ten generations from Adam to Noah, to show how long-suffering God is. . . ," and "Ten trials inflicted upon Abraham, our father . . . , to show you how great is His love for Abraham . . ." (M. Abot 5:2, 3). These sayings do not propose interpretations of history or draw conclusions based upon carefully examined events. They are compositions of another order entirely, monothetic taxonomy. Nor can we automatically treat the little liturgy tacked on at the end, in Judah b. Tema's name (M. Abot 5:20), as a messianic prayer: "May it be found pleasing . . . that you rebuild your city quickly in our day and set our portion in your Torah." The "you" here is God; the Messiah plays no role, so we can hardly treat Judah's prayer as an explicit plea for the coming of the Messiah.

As we shall now notice, the last judgment, moreover, is linked to the death of each individual. It is not represented as a world-historical event encompassing in one cataclysmic trial the whole of humanity. Moreover, if the Messiah is supposed to play a part in the sequence of events leading to the last judgment, the framers of Abot have never heard of it. So the issue is reduced to the fate of each individual, an enduring, existential fact, not a historical-eschatological one. When we consider how the last judgment figures in the teleology of Abot, the picture is clear.

M. ABOT 3:15–16, 4:16–17

3:15   I   A. [R. Aqiba says,] "Everything is foreseen, and free choice is given.

      II   B. "In goodness the world is judged.

III   C. "And all is in accord with the abundance of deed[s]."

3:16   A. He would say, "All is handed over as a pledge.

B. "And a net is cast over all the living.

C. "The store is open, the storekeeper gives credit, the account book is open, and the hand is writing.

D. "(1) Whoever wants to borrow may come and borrow.

E. "(2) The charity collectors go around every day and collect from a man whether he knows it or not.

F. "(3) And they have grounds for what they do.

G. "(4) And the judgment is a true judgment.

H. "(5) And everything is ready for the meal."

4:16   A. R. Jacob says, "This world is like an antechamber before the world to come.

B. "Get ready in the antechamber, so you can go into the great hall."

4:17   A. He would say, "Better is a single moment spent in penitence and good deeds in this world than the whole of the world to come.

B. "And better is a single moment of inner peace in the world to come than the whole of a lifetime spent in this world."

Neither saying takes up the large issues of interpreting events and the meaning and end of Israel's history. Indeed, the organizing category is not Israel as a nation and society, but the individual Israelite and his or her private fate. Aqiba emphasizes the exquisitely delicate balance maintained by each Jew, enjoying free choice, before a God who knows what will be, and likewise by Israel's experiencing God's deep love in full awareness that God rewards good and punishes evil. Jacob speaks to individuals who live and die, and who therefore need to be taught how to live so as to accept death when it comes. These are the critical questions. So, while Abot does present sayings that indicate beliefs about a last judgment (e.g., "Your employer can be depended upon to pay your wages for what you do, and know what sort of reward will be given to the righteous in the coming time" [M. Abot 2:16]), the view of Abot concerning the last judgment of the individual is distinct from a myth of the collective end of history and the coming of the Messiah. The "full account" will be given "before the King of kings of kings" (M. Abot 3:1). This is simply after death, and is not a setting for the last judgment faced by an individual in which the end of history and the coming of the Messiah enjoy any part whatever.

We see a correlation between the presence of the doctrine of history, on the one side, and the exploration of the image and myth of the Messiah on the other. The "if, then" construct is decisive. If matters are phrased in terms of, "If you do such and such, then so and so will (or will not) *happen*," inevitably in any system of Judaism, the Messiah will make his appearance. What, then, is the alternative to such a (to our eyes) systemically natural, mythic-eschatological mode of working out the critical issue of teleology? When we consider how the framers of Abot provide an equivalent component of their system as a whole for the sixty-two tractates before them, we see a different way. The program of sagacity and sanctification answers the same question dealt with in the messianic-salvific system of events pointing toward (or away from) salvation in time and at the end of time. The system that evokes the Messiah as savior (not as priest and only incidentally as a general) has its own teleology, as we shall see. Abot, on behalf of the Mishnah, deals with the matter of teleology too. But each frames and answers the question in a way distinctive to itself.

We may hardly be surprised, therefore, that the sayings in Abot, as much as those in the rest of the Mishnah, nowhere allude to the person of the Messiah, to when he will come, to the meaning of what happens beforehand, or to what we have to do to bring him. The fundamental issues addressed by mishnaic "Judaism" are simply not messianic. That explains why we find no attention given at all to the large questions of the meaning of history and of the destiny of Israel at this time or at any other.

DOCUMENTS OF SUCCESSION (II):
TOSEFTA

Closely associated with the Mishnah and completely dependent upon its organizational structure and rhetorical patterns, the Tosefta repeats the picture revealed by the Mishnah. That would not be surprising were it not for one fact. The Tosefta came to closure about two hundred years later than the Mishnah. Whatever else was happening, the circles responsible for the systematic exegesis, exposition, and supplement to the Mishnah provided by the Tosefta presented things much the same as the framers did in the Mishnah. If, therefore, within the rabbinical estate, new currents flowed and new issues stimulated new movement, the exegetes represented by the Tosefta did not use the Mishnah as the arena of fresh discourse.

We shall observe the same tendency in the Talmud of the Land of Israel. That is, where the exegetes of the Mishnah represented by that Talmud discuss the Mishnah's meaning in particular, they do not introduce issues or conceptions essentially at odds with the Mishnah. When, on the other hand, they construct units of discourse entirely autonomous of the Mishnah, they freely deal with whatever they wish, including in a substantial way the Messiah myth and other associated concepts of Israelite history.

So, while we witness some interesting developments in the Tosefta, we find no surprises. The Messiah proves no more important than before. Mere events do not rise to the level of a history interpreted and projected. Rather, noteworthy and distinctive events sink beneath the surface of an ahistorical framework. In that setting extraordinary happenings are made to seem ordinary and subject to orderly rules. So once again there is no Messiah and no doctrine of Israel's history and destiny. A Judaism which is centered on other things emerges from two hundred years of study of the Mishnah as revealed in the Tosefta.

We find in the Tosefta no tendency to introduce, into mishnaic contexts in which they otherwise are absent, the issues of the Messiah and the meaning and end of history. What we do find is a restatement and expansion of the Mishnah's handling of these matters. Since the Mishnah knows as anointed authorities the high priest and the high priest who leads the troops, the Tosefta repeats the same use of the adjective "anointed" and the noun "anointed one." T. Hor. 1:8O, for example, speaks of the anointed high priest who inadvertently commits idolatry and how the sin is expiated; the word "messiah" means the same at T. Hor. 2:3, 4 and T. Zeb. 10:2. "The Messiah" to the authors of the Tosefta is only a high priest who is consecrated for his office by being anointed in oil. That is the only meaning the noun with the definite article receives (cf. for example, T. Sheb. 1:6, 10; 2:4).

To be sure, just as, in a routine setting, the Mishnah knows about the "days of the Messiah" (M. Ber. 1:5, in the contrast to "the present age"), so the Tosefta goes over the same ground in covering the same passage (T. Ber. 1:10). There is a further reference to what will happen to the nations in the time of the Messiah (T. Ta. 3:1). The allusion to addition of an eighth string to the seven strings of the harp (T. Ar. 2:7B) in the time of the Messiah, with three more (ten strings in all) "in the future which is coming," suggests that the days of the Messiah form a differentiated interim period, between this age and the age to come. But nothing is made of the matter, which is treated as an established fact not requiring further amplification.

The eschatological theory associated with "the world to come" remained essentially indifferent to the matter of the coming of the Messiah. That is hardly surprising, considering the priestly use which both the Mishnah's and the Tosefta's authorities make of "*the* Messiah." When the Mishnah catalogues those who may or may not enjoy a "portion in the world to come" (M. San. 10:1F), the complement of the Tosefta serves to augment and clarify what the Mishnah states (T. San. 12:9–11, 13:1–5). Various kinds of sinners as well as those who attacked and destroyed the Temple of Jerusalem will remain in Gehenna without hope of redemption. In all of this, the Messiah in the sense of redeemer and savior plays no part whatsoever.

T. SANHEDRIN 13:5

A. But heretics, apostates, traitors, Epicureans, those who deny the Torah, those who separate from the ways of the community, those who deny the resurrection of the dead, and whoever both sinned and caused the public to sin,

B. for example, Jeroboam and Ahab,

C. and those who sent their arrows against the land of the living and stretched out their hands against the "lofty habitation" [the Temple],

D. Gehenna is locked behind them, and they are judged therein for all generations,

E. since it is said, *And they shall go forth and look at the corpses of the men who were transgressors against me. For their worm dies not, and their fire is not quenched. And they shall be an abhorring unto all flesh* [Isa. 66:24].

F. Sheol will waste away, but they will not waste away,

G. for it is written, *and their form shall cause Sheol to waste away* [Ps. 49:14].

55

H. What made this happen to them? Because they stretched out their hand against the "lofty habitation" [the Temple].

We see yet elsewhere this same tendency to leave untouched the opportunities that might have invited exegesis in terms of the time or circumstance of the coming of the Messiah. In a striking instance, when there *is* reference to the possibility of miraculously obtaining permission to rebuild the Temple (T. Pisha 8:4), the passage in no way resorts to the messianic myth in order to express the course of such an event. So it is entirely possible to speak even about the restoration of the cult without invoking the messianic myth. The established liturgy of the synagogue, we shall note in due course, hardly concedes that possibility.

Along these same lines, several passages explicitly refer to the rebuilding of Jerusalem and of the Temple. None of them alludes to any role whatsoever for the Messiah, nor is there a prayer that he will come and do these things.

T. BABA BATRA 2:17

2:17   E. A man may plaster his entire house with plaster,
F. but he leaves a small bit unplastered as a memorial to Jerusalem.
G. A woman puts on all her makeup but leaves off some small thing as a memorial to Jerusalem,
H. since it is said, *If I forget you, O Jerusalem, let my right hand wither! Let my tongue cleave to the roof of my mouth, if I do not remember you, if I do not set Jerusalem above my highest joy!* [Ps. 137:5–6].
I. Whoever mourns for Jerusalem in this world will rejoice in her in the world to come,
J. since it says, *Rejoice with Jerusalem and be glad for her, all you who love her; rejoice with her in joy, all you who mourn over her* [Isa. 66:10].

T. MENAHOT 13:22–23

13:22   A. Said R. Yohanan b. Torta, "On what account was Shiloh destroyed? Because of the disgraceful disposition of the Holy Things which were there.
B. "As to Jerusalem's first building, on what account was it de-

stroyed? Because of idolatry and licentiousness and bloodshed which was in it.

C. "But [as to] the latter [building] we know that they devoted themselves to Torah and were meticulous about tithes.

D. "On what account did they go into exile? Because they loved money and hated one another.

E. "This teaches you that hatred of one for another is evil before the Omnipresent, and Scripture deems it equivalent to idolatry, licentiousness, and bloodshed."

13:23 A. But as to the final building which is destined to be built —may it be in our lifetime and in our days!—what is stated?

B. *And it shall come to pass in the latter days that the mountains of the house of the Lord shall be established as the highest of the mountains, and shall be raised above the hills; and all the nations shall flow to it, and many people shall come and say, "Come, let us go up to the mountain of the Lord, to the house of the God of Jacob"* [Isa. 2:2–3].

C. *For there shall be a day when watchmen will call in the hill country of Ephraim: "Arise, and let us go up to Zion our God"* [Jer. 31:6].

None of these passages, we see, alludes to the Messiah when treating the restoration of the Temple and recovery of the holy city. That is not to suggest that the framers of the Tosefta had never heard of the Messiah, the days of the Messiah, or the rule of the Messiah. The rule of the house of David is going to be forever: "David and Solomon were anointed from a horn, because their dominion is an eternal dominion" (T. San. 4:9J). Accordingly, people knew the commonplace fact that the Messiah would come and rule Israel. That makes all the more striking the failure of the framers of the passages at hand to resort to the myth at a point at which, in time to come or elsewhere in their own day, it would be entirely conventional to do so. We may say with some confidence that the philosophers of the Tosefta did *not* regard as an essentially messianic exercise the vast stretches of mishnaic law about the Temple and its cult. These laws do not describe, especially when the Messiah comes, how things would be done. On the contrary, we see that it is entirely feasible to discuss the restoration of the cult and rebuilding of Jerusalem without making reference to the issue of the Messiah at all, even though people regarded these events as marking the end of history as it then was known—in "the age to come."

In complementing the Mishnah's blessings for special occasions, the Tosefta's framers supply further items deriving from the natural world on the one side and the supernatural on the other, omitting all reference to blessings, one may say when dealing with events of historical or messianic character. The pertinent passage is as follows:

T. BERAKHOT 6:3–6
(TRANSLATED BY TZVEE ZAHAVY)

6:3   A. He who sees a Negro, or an albino, or [a man] red-spotted in the face [*gyhwr*, Jastrow], or [a man] white-spotted in the face [a man afflicted with psoriasis, or elephantiasis], or a hunchback, or a dwarf [E, *ed. princ.* omit: or a deaf man, or an imbecile, or a drunk] says, "Blessed . . . [is he] who varies creatures [viz., who creates such varied creatures]."

B. [He who sees] an amputee, a lame man, a blind man, or a man afflicted with boils, says, "Blessed be the true judge" [cf. M. Ber. 9:2].

6:4   A. One who sees handsome people or handsome trees says, "Blessed be He who has [created] such handsome creatures."

6:5   A. One who sees the rainbow in the cloud says, "Blessed . . . who is faithful to his covenant, who remembers the covenant."

6:6   A. One who was walking in a path between graves says, "Blessed . . . who knows the number of you. He will judge and he will raise you to judgment. Blessed . . . whose word is trustworthy, who resurrects the dead."

B. One who sees the sun, or the moon, or the stars, or the constellations says, "Blessed . . . who made creation."

C. R. Judah says, "One who recites a blessing for the sun, behold this is heresy" [cf. T. Ber. 6:20].

D. And so R. Judah would say, "He who sees the sea regularly, and something about it has changed, must recite [a blessing]" [cf. M. Ber. 9:2].

What we see, therefore, is that the framers of Tosefta stay well within the boundaries established by the Mishnah. Where the Mishnah's passage makes no reference to the Messiah or to other important historical events, the Tosefta's counterpart adds none.

When we turn to the Tosefta's doctrine of Israel's history and destiny, we find, once again, that our question is hardly symmetrical to the Tosefta's answers. Just as the Mishnah's philosophers drew into their own system and treated as commonplace and as subject to law what to historical minds appear as one-time and perplexing events, so do the Tosefta's exegetes of the Mishnah. Where the opportunity exists to treat as historically suggestive a passage provided by the Mishnah, the Tosefta's authors do nothing of the kind. Indeed, we may point to the very opposite, to a rejected opportunity to treat a passage in a historical and messianic setting. In the following explicit reworking of a familiar passage, the Tosefta's seers provide a chronology. The construction absolutely demands one more step: the date of the end. But then the authors do not tell us when time will end or when the final Temple will be built! Accordingly, the occasion is not only lost; it is avoided. That is why the passage at hand, commenting on M. Zeb. 14:4–8, is not materially revised into a more suggestive picture of history than the Mishnah had provided to begin with.

T. ZEBAHIM 13:6

A. The days of the tent of meeting which was in the wilderness were forty [years] less one,
  and in Gilgal, fourteen years,
  and in Shiloh, three hundred and seventy years less one,
  and in Nob and Gibeon, fifty-seven.
B. In the Eternal House, four hundred and ten years from the time that it was built the first time, four hundred and twenty years from the time that it was built the last time.

What we find particularly striking in this passage is that the occasion clearly arises here for calculating the end time, when the Messiah will come. Yet the framers of the Tosefta's complement do not use the opportunity to treat as a messianic and eschatological discourse what is an open invitation for just that kind of inquiry. In all, therefore, those responsible for the formation and arrangement of materials in the Tosefta stayed well within the narrow conceptual framework of the document upon which they proposed to comment.

We must not suppose that to the compositors of the Tosefta, events in history proved utterly useless. Quite to the contrary, they made numerous references to things that had happened. Some of these things are exemplary, but private, events in the life of sages.

Others serve as precedents in the study of the law. Both kinds of stories prove far more numerous in the Tosefta than in the Mishnah. Where the Mishnah presents few precedents or examples of case law, the Tosefta frequently does so. Exemplary deeds of individual sages very often find their way into the Tosefta's complement to the Mishnah. (A detailed catalogue of these items would not advance our inquiry.) The presence of Roman troops is acknowledged (T. Shab. 13:9B), and what was done "in the time of danger," meaning during the pacification of the country after Bar Kokhba's war, more than seldom is invoked in law (e.g., T. Er. 5:240). The destruction of the Temple and reasons for it also come under discussion. Yet, in this last matter, the discussion is hyperbolic and inconsistent. The reference to the "reason" for the destruction (the moral quality of the community) noted above is matched by the view that "the excessive fastidiousness of Zechariah b. Aqilas is what burned the Temple" (T. Shab. 16:7E). In other words, even within the repertoire of historical insights and conventional arguments available at that time, the sages of the Tosefta hardly undertook mature and systematic inquiry into the great events of their age. On the contrary, these events were made into the setting for events the sages themselves regarded as important. To give one such instance:

T. SANHEDRIN 2:8

G. Said R. Simeon, "R. Aqiba was imprisoned, and he intercalcated three years one after the other."
H. They said to him, "From there do you derive proof? But it was because the court was in session and was reckoning the need for one year after another, in its proper time."

The reason for Aqiba's imprisonment is unimportant; his fate (perhaps well-known) is treated as inconsequential for the purposes of discourse. That is entirely natural. In the following series of cases, we find reference to what surely were events in the aftermath of Bar Kokhba's defeat. But the circumstances are important only because of the substance of the law at hand:

T. YEBAMOT 14:7-8

14:7 J. Said Rabban Simeon b. Gamaliel, "A band of prisoners went to Antioch, and upon their return they said, 'Of our group only

So-and-so, a Jew, was killed.' And the case came before sages, who permitted his wife to remarry."

14:8 A. Sixty men went down to the fortress at Betar and not a single one of them came back. And the matter came before sages, who permitted their wives to remarry.

In all, therefore, the Tosefta's authors, like those of the Mishnah, easily absorbed into their framework of discussion and analysis whatever details of important historical events they had in hand.

It may be argued that narratives, fables, or tales found no legitimate place in the Tosefta, which was, after all, concerned with other things. Yet the document does contain a sizable corpus of stories. Many of these stories deal not only with the private doings of sages (exemplary of law or virtue, to be sure) or precedents for the law and allusions to settings in which cases were decided. We also have an extended series of accounts that, in other hands and for other purposes, might have served as a rich account of consequential events. We could readily string these together into a sizable narrative. Accordingly, the framers of the Tosefta included in their document materials of rich potential for historical writing. As we shall see, the authors furthermore provided a measure of philosophizing on the meaning of history and the message of Israel's destiny. So, in this document, as in others of its age, raw materials for writing and reflection on Israel's history and destiny lay at hand. Further, the occasion—reflection on Israel's condition—for reshaping them into historical lessons and doctrines remained constant. Israel's sorry condition had scarcely changed, but nothing was done. The reason, we need hardly repeat, was that the system of the Mishnah governed the ways and directions in which the framers of the Tosefta proposed to pursue their task. Whatever else they or their contemporaries did in the composition of other books, in this book, at least, the mishnaic system would make its appearance; even if amplified, expanded, and even reshaped, it was still essentially intact and unrevised.

Out of a rather sizable selection of potential candidates, let us now briefly examine some of the stories that, in other hands, might have been transformed into history. First, we take up tales that tell us about the Tosefta's awareness of Jesus as a person and the supernatural powers and standing attributed to him by his followers. These stories deal with two aspects of the life of Jesus: his teachings and his miracles. As to the latter:

T. SHEHITAT HULLIN 2:22–24

2:22　A. R. Eleazar b. Damah was bitten by a snake.

B. And Jacob of Kefar Sama came to heal him in the name of Jesus, son of Pantera.

C. And R. Ishmael did not allow him [to accept the healing].

D. They said to him, "You are not permitted [to accept healing from him], Ben Dama."

E. He said to him, "I shall bring you proof that he may heal me."

F. But he did not have time to bring the [promised] proof before he dropped dead.

2:23　A. Said R. Ishmael, "Happy are you, Ben Dama. For you have expired in peace, but you did not break down the hedge erected by sages.

B. "For whoever breaks down the hedge erected by sages eventually suffers punishment, as it is said, *He who breaks down a hedge is bitten by a snake* [Qoh. 10:8]."

2:24　A. R. Eliezer was arrested on account of *minut*. They brought him to court for judgment.

B. That *hegemon* said to him, "Should an elder of your standing get involved in such things?"

C. He said to him, "The Judge is reliable in my view" [I rely upon the Judge].

D. That *hegemon* supposed that he referred to him, but he referred only to his Father in heaven.

E. He [the *hegemon*] said to him, "Since you have deemed me reliable for yourself, so thus I have ruled: Is it possible that these grey hairs should err in such matters? ['Obviously not, therefore':] [you are] *'Dimissus'* [pardoned]. Lo, you are free of liability."

F. And when he left court, he was distressed to have been arrested on account of matters of *minut*.

G. His disciples came to comfort him, but he did not accept their words of comfort.

H. R. Aqiba came and said to him, "Rabbi, may I say something to you so that you will not be distressed?"

I. He said to him, "Go ahead."

J. He said to him, "Perhaps some one of the *minim* told you something of *minut* which pleased you."

K. He said to him, "By heaven! You remind me. Once I was strolling in the camp of Sepphoris. I bumped into Jacob of Kefar Sikhnin, and he told me a teaching of *minut* in the name of Jesus ben Pantiri, and it pleased me.

"So I was arrested on account of matters of *minut*, for I transgressed the teachings of Torah: *Keep your way far from her and do not go near the door of her house . . .*" [Prov. 5:8].

L. For R. Eliezer did teach, "One should always flee from what is disreputable and from whatever appears to be disreputable."

The important aspect of these stories is clear. The raw materials for a sustained account of the problem posed by the growth, presumably among Jews, of Christian belief surely lie before us. A kind of "anti-gospel," narrating nasty stories about Jesus, could have been constructed; later on it was. Along these same lines, a systematic narrative of several rabbis' opposition to Jesus and his teachings, pursuing lines of consistent discourse, surely could have emerged even from the mere stringing together of tales such as these. But while narrative—which led to reflections on history and its periods, patterns, and meaning—served others as a mode of response to the issue at hand, a sustained narrative proved useless to the framers of the Tosefta. The stories remained detached and episodic. What drew materials together into protracted and pointed discourse for the Tosefta's authors was something other than the sequence of events which produced ineluctable truths.

That other context lay within the walls of the holy Temple in the mode of thought and description and analysis of deeds in patterns. Nearly all of the *Geschichten* at hand deal with that one place. These fall into several categories, of which one or two examples for each suffice. First, we take up supernatural events in the cult.

T. SOTAH 13:8

C. In the year in which Simeon the Righteous died, he said to them, "This year I am going to die."

D. They said to him, "How do you know?"

E. He said to them, "On every Day of Atonement there was a certain elder, dressed in white and cloaked in white, who would go in with

me and come out with me. This year, however, while he went in with
me, he never came out."
F. After the festival he fell ill for seven days and then died.

T. KIPPURIM 1:8, 2:4

1:8   G. The Boethusians maintained that he should burn the incense
while he is still outside, as it says, [And put the incense on the
fire before the Lord, that] the cloud of the incense may cover
[the mercy seat which is upon the testimony] [Lev. 16:13].
H. Sages said to them, "Now has it not also been stated, And put
the incense on the fire before the Lord?
I. "From this it follows that whoever offers up incense offers up
incense only inside.
J. "If so, why is it said, The cloud of the incense may cover?
K. "This teaches that he puts into it something which causes
smoke to rise.
L. "If therefore he did not put in something which makes smoke
rise, he is liable to the death penalty."
M. Now when this Boethusian went forth, he said to his fathers,
"In your entire lives you would [merely] expound the Scripture,
but you never did the deed properly, until I arose and I went in
and did it right."
N. They said to him, "Even though we do expound matters as
you say, we do not do things in the way in which we expound
them. We obey the words of sages.
"I shall be very much surprised at you if you live for very
long."
O. Not thirty days passed before they put him into his grave.

2:4   A. All the gates which were there were covered with gold except
for Nicanor's gates,
B. for a miracle was done with them.
C. There are those who say it is because their copper is bright.
D. R. Eliezer b. Jacob says, "It was Corinthian bronze and shone
like gold ['it is as pretty as gold']."
E. Now what is the miracle which was done with them?
F. They say: When Nicanor was bringing them from Alexandria,
in Egypt, a gale rose in the sea and threatened to drown them.
They took one of them and tossed it into the sea, and they
wanted to throw in the other but Nicanor would not let them. He
said to them, "If you throw in the second one, throw me in with
it." He was distressed all the way to the wharf at Jaffa. Once they

reached the wharf at Jaffa, the other door popped up from underneath the boat.

G. And there are those who say one of the beasts of the sea swallowed it, and when Nicanor came to the wharf at Jaffa, it brought it up and tossed it onto land.

H. And concerning it, it is explicitly stated in tradition, *The beams of our house are cedar, our rafters are pine* [Song 1:17].

These three stories show us how supernatural intervention in the lives of the priests was routinely represented.

A second type of story about the cult involved noteworthy events in the lives of priests. Here are three such tales.

T. KIPPURIM 1:4, 1:21–22, 3:20

1:4   H. Said R. Yose, "Joseph b. Elim of Sepphoris served in the place of the high priest for one hour.

I. "And from that time onward he was not valid either as a high priest or as an ordinary priest.

J. "When he went forth [from his high priesthood of one hour], he said to the king, 'The bullock and ram which were offered today, to whom do they belong? Are they mine, or are they our high priest's?'

K. "The king knew what to answer him.

L. "He said to him, 'Now what's going on, Son of Elim! It is not enough for you that you have served in the place of the high priest for one hour before Him who spoke and brought the world into being. But do you also want to take over the high priesthood for yourself?'

M. "At that moment Ben Elim realized that he had been separated from the priesthood."

1:21   D. Ishmael b. Phiabi's mother made for him a tunic worth a hundred *maneh*.

E. And he would stand and make offerings on the altar wearing it.

1:22   A. Eleazar b. Harsom's mother made for him a tunic for twenty thousand, and he would stand and make offerings on the altar while wearing it.

B. But his brethren, the priests, called him down,

C. because [it was so sheer that] he appeared naked while wearing it.

3:20   Simeon b. Qimhit went forth to speak with an Arab king, and spit spurted out of his [the king's] mouth and fell on his clothes. His brother went in and served in his stead as high priest. The mother of these [men] witnessed two [officiating] high priests [who were her sons] on the same day.

We observe that if anyone wanted to compose a history of the cult, including noteworthy events "on some one day," the materials lay at hand. But these stories remain episodic and didactic in an atemporal sense. They convey the message that what happens in the Temple is important in and of itself; there is no larger moral lesson in most of the tales, and no historical interest in any of them.

Third, stories about conflict in the cult, with special reference to the performance of Temple rites, find their way into the Tosefta. Such conflict stories are represented by the following:

T. HAGIGAH 2:11–12

2:11   A. Hillel the Elder laid hands on a whole-offering in the court-yard [cf. M. Hag. 2:3B], and the disciples of Shammai ganged up on him.

B. He said to them, "Go and see it, for it is a female, and I have to prepare it as sacrifices of peace-offerings are prepared."

C. He put them off with a bunch of words, and they went their way.

D. But the power of the House of Shammai forthwith became strong, and they wanted to decide the law permanently in accord with their opinion.

E. Now there was present Baba b. Buta who was one of the disciples of the House of Shammai, but who acknowledged that the law is in accord with the opinions of the House of Hillel in every last detail.

F. He went and brought the whole *Qedar* flock and set them up right in the courtyard and announced, "Whoever is required to bring whole-offerings and peace-offerings, let him come and take a beast and lay on hands" [cf. M. Hag. 2:3B].

G. So [everybody] came along and took a beast and offered up whole-offerings, having laid on hands.

H. On that very day the law was confirmed in accord with the opinion of the House of Hillel,

I. and not a single person griped about it.

2:12 A. Another disciple of the disciples of the House of Hillel laid hands on a whole-offering.
B. One of the disciples of Shammai found him out.
C. He said to him, "What's this laying on of hands?!"
D. He said to him, "What's this shutting up?!"
E. And he shut him up by force.

The importance of the narrative for our inquiry is simply its existence. The framers of the Tosefta clearly had ample materials at hand for the composition of a sacred history of the cult, including attention to points of conflict and resolution. But instead these materials were systematically introduced only where they illustrated points of law. So they were treated as nothing more than precedents. No one composed either a history of the cult or even a Hillel gospel; events once more remain subordinate.

The fourth type of story about the Temple involved its destruction, on the one side, and reasons for God's rejecting the cult, on the other. The first of the following stories provides a picture of why God's presence abandoned the cult. The second and third present accounts of the aftermath of the destruction.

T. SHEBUOT 1:4

A. Two priests who were brothers were running neck and neck up the ramp, and one of them got within four cubits of the altar before the other.
B. He took the knife [for killing the sacrificial animal] and stuck it into his heart.
C. R. Sadoq came and stood on the steps of the portico of the Temple mount and said, "Hear me out, O brothers of ours, House of Israel!
D. "Lo, it says, *When a corpse is found . . . [and it is not known who killed him], and your elders and judges go forth and measure . . . [to which village is the corpse nearer, and that village has to bring a heifer in penitence]* [Deut. 21:1–2].
E. "Now as to us—whither and whence shall we measure? To the sanctuary? Or to the courtyard?"
F. All the people groaned and wept after what he said.
G. Then the father of the youth came and said to them, "My brothers, may I be atonement for you!
H. "My son is still writhing, so the knife has not yet contracted corpse-uncleanness!"

I. This teaches you that the uncleanness of the knife was more disturbing to them than bloodshed,

J. and so Scripture says, *And also Manasseh shed very much innocent blood [until he had filled the whole of Jerusalem from one end to another]* [1 Kings 21:16].

K. On this basis it is said that for the sin of bloodshed the presence of God flew away, and the sanctuary was contaminated.

T. KIPPURIM 2:6, 2:8

2:6   A. The members of the house of Abtinas were experts in preparing the incense for producing smoke [cf. M. Yom. 3:11C], and they did not want to teach others how to do so.

B. Sages sent and brought experts from Alexandria, in Egypt, who knew how to concoct spices in much the same way.

C. But they were not experts in making the smoke ascend [as well as the others had done].

D. The smoke coming from the incense of the house of Abtinas would ascend straight as a stick up to the beams, and afterward it scattered in all directions as it came down.

E. That of the Alexandrians would scatter as it came down forthwith [not rising properly].

F. Now when the sages realized this, they said, "The Omnipresent has created the world only for his own glory, as it is said, *The Lord has made everything for his own purpose* [Prov. 16:4]."

G. Sages sent to them [the members of the house of Abtinas], but they declined to come until the sages doubled their wages.

H. "They had been receiving twelve *manehs* every day, and now they went and got twenty-four," the words of R. Meir.

I. R. Judah says, "They had been getting twenty-four every day. Now they went and got forty-eight *manehs*."

J. Sages said to them, "Now why were you unwilling to teach [others]?"

K. They said to them, "The members of father's house knew that the Temple is destined for destruction, and they did not want to teach others their art, so that people would not burn incense before an idol in the same way in which they burn incense before the Omnipresent."

2:8   A. Agdis b. Levi knew a certain mode of singing, and he did not want to teach it to others [M. Yom. 3:11D].

B. Sages said to him, "Why did you not want to teach it to others?"

C. He said to them, "The members of father's house knew that the Temple was destined for destruction, and they did not want to teach their mode of singing to others, so that they should not sing before an idol the way in which they say [sing] before the Omnipresent."

This same matter of the gradual decline of the Temple's supernatural standing forms a bridge to the next issue, the interpretation of the destruction of the Temple in the larger setting of Israel's history and destiny. In the present context we may hardly be astonished to find that historical explanation is framed by the actions of individuals, having been reduced by the imagination of rabbinical moralizers from its large political and social framework to the dimensions of the private life of ordinary Israelites. That sort of thinking is to be expected. But it has an interesting and suggestive side. God's relationship to Israel, worked out in particular in Israel's history, is governed by Israel's relationship to God. That is the fundamental mode of explaining and drawing meaning from what has happened: the "philosophy of history" of the Tosefta (among all other documents). The main point is that at each step, Israel provoked an equal, and opposite, divine response: not too much, not too little, but always the just and measured reply. So we find the Toseftan exegetes' treatment of the familiar passage at M. Sot. 9:9ff. We recall that for the framers of the passage the destruction of the Temple signaled also the removal of men of virtue from Israel's social life; the sacred Temple and the sacred community corresponded to one another in life as in death. The point of that set of facts as presented by the Mishnah is made explicit in the following complement supplied by the Tosefta:

T. SOTAH 10:1–2

10:1   A. When righteous people come into the world, good comes into the world and retribution departs from the world.
B. And when they take their leave from the world, retribution comes into the world, and goodness departs from the world.

10:2   A. When bad people come into the world, retribution comes into the world, and goodness departs from the world.
B. And when they depart from the world, goodness comes back into the world, and retribution departs from the world.
C. How do we know that, when righteous people come into the world, goodness comes into the world, and retribution departs

69

from the world? Since it is said, *And he called him Noah, saying, "This one will comfort us in our work and in the toil of our hands"* [Gen. 5:29].

D. And how do we know that, when they take their leave of the world, retribution comes into the world and goodness departs from the world? Since it is said, *The righteous man perishes and no one lays it to heart* [Isa. 57:1], and it says, *He enters into peace, they rest in their beds who walk in their uprightness* [Isa. 57:2]—He goes in peace to the grave. And it says, *But you, draw near hither, sons of the sorceress, offspring of the adulterer and the harlot* [Isa. 57:3].

E. And how do we know that when bad people come into the world, retribution comes into the world and goodness departs from the world? Since it is said, *When the wicked comes, then comes also contempt, and with ignominy, reproach* [Prov. 18:3].

F. And how do we know that, when he departs from the world, goodness comes into the world and retribution leaves the world? Since it says, *And when the wicked perish, there is exultation* [Prov. 11:10]. And it says, *So that the Lord may turn from the fierceness of his anger and show you mercy and have compassion on you* [Deut. 13:17].

The presence or absence of virtuous men found a response in heaven. So too was the decline in the supernatural cult marked by the decline in the social morality of Israel. Each rite removed from the cult was found no longer serviceable, given the corresponding development in the life of the community. While the cited passage of the Mishnah surely implies that view, the Toseftan counterpart here made it explicit:

T. SOTAH 14:1–4

14:1 A. Rabban Yohanan b. Zakkai says, "'When murderers became many, the rite of breaking the heifer's neck was annulled [M. Sot. 9:9A],'

B. "for the heifer whose neck is to be broken is brought only in case of doubt.

C. "But now there are many who commit murder in public.

14:2 A. "When adulterers became many, the ordeal of the bitter water was annulled,

B. "for the ordeal of the bitter water is performed only in a case of doubt.

C. "But now there are many who see [their lovers] in public."

14:3 A. When hedonists became many, fierce wrath came upon the world, and the glory of Torah ceased.

B. When those who went about whispering in judgment multiplied, conduct deteriorated, the laws were perverted, and the Holy Spirit ceased in Israel.

14:4 A. When those who displayed partiality in judgment multiplied, the commandment, *You shall not respect persons in judgment* [Deut. 1:17] was annulled, and *You shall not be afraid of anyone* [Deut. 1:17] ceased.

B. And they removed the yoke of heaven from themselves, and accepted the authority of the yoke of mortal man.

When God's rule was rejected by Israel, man's rule (Rome's dominion) took its place. This conviction would be restated in messianic-mythic terms. The conviction that the presence of virtuous men guaranteed God's dwelling in the Temple, their absence, God's departure, indeed can have served a variety of messianic purposes. For one thing, it could be maintained that when there were enough truly righteous Israelites, the Messiah would come. For another, people could suppose that truly virtuous men themselves would conform to the model of the Messiah and would be messiahs. Sages, in particular, could be seen as near-term messiahs, pointing toward the messianic denouement at the end. The passage at hand invites the sort of extension and amplification just now suggested. In time to come, both positions would emerge within the kind of Judaism whose earlier stages here are present. That makes all the more striking the failure of sages in the Tosefta to draw, or even hint at, conclusions such as these. Even where the raw materials for a messianic statement in the Tosefta proved abundant, no one used them.

Accordingly, the Tosefta's authorities brought to the surface the theory of Israel's history and destiny which was implicit in the Mishnah. This was, pure and simple, the view that events provide a barometer of the supernatural standing of Israel. But that matter itself is governed by patterns of life and behavior. Accordingly, manifest history is secondary to latent history expressed in social facts. The reason people in this line of rabbinical development did not write history is that they did not think history was important. They wrote law books because they thought that the rules they taught would prove decisive in settling the important question confronting the holy people: how to sustain the sanctification of Israel.

The holiest dimension and aspect of the life of Israel forms the focus of the bulk of the *Geschichten* which the framers of the Tosefta chose to draw together. So far as a history is possible, it consists of episodes concerning the Temple and its cult, with an account of its counterpart (given the character of the sages' movement) in the life of the holy community. If that is the case, we have to ask ourselves the obvious question: how can we speak of a doctrine of history in a document that knows of only one event, the destruction of the Temple? How can there be history without a broad repertoire of historical events demanding classification and interpretation? The answer, of course, is that under such circumstances, in the framework of such convictions, there can no history at all.

We close our inquiry with a stunning example of how the system constructed by the founders of the Mishnah treats the already available historical-apocalyptic materials of Scripture. This passage shows us what the Tosefta's authorities did with the most historical of all scriptural materials, the apocalypse. The climax of scriptural historiography comes in apocalyptic interpretations of natural symbols in terms of concrete historical events, and of events in terms of symbols. Such an interpretation is provided in the book of Daniel. To appreciate the Tosefta's transformation of the apocalyptic vision, we shall follow the entire discussion in context. What we see is the interpretation of the apocalyptic vision of history wholly in terms of what happens within the circles of sages' debates, a truly stunning metamorphosis.

T. MIQVAOT 7:11

A. A cow which drank purification water, and which one slaughtered within twenty-four hours—

B. This was a case, and R. Yose the Galilean did declare it clean, and R. Aqiba did declare it unclean.

C. R. Tarfon supported R. Yose the Galilean. R. Simeon ben Nanos supported R. Aqiba.

D. R. Simeon b. Nanos dismissed [the arguments of] R. Tarfon. R. Yose the Galilean dismissed [the arguments of] R. Simeon b. Nanos.

E. R. Aqiba dismissed [the arguments of] R. Yose the Galilean.

F. After a time, he [Yose] found an answer for him [Aqiba].

G. He said to him, "Am I able to reverse myself?"

H. He said to him, "Not anyone [may reverse himself], but you [may do so], for you are Yose the Galilean."

I. [He said to him,] "I shall say to you: Lo, Scripture states, *And they shall be kept for the congregation of the people of Israel for the water for impurity* [Num. 19:9].

J. "Just so long as they are kept, lo, they are water for impurity, but not after a cow has drunk them."

K. This was a case, and thirty-two elders voted in Lud and declared it clean.

L. At that time R. Tarfon recited this verse:

M. "*I saw the ram goring westward and northward and southward, and all the animals were unable to stand against it, and none afforded protection from its power, and it did just as it liked and grew great* [Dan. 8:4];

N. "[This is] R. Aqiba.

O. "'*As I was considering, behold, a he-goat came from the west across the face of the whole earth, without touching the ground; and the goat had a conspicuous horn between his eyes.*

P. "'*He came to the ram with the two horns, which I had seen standing on the bank of the river, and he ran at him in his mighty wrath. I saw him come close to the ram, and he was enraged against him and struck the ram and broke his two horns*'; this is R. Aqiba and R. Simeon b. Nanos.

Q. "'*And the ram had no power to stand before him*'; this is R. Aqiba.

R. "'*But he cast him down to the ground and trampled upon him*'; this is R. Yose the Galilean.

S. "'*And there was no one who could rescue the ram from his power*'; these are the thirty-two elders who voted in Lud and declared it clean.'"

In the sages' debates Daniel's vision of the kingdoms now is turned into an account of the clash of titans. The history of nations, their wars and kings and victories, moves from the world of material reality to the realm of mind constructed in the fantastic law systems of the Mishnah and the Tosefta. History in the ordinary sense of the word is not merely rejected or ignored; it is transformed. The process inaugurated in the Mishnah's reduction of unique events to their monothetic taxa and absorption of these events within a system of predictable classification here reaches its climax. People who know what history really consists of will then recognize that sages make history. They make history in their thoughts and their rules. In such a context as this, there is no place for either history or an end of history, nor will the Messiah find his services required.

ESCHATOLOGY WITHOUT MESSIAH; TELEOLOGY BEYOND TIME

At issue is the direction of eschatology in the foundation document and in its continuations. It is not merely whether, or how frequently, the figures of the Messiah and Elijah make an appearance, how often "the days of the Messiah" come under discussion, or how many references we find to "the end of days" or events we regard as historical. We focus upon how the system which was laid out in the Mishnah takes up and disposes of those critical issues of teleology which were worked out through messianic eschatology in other, earlier versions of Judaism. These earlier systems resorted to the myth of the Messiah as savior and redeemer of Israel, a supernatural figure engaged in political-historical tasks as king of the Jews, even a God-man facing the crucial historical questions of Israel's life and then resolving them—Christ as king of the world, of the ages, even of death itself. Although the figure of a Messiah does appear, when the framers of the Mishnah spoke of "the Messiah," they meant a high priest designated and consecrated to office in a certain way, and not in some other way. The reference to "days of the Messiah" constitutes a conventional division of history at the end time but before the ultimate end. But that category of time plays no consequential role in the teleological framework established within the Mishnah. Accordingly, the Mishnah's framers constructed a system of Judaism in which the entire teleological dimension reached full exposure while hardly invoking the person or functions of a messianic figure of any kind. Perhaps in the aftermath of Bar Kokhba's debacle, silence on the subject served to express a clarion judgment. I am inclined to think so. But, for the purpose of our inquiry, the main thing is a simple fact, now fully expounded and illustrated.

The issue of eschatology, framed in mythic terms, draws in its wake the issue of how, in the foundation document of Judaism, history comes to full conceptual expression. "History" as an account of a meaningful pattern of events, a making sense of the past and giving guidance about the future, begins with the necessary conviction that events matter, one after another. The Mishnah's framers present us with no elaborate theory of events, a fact fully consonant with their systematic points of insistence and encompassing concern. Events do not matter, not one by one.

The philosopher-lawyers exhibited no theory of history either. Their conception of Israel's destiny in no way called upon historical categories of either narrative or didactic explanation to describe and account for the future. The small importance attributed to the figure of the Messiah as a historical-eschatological figure, therefore, fully accords with the larger traits of the system as a whole. Let me speak with emphasis: *If what is important in Israel's existence were sanctification, an ongoing process, and not salvation, understood as a one-time event at the end, then no one would find reason to narrate history.* Few then would form the obsession about the Messiah so characteristic of Judaism in its later, rabbinic mode. But, as we shall see, the Messiah then would wear a rabbinical cloak and draw Israel to accept the Talmud's irenic conception of the holy life. Salvation comes through sanctification, just as M. Sot. 9:15 indicates. The salvific figure, then, becomes an instrument of consecration and so fits into a system quite different from the one originally built around the Messiah.

When, in analyzing the foundations of Judaism, we move from species and eschatology upward to genus and teleology, we find ourselves addressing the motives and goals of the mishnaic system. The system is so constructed as *not* to point toward a destination at the end of time. But still it does speak of last things. Accordingly, we ask, where, if not in the eschaton, do things end? The answer provided by Abot, the Mishnah's first apologetic, is clear: "Where do we head? Where do we go? Below, below, below." Death is the destination. In life we prepare for the voyage. We keep the law in order to make the move required of us all. What is supposed in Abot to make the system work, explaining why we should do the things the Mishnah says, is that other end, the end to which history and national destiny prove remote, or, rather, irrelevant. Abot constructs a teleology beyond time, providing a purposeful goal for every individual. Life is the antechamber, death the destination; what we do is weighed and measured. When we die, we stand on one side of the balance, while our life and deeds stand on the other.

The Mishnah's teleology as supplied by Abot presents a curious contrast to the focus of the Mishnah itself. Abot addresses the life of the individual, but only incidentally the construct of the nation. But the system of the Mishnah, for its part, designs a whole society, one component after another. Mishnaic discourse speaks of the individual in the context of a national life of collective sanctification. Self-evidently, tensions between individual and community reach ready resolution; that is hardly the point. The main thing is that the Mishnah addresses not the stages or phases of individual life but the constituents of the life of village and Temple, the former shaped, where possible, into the counterpart and mirror image of the latter. For the system of sanctification imagined in the Mishnah, the individual is not a principal building block. The householder and his *ménage* form the smallest whole unit of social construction. So, as I said, the teleology contributed by Abot to the mishnaic system turns out to be no more appropriate than the one that might have, but did not, come out of messianic eschatology. Yet the world beyond historical time to which Abot makes reference provides precisely the right metaphysical setting for the system of order and stasis, of proper and correct classification, that underlay, as foundation and goal, the Mishnah's own detailed statements.

While, as I said, we do not know when the Tosefta came to closure, it clearly was after the conclusion of the Mishnah and, people generally suppose, long afterward. But if, in the intervening two hundred or more years between the conclusion of the Mishnah and the completion of the Tosefta, important developments had changed the direction of reflection within rabbinical circles, the Tosefta hardly suggests so. On the contrary, the Tosefta exhibits (with still greater intensity and clarity) precisely the traits of mind and conception discerned, to begin with, in the Mishnah. That fact is valuable evidence for the direction the mishnaic system might have taken, had the heirs and successors of the Mishnah chosen to walk only in the paths already indicated in the document entrusted to them. To speak in hypostatization, the Tosefta through its loyalty to the Mishnah betrayed the Mishnah. It did not allow the Mishnah to serve as a resource, or to enrich, enhance, and guide the ages to come. Rather, the Tosefta treated the Mishnah as the last word. So the framers of the Tosefta took as their task the labor of explaining, in the names of the authorities of the Mishnah, the things which the Mishnah's original authorities had said. What they added was in imitation of the Mishnah's language. When they extended or amplified or even revised, it was always within the lines laid forth by the Mishnah's original thinkers.

That is why, at the end, we come to the absurdity of the reduction of an apocalyptic vision of the wars of great empires to the paltry dimensions of an academic argument about nothing of material consequence. Were it not for the document's prevailing seriousness, we might be inclined to see Tarfon's reading of Daniel 8:4 as a remarkably subtle and ironic judgment, a joke. But it was not a joke. The disproportion between Daniel's images and Tarfon's interpretation strikes us, but it struck no one before us. What we learn from the Tosefta is the way forward from the Mishnah onward, as it was explored by some in the third and fourth centuries. The Tosefta tells us what people might have done.

But, we realize full well, the Tosefta does not point toward the character of Judaism as it was to emerge from late antiquity: richly eschatological, obsessed with the Messiah and his coming, and engaged by the history of Israel and the nations. The Tosefta, in line with the Mishnah, allowed no glimpse at a doctrine of Israel's history and destiny because the framers had nothing to show. But Judaism at the end did indeed provide an ample account and explanation of Israel's history and destiny. These emerged as the generative problem of Judaism, just as they framed the social reality confronted by Jews wherever they lived. So, to seek the map that shows the road from the Mishnah, at the beginning, to the fully articulated Judaism of the end of the formative age in late antiquity, we have to look elsewhere. As to the path from the Mishnah to tractate Abot and through the Tosefta, this is not the way.

It never could have been the way because, in my view, the Mishnah with its documents of continuation and succession proposed to ignore the actualities of the social condition of Israel. The critical issues confronting the Jewish nation emerged from its sorry political condition. In the most commonplace sense of the word, these were *historical* issues. Any sort of Judaism that pretended the history of Israel could be reduced to lists of events sharing the same taxonomic traits. That the destiny of Israel might be absorbed into an essentially imaginary framework of sanctification attained through the human heart and mind, demanded what the Jewish nation could not give. For people could not pretend to be other than who they were

77

and what they were. Israel constituted a defeated people, driven from its holy place, yet reminded, every time it opened its ancient Scriptures, of God's special love for it and of its distinctive destiny among nations. Israel lived out an insufferable paradox between God's word and world, between promise and postponed fulfillment. So the critical issue confronting any sort of Judaism to emerge in late antiquity reached definition and attained urgency in the social reality, the everyday experience, of Israel: When? By whom? To the Jewish nation history proved very real indeed. The political question of Israel's destiny settled by the myth of the promise of the Messiah's coming salvation—a concrete, national, and historical salvation—could not be wished away. It demanded response: how long, O Lord? So, as is clear, the Mishnah's system would have to undergo revision and reformation. The labor of renewal would demand fresh and original thinkers: exegetes of a remarkably subtle capacity.

2

The Messiah in
the Documents of Exegesis
and Expansion: The Talmud of
the Land of Israel

Formed as a systematic exegesis of the Mishnah and brought to closure at ca. A.D. 400, the Talmud of the Land of Israel (also known as the Yerushalmi or the Palestinian Talmud) in no way takes so subordinate a position toward the Mishnah as does the Tosefta. That negative statement prepares us for a positive one. The Talmud of the Land of Israel picks and chooses what it wishes out of the larger program of topics covered by the Mishnah, treating only thirty-nine of the Mishnah's sixty-two tractates (leaving Abot out). What the Yerushalmi in general accomplishes with the tractates is less important. The main point is that the framers of the Yerushalmi exhibited independent judgment in determining the things they chose and did not choose to pursue. Their system, in consequence, is not symmetrical with that of the Mishnah.

The Mishnah describes a world and presents rules for it. We may say, in simple language, that the Mishnah is about "life." The Mishnah describes the life of Israel, viewed from one perspective. But the Talmud, for its part, is not so much about "life," in general, as it is about the Mishnah, in particular. Whatever the framers of the Talmud's units of discourse wished to say, they expressed in relationship something they found in the Mishnah.

The Talmud nonetheless follows a distinctive program of topics. At issue is that which the Mishnah does not choose to treat, but the Talmud for its part wishes to discuss. The principal example so far as we are concerned is the absence, in the Mishnah, of a taxon defined by the issue of Israel's history, its form, direction, meaning, and end. These fall wholly outside of the Mishnah's frame of reference. On that protean topic the Mishnah offers no tractate, no chapter, scarcely even a reference. Not only do we find a lack of attention given to that classical issue of the Israelite worldview, but we do not even know how we might find appropriate, specifically mishnaic, language or categories for discussion of the issue. Suitable words elude us. Whatever discourse we do find in the Talmud pertinent to this formidable and urgent topic therefore lies wholly outside the symbolic and even linguistic-conceptual framework of the Mishnah. As a result, it is principally when the Talmud ignores the Mishnah that it addresses questions important to the present inquiry.

Let us now briefly review the two types of discourse which compose the Yerushalmi. These are, as already is clear, passages that take up the exegesis of the Mishnah, and passages that do not. A severely limited repertoire of intellectual initiatives was available to the authorities of our Talmud. Approaching a given rule of the Mishnah, a sage would do one of two things: he would either explain the meaning of the passage or amplify and expand the meaning of the passage. Of the two sorts, the work of explicating the plain meaning of a law predominates. What the framers of the Talmud wanted to say—whatever else was their aspiration—was what they thought the Mishnah meant in any given passage. We need not elaborate the modes of exegesis of the Mishnah, since these make no contribution to the present topic.

We come, next, to the modest corpus of discourse in the Talmud in which the principal goal was to introduce conceptions or discussions outside of those originating in the Mishnah. When we collect all the units of discourse, or larger parts of such units, in which exegesis of the Mishnah or expansion upon the law of the Mishnah is lacking, we find four types.

First are theoretical questions of law not associated with a particular passage of Mishnah. There is some tendency to move beyond the legal boundaries set by the Mishnah's rules themselves. More general inquiries are taken up. These of course remain within the framework of the topic of one tractate or another, although there are some larger modes of thought characteristic of more than a single tractate. But these items tend not to leave the Mishnah far behind.

Second, we find exegesis of Scripture separate from that of the

Mishnah. It is under this rubric that we find the most important instances in which the Talmud presents materials essentially independent of the Mishnah. Here we find problems or themes, worked out through what is said about a biblical figure, which express ideas and values simply unknown to the Mishnah.

Third, there are historical tales. The Talmud contains a fair number of statements about something happening or narratives about how something happened. While many of these are replete with biblical quotations, they generally do not provide exegesis of Scripture, which itself serves merely as an illustration or reference point.

Finally, we find stories about, and rules for, sages and disciples who are not connected with the discussion of a Mishnah passage. The Mishnah contains very few tales about rabbis, which serve principally as precedents for, or illustrations of, rules. The Talmud by contrast contains a sizable number of stories about sages and their relationships to other people. These tales rarely serve to illustrate a rule or concept of the Mishnah. The main, though not the only, characteristic theme is the power of the rabbi, the honor due to the rabbi, and the tension between the rabbi and others, whether that be the patriarch, the heretic, or the Gentile.

Units of discourse (or large segments of such units) independent of the interests of the Mishnah are not numerous. Varying in bulk from one tractate to the next, they do not add up to much more than ten percent of the whole. We do find extensive passages that leave the Mishnah far behind, but they normally are of two kinds: exegesis of narrative or theological passages of Scripture, and fables about heroes. Accordingly, when the Talmud presents us with ideas or expressions of a world related to, but fundamentally separate from, that of the Mishnah—that is, when the Talmud wishes to say something other than what the Mishnah means—it will take up one of two modes of discourse. We find either exegesis of biblical passages, with the value system of the rabbis read into the scriptural tales; or stories about holy men and paradigmatic events, again through tales told so as to serve a didactic and paranetic purpose.

If, therefore, we want to point to what is distinctively talmudic in the Talmud of the Land of Israel, it is the exegesis of Scripture, on the one side, and the narration of historical or biographical tales about holy men, on the other. Since much of the biblical exegesis turns upon holy men of biblical times, we may say that when the

Talmud speaks for itself alone, as distinct from addressing the problems of the Mishnah, it tells about holy men now and then. But what is genuinely new in the Talmud, in contrast to the Mishnah, is the inclusion of an extensive discourse on the meaning of Scripture. That fact is decisive for our inquiry.

The Talmud of the Land of Israel therefore stands essentially secondary to two prior documents: the Mishnah and Scripture. The Mishnah is read in the Talmud within the framework of meaning established by the Mishnah itself. Scripture is read as an account of a world remarkably like that of the talmudic rabbis. When the rabbis speak for themselves, and as distinct from the Mishnah, it is through scriptural exegesis. To them any other manner of reading Scripture would have been unthinkable. They took for granted that they lived in a single timeless plane along with Scripture's heroes and sages. The Talmud thus is a composite of three kinds of materials: exegesis of Mishnah, exegesis of Scripture, and accounts of the men who provide both. Perhaps one might wish to see the Talmud as a reworking of its two antecedent documents: the Mishnah (lacking much reference to Scripture) and the Scripture itself. The Talmud brings the two together in a synthesis of its own making, both reading Scripture into Mishnah and reading Scripture alongside of, but separate from, Mishnah.

Let us now return to the point at which we started and characterize this Talmud's relationship to the Mishnah. What the Mishnah provided was not received in a spirit of humble acceptance. Important choices were made about what to treat and also what to ignore. The exegetical mode of reception need not have obscured the main lines of the Mishnah's system. But it surely did so. Discrete reading of sentences, or, at most, paragraphs, while denying all context and avoiding all larger generalizations except for those transcending the specific lines of tractates, this approach need not have involved the utter reversal of the definitive elements of the Mishnah's integrated worldview (its "Judaism"). But doing these things did facilitate the revision of the whole into a quite different pattern. To use a different metaphor, they shifted the orbit of the Mishnah from one path to another. The Mishnah centered on the priesthood and the Temple. The Talmud took over and deflected the whole into an orbit around the rabbi and his relationship to the disciple, the rabbi and his activities in the court, and the rabbi and his opinions in the school.

The simplest way to overcome gravity is to reduce the critical mass of the whole. Chopping the Mishnah into bits and pieces accomplished just that. While the Mishnah was set forth by Judah the Patriarch (called simply "Rabbi") as a profoundly unified and harmonious document, the Talmud insists upon obliterating the marks of the Mishnah's coherence. It treats in bits and pieces what was originally meant to speak wholly and cogently. The Mishnah, furthermore, delivered its message in the way chosen by Rabbi, and the authors of the Tosefta followed suit. That is to say, by producing the document as he did, Rabbi left no place for the very enterprise of episodic exegesis undertaken so brilliantly by his immediate continuators and heirs. True, a rather limited process of explanation and gloss of words and phrases, accompanied by a systematic inquiry into the wording of one passage or another, got under way probably at the very moment and within the very process of the Mishnah's closure. But insofar as the larger message and meaning of the document are conveyed in the ways Rabbi chose—through formalization of language and by means of contrasts and successive instances of the same general proposition—the need for exegesis was surely not generated by Rabbi's own program for the Mishnah. Quite to the contrary, Rabbi chose for his Mishnah a mode of expression, and defined for the document a large-scale structure and organization, which, by definition, were meant to stand independently. Rabbi's Mishnah speaks clearly for itself.

For the Mishnah did not merely come to closure. At the moment of conclusion it also formed a closed system—that is, a whole, complete statement—and the Tosefta accommodated itself to that system. How so? First, the Mishnah presents a complete picture and makes no provision for commentary and amplification of brief allusions, as does the Talmud. Second, the Mishnah refers to nothing beyond itself. It promises no information other than what is provided within its limits. Third, the Mishnah raises no questions for ongoing discussion beyond its decisive, final statement of enduring realities and fixed relationships. The Talmud makes precisely the opposite judgment. The Talmud's first initiative was to reopen in new language and taxa the Mishnah's closed system at the very moment of its completion and perfection. What is talmudic about the Talmud of the Land of Israel is its daring assertion that that which was concluded and completed demanded further clarification. Once this assertion was accepted, nothing else mattered.

What was to be clarified was obvious. What was to be continued—that is, subjected to close exegesis—had to go forward from the starting point along an essentially straight line. The message was clear in the Talmud's assertions about the Mishnah's laws. At every point, from the simplest gloss to the most far-ranging speculative inquiry, it was conveyed in the very medium of the Talmud: a new language, focused upon a new grid of discourse. The language was anything but patterned, and thus anything but Mishnaic. The grid of discourse lay across, rather than within, the inner boundaries of the Mishnah itself—a fundamental revolution in thought. Accordingly, the Talmud's distinctive traits lay not in the depths of what was said, but on the very surface, in its literary formulation.

The upshot is that where the Talmud of the Land of Israel treats the Messiah and other topics of our inquiry, it does so not in its exegesis of the Mishnah but in its own discussions autonomous of the Mishnah. What the Talmud has to say about the Messiah and associated issues, moreover, derives from the vast heritage of conviction and symbolic embodiments of hope and expectation. How the Talmud makes use of these available facts leads us deep into the inner workings of the Talmud's own systematic structure.

I must further emphasize that the system of belief and behavior in the Talmud of the Land of Israel—that is, the Judaism in the process of formation in the canon of rabbinical writings—is not fully spelled out in that one document. To the contrary this Talmud points toward a larger worldview, of which only part is expressed overtly in this Talmud. So the Talmud of the Land of Israel is only one component of a larger corpus of writings, and finds completion beyond itself in the greater canon of rabbinical compositions. In this paradoxical way, the Talmud stands asymmetrically not only over against the Mishnah, which it purports to explain, but also in respect to the larger canon of rabbinical Judaism, of which it forms only one part, in some ways distinct but in no way distinctive.

What the Yerushalmi shares with the rest of its sector of the rabbinic canon, above all, is the very subject of our present discussion: the Messiah myth. We shall now trace the evidence that, in the third and fourth centuries, rabbis took into their system the figure of the Messiah and the hopes associated with his coming. In this way they reconstructed the system of the Mishnah into something strikingly new and far more pertinent than anything the Mishnah's authors had imagined. As the document of legal philosophers or jurisprudents drew even closer to the everyday life of the Jewish nation, and brought order and regularity to disorder and chaos, so too did the character of the philosophical legal system change.

In the encounter between the Mishnah's vision of how things ought to be and the Jews' perception of who they were and what their history meant, the pure vision of holy Israel rested upon the raw reality of suffering Israel. So the Talmud's sages, both in the Land of Israel and in Babylonia, effected the union of the two—Mishnah's Israel in stasis and in holy order, and the reality of Jewish life in turmoil and anguished disarray. The offspring of that union was the incorporation of the Messiah myth into what had been the mishnaic system, and the reciprocal reframing of the myth for the reformation of that system. In this and subsequent chapters, we review stories and statements that testify to that process of transformation and reform.

THE MESSIAH IN THE TALMUD
OF THE LAND OF ISRAEL

When the framers of the Talmud of the Land of Israel addressed the exegesis of the Mishnah in particular, they did not introduce topics that the Mishnah's authors had ignored. Accordingly, in the Yerushalmi we find no tendency to raise questions of messianic importance when the Mishnah's statements come under discussion. In those units of discourse in which the Mishnah frames the talmudic issue, that is, approximately 90 percent of the Talmud of the Land of Israel, we find ourselves exactly where we were to begin with in the Mishnah and the Tosefta. But in those units of discourse in which, for one reason or another, the framers of the Talmud took up topics of their own, a set of conceptions new to this particular canon and its Judaism made an appearance. In the contrast between its two types of material—exegesis of the Mishnah, on the one side, and independent discourse, on the other—the character of the Yerushalmi becomes clear. It forms a bridge from the world of the Mishnah to the age of the fully realized rabbinic Judaism of the fifth- and sixth-century writings, that is, to the compositions of scriptural exegesis (Midrash) and the Babylonian Talmud.

Our survey of the way in which the Messiah myth comes to expression in the Talmud of the Land of Israel begins with the differentiation between the two types of material of which that Talmud is composed. These are the exegesis and expansion of a discrete passage of the Mishnah, on the one side, and freewheeling discourse on fresh topics, on the other. In the Yerushalmi, we find no tendency whatever to introduce questions of messianic import even into the discussion of Mishnah passages that seem to invite such interest. We begin with the single most important example of that striking phenomenon, the one passage in the Mishnah in which the Messiah ought to have found a place but did not do so: M. Sot. 9:15–16. In the Yerushalmi's exegesis of the passage, it evidently occurred to no one to introduce the absent, but surely awaited, figure. Despite the prevalent notion that the Messiah would raise the dead, that idea proved of no importance to the exegetes of the passage that discusses the resurrection of the dead. Let us now see how the Yerushalmi's exegetes of the Mishnah believed the passage should be expanded. (To distinguish the mishnaic passage from the talmudic amplification, I present in this chapter the Mishnah in italics. Verses of Scripture likewise are given in italics.)

Y. SHEQALIM 3:3

[VI. A] *And so does R. Pinhas b. Yair say, "Heedfulness leads to cleanliness, cleanliness leads to cleanness, cleanness leads to abstinence, abstinence leads to holiness, holiness leads to modesty, modesty leads to the fear of sin, the fear of sin leads to piety, piety leads to the Holy Spirit, the Holy Spirit leads to the resurrection of the dead, and the resurrection of the dead comes through Elijah, blessed be his memory, Amen"* [M. Sot. 9:15].

[B] *Heedfulness leads to cleanliness*: as it is written, *"And when he has made an end of atoning for the holy place and the tent of meeting and the altar, he shall present the live goat"* [Lev. 16:20].

[C] *Cleanliness leads to cleanness*: as it is written, *"And the priest shall make atonement for her, and she shall be clean"* [Lev. 12:8].

[D] *Cleanness leads to holiness*: as it is written, *"And cleanse it and hallow it from the uncleanness of the people of Israel"* [Lev. 16:19].

[E] *Holiness leads to modesty*: as it is written, *"For thus says the high*

*and lofty One who inhabits eternity, whose name is Holy: 'I dwell in
the high and holy place, and also with him who is of a contrite and
humble spirit, to revive the spirit of the humble, and to revive the
heart of the contrite'"* [Isa. 57:15]. So you find purity and humility.
[F] *Modesty leads to the fear of sin:* as it is written, *"The reward for
humility and fear of the Lord is riches and honor and life"* [Prov.
22:4].
[G] *The fear of sin leads to piety:* as it is written, *"But the steadfast
love of the Lord is from everlasting to everlasting upon those who fear
him, and his righteousness to children's children"* [Ps. 103:17].
[H] *Piety leads to the Holy Spirit:* as it is written, *"Of old thou didst
speak in a vision to thy faithful one"* [Ps. 89:19].
[I] *The Holy Spirit leads to the resurrection of the dead:* as it is written, *"Thus says the Lord God to these bones: Behold, I will cause
breath to enter you, and you shall live"* [Ezek. 37:5].
[J] *The resurrection of the dead comes through Elijah, blessed be his
memory:* as it is written, *"Behold, I will send you Elijah, the prophet,
before the great and terrible day of the Lord comes"* [Mal. 4:5].
[K] It has been taught in the name of R. Meir, "Whoever lives permanently in the Land of Israel, speaks the Holy Language, eats his produce in a state of cultic cleanness, recites the *Shema* morning and
night—let him be given the news that he belongs to the world to
come."

Here we see a remarkable fact. The exegetes remained wholly
subservient to the points emphasized in the Mishnah. They merely
supplied prooftexts for the Mishnah's factual allegations. That conventional approach to the exegesis of the Mishnah is startling when
we consider the prevalent conception of a Messiah who would play a
critical role in Israel's salvation at the end of time and in the resurrection of the dead. It means that, where the Mishnah failed to introduce a current notion, the later exegetes likewise chose not to do
so. So this passage is treated without the slightest inclination to
make conceptual innovations.

What conclusions can we draw from these facts? The first and obvious one is that the authors of the Talmud showed remarkable re-
straint in the exegesis of the Mishnah passage. Whatever they themselves may have thought important, they took up only the issues
already present in the program of the Mishnah's own framers.

Second, if at the time this passage was composed everyone knew that the Messiah in particular would raise the dead, then the omission of the Messiah from the Mishnah's list must have proved striking. In the case of so collective, hence official, a process as the exegesis of the Mishnah, moreover, with consequences for the concrete control of Israel's life, the record surely required correction. It must follow that, whatever beliefs were in circulation within the framework of the consensus prevailing in the circles of masters and disciples, judges and administrators represented in the Yerushalmi, no firm and final judgment had yet been made. By contrast, we shall see how the Scriptures were rewritten to make King David into Rabbi David. That was because all agreed that any great Israelite figure must appear in the model of the rabbi. There was no hesitation in rewriting the ancient records, but, in the present instance, the rabbis clearly saw no reason to do this. Now, if people generally agreed that the figure of the Messiah must be mentioned whenever the end of time came under discussion, then it surely would have appeared in this fundamental passage. The absence of the Messiah here, then, proves one of two things. First, the third- and fourth-century rabbis in the Land of Israel did not perceive the Messiah as the central figure of the eschatological drama; or, second, the Messiah was simply not linked to resurrection of the dead. It adds up to the same thing.

Even if doctrine had not yet been finalized in these circles, still the theme of the Messiah was familiar. As an established myth of the age, the conventional figure appears here and there in the Talmud's discourse. Let us first give a brief account of how this familiar notion makes its appearance and, second, proceed to what I think are the important initiatives in this regard.

When we turn to what by the time of the Mishnah's completion was an entirely conventional repertoire of ideas, we find familiar notions not much developed. Everyone knew, for one thing, that the Messiah would come at the end of time and raise the dead. These commonplace ideas were widely held beyond the circle of sages behind Mishnah or the Talmud of the Land of Israel. They therefore appear routinely. So, for example, when the slaughter of Jewish women by Trajan's forces marked the end of Israel's prosperity, "At that moment the horn of Israel was cut off, and it is not destined to return to its place until the son of David will come" (Y. Suk. 5:1 VII L). The allusion to restoration of Israel's prosperity with the coming of the Messiah merely repeats an ancient conviction. Along the same lines, we find other references of a routine character: "It was like what someone says, 'Until the dead will live!' . . . 'until David's son will come,'" (Y. Qid. 4:1 II/I), meaning, "a long time from now." Again, a reference to "the resurrection of the dead when the Messiah comes" (Y. Ket. 12:3 VIII H) produces no surprise. Nor does the word "messiah" always refer to *the* Messiah, who will come at the end of time and raise the dead. We find that same variety of usage that the Mishnah's authors allow. For instance, "When R. Meir lay dying in Asya, he said, 'Tell the sons of the Land of Israel that your Messiah is coming home for burial'" (Y. Ket. 12:4 XIII A). Indicative of the place of the messianic hope within the estate responsible for this document are three facts.

First, the sages of the Talmud of the Land of Israel were not merely reporting widespread views of others. They shared fully the expectation that the Messiah would come. They hoped it would happen in their own time. They prepared for his coming. The following stories leave no doubt that the myth of the Messiah's coming at the end of time to raise the dead and restore all Israel to its Land found full affirmation among authorities of the present document.

Y. NAZIR 7:1

[X C] R. Hezekiah, R. Jeremiah, and R. Hiyya in the name of R. Yohanan: "It is a religious duty to see the great men of the realm. For when the dynasty of the house of David will come, one must know how to distinguish one dynasty from the other."

Y. KETUBOT 12:3

[III A] R. Jeremiah gave instructions, "Shroud me in white shrouds. Dress me in my slippers, and put my sandals on my feet, and place my staff in my hand, and bury me by the side of a road. If the Messiah comes, I shall be ready."

[VIII G] R. Simeon b. Levi said, "*I walk before the Lord in the land of the living* [Ps. 116:9]. And is not 'the land of the living' only the areas around Tyre and Caesarea and their environs? Everything is there. Everything is abundant there."

[H] R. Simeon b. Levi in the name of Bar Qappara: "It is the land in which the dead will first come to life in the time of the Messiah."

[I] What is the scriptural basis for this view?

[J] "*[Thus says God, the Lord, who created the heavens and stretched*

89

them out, who spread forth the earth and what comes from it,] who gives breath to the people upon it [and spirit to those who walk in it]" [Isa. 42:5].

[K] If that is the case, then our rabbis in Babylonia have lost out!

[L] Said R. Simai, "The Holy One, blessed be he, will cave the ground before them, and they will roll like wineskins. Once they reach the Land of Israel, their souls are with them."

[M] What is the scriptural basis for this view?

[N] *"And I shall put my spirit within you, and you shall live, and I will place you in your own land; then you shall know that I, the Lord, have spoken, and I have done it, says the Lord"* [Ezek. 37:14].

The importance of the first two sayings is that they show us the routine place of the messianic myth among the cited sages. The third item tells us that an effort had now begun to accommodate the myth to a second and separate one, the Torah myth of the talmudic sages themselves. For at issue, we see, is how the rabbis in Babylonia, marked by the special merit of mastery of Torah traditions, would participate in the messianic miracle of resurrection.

Second, what appears to have gotten under way is the process whereby the prevailing notion of a Messiah who would raise the dead at the end of time entered the system of the sages. It was one thing to refer to conventional facts; it was quite another to adopt these facts and use them in a way particular to the rabbinic estate. As we saw, the Mishnah's authors, its first apologists in Abot and the framers of the Tosefta, found remarkably slight use for the Messiah myth. Obviously, they took it as fact. But among the available facts—those provided by Scripture, for example—they selected some and not others for expansion and development. In the document at hand we first observe how sages imposed the distinctive stamp of their own viewpoint on the commonplace conviction of the Israelite community at large. They did so, in particular, by investing the principal messianic figure, David, with the definitive characteristics of the rabbi. As I said, King David came to the fore as Rabbi David. In consequence, the figure of *the* Messiah—as distinct as *a* messiah, such as an anointed priest or a priestly military commander—emerged into mainstream Judaism as it took shape in these documents.

Let us see how the general and leader enters the study circle and, in the speeches which Scripture put in his mouth and in the stories ancient narrators tell about him, how he "talks Torah" and "does Torah deeds." To be sure, the process of rabbinization of the messianic myth surely was not uniform. Not every reference to David served to amplify the myth of the Messiah. In a great many places where David comes under discussion in the Yerushalmi, the historical, not the mythical, figure is at issue. A number of stories about David as king are amplified without introducing the messianic motif, but, as we shall now see, David as rabbi emerges. This means, as I just said, that the storytellers now proposed to make over in their own image the figure of the Messiah. The Messiah would be a rabbi. But it is impossible to say whether we deal with *the* Messiah—the one at the end of time who will raise the dead—or *a* messiah in the Mishnah's use of the title.

Y. SANHEDRIN 2:5

[III H] [To understand the following, we must refer to 2 Sam. 23:15–16: *"And David longed and said, 'O that some one would give me water to drink from the well of Bethlehem which is by the gate!' And the three mighty men broke through the house of Philistines, and drew water out of the well of Bethlehem that was by the gate."* Now "water" here is understood to mean Torah or "learning," "gate" the rabbinical court, and David is thus understood to desire instruction. At issue is the battlefield in which the Philistines had hidden themselves. What troubled David now is at issue.] David found it quite obvious that he might destroy the field of grain and pay its cost.
[I] Could it be obvious to him that he might destroy the field and *not* pay its cost [to the Israelite owners]? [It is not permissible to rescue oneself by destroying someone else's property unless one pays compensation. So that cannot be an issue at all.]
[J] [If he did have to pay, as he realized, then what he wanted to know "at the gate" was] which of them to destroy, and for which of the two he should pay compensation [since he did not wish to destroy both fields such as, at G, Samuel says were there].
[K] [These are then the choices] between the one of lentils and the one of barley.
[L] The one of lentils is food for man, and the one of barley is food for beast. The one of lentils is not liable, when turned into flour, for a dough offering, and the one of barley is liable, when turned into flour, for a dough offering. As to lentils, the *omer* [sheaf to be offered from Passover to Pentecost] is not taken therefrom; as to barley the *omer* is taken therefrom. [So these are the three choices before David, and

since there were two fields, he wanted to know which to burn and for which to pay compensation.]

[IV A] It is written, *"And David said longingly, 'O that someone would give me water to drink from the well of Bethlehem [which is by the gate]"* [1 Chron. 11:17].

[B] R. Hiyya bar Ba said, "He required a teaching of law."

[C] *"Then the three mighty men broke through [the camp of the Philistines]"* [1 Chron. 11:18].

[D] Why three? Because the law is not decisively laid down by fewer than three.

[E] *"But David would not drink it; [he poured it out to the Lord, and said, 'Far be it from me before my God that I should do this. Shall I drink the lifeblood of these men? For at the risk of their lives they brought it']"* [1 Chron. 11:18–19].

[F] David did not want the law to be laid down in his name.

[G] *"He poured it out to the Lord"*—establishing [the decision] as [an unattributed] teaching for the generations [so that the law should be authoritative and so be cited anonymously].

Y. SHEQALIM 2:4

[VI O] And was it so important to R. Yohanan that people say traditions in his name? [Indeed it was,] for David himself prayed for mercy for himself, as it is said, *"Let me dwell in thy tent for ever! Oh to be safe under the shelter of thy wings! Selah"* [Ps. 61:4].

[P] And did it enter David's mind that he would live for ever?

[Q] But this is what David said before the Holy One, blessed be he, "Lord of the world, may I have the merit that my words be stated in synagogues and in school houses."

The representation of David as a master of Torah was not only implicit; the fact that David was a rabbi was made quite explicit.

Y. BERAKHOT 1:1

[XII Q] And what would David do? R. Pinhas in the name of R. Eleazar b. R. Menahem [said], "He used to take a harp and lyre and set them at his bedside. And he would rise at midnight and play them so that the associates of Torah should hear. And what would the associates of Torah say? 'If King David involves himself with Torah, how much more so should we!'"

The Talmud of the Land of Israel thus presents clear evidence that the Messiah myth had come into a process of absorption and assimilation within the larger Torah myth which was characteristic of Judaism in its formative and later literature.

Third, we find a clear effort to identify the person of the Messiah and to confront the claim that a specific, named individual had been, or would be, the Messiah. This means that the issue had reached the center of lively discourse at least in some rabbinic circles. Two contexts framed discussion, the destruction of the Temple and the messianic claim of Bar Kokhba.

As to the former, we find a statement that the Messiah was born on the day the Temple was destroyed. Accordingly, once the figure of the Messiah has come on stage, there arises discussion on who, among the living, the Messiah might be. The identification of the Messiah begins, of course, with the person of David himself: "If the Messiah-King comes from among the living, his name will be David. If he comes from among the dead, it will be King David himself" (Y. Ber. 2:3 V P). A variety of evidence announced the advent of the Messiah as a figure in the larger system of formative Judaism. The rabbinization of David constitutes one kind of evidence. Serious discussion, within the framework of the accepted document of mishnaic exegesis and the law, concerning the identification and claim of diverse figures asserted to be messiahs, presents still more telling proof.

Y. BERAKHOT 2:4
(TRANSLATED BY T. ZAHAVY)

[A] Once a Jew was plowing and his ox snorted once before him. An Arab who was passing and heard the sound said to him, "Jew, loosen your ox and loosen the plow and stop plowing. For today your Temple was destroyed."

[B] The ox snorted again. He [the Arab] said to him, "Jew, bind your ox and bind your plow, for today the Messiah-King was born."

[C] He said to him, "What is his name?"

[D] "Menahem."

[E] He said to him, "And what is his father's name?"

[F] The Arab said to him, "Hezekiah."

[G] He said to him, "Where is he from?"

[H] He said to him, "From the royal capital of Bethlehem in Judea."

[I] The Jew went and sold his ox and sold his plow. And he became a peddler of infant's felt-cloths [diapers]. And he went from place to place until he came to that very city. All of the women bought from him. But Menahem's mother did not buy from him.

[J] He heard the women saying, "Menahem's mother, Menahem's mother, come buy for your child."

[K] She said, "I want to bring him up to hate Israel. For on the day he was born, the Temple was destroyed."

[L] They said to her, "We are sure that on this day it was destroyed, and on this day of the year it will be rebuilt."

[M] She said to the peddler, "I have no money."

[N] He said to her, "It is of no matter to me. Come and buy for him and pay me when I return."

[O] A while later he returned to that city. He said to her, "How is the infant doing?"

[P] She said to him, "Since the time you saw him a spirit came and carried him away from me."

[Q] Said R. Bun, "Why do we learn this from [a story about] an Arab? Do we not have explicit scriptural evidence for it? *Lebanon with its majestic trees will fall* [Isa. 10:34]. And what follows this? *There shall come forth a shoot from the stump of Jesse* [Isa. 11:1]. [Right after an allusion to the destruction of the Temple the prophet speaks of the messianic age.]"

This is a set-piece story, adduced to prove that the Messiah was born on the day the Temple was destroyed. Its importance for our purpose is to indicate that elaborate materials on the Messiah—on his coming, his name, and the like—found a comfortable place within the rabbinic canon. The contrast to the character of discourse in the Mishnah, the Tosefta, and Abot is stunning. From perfunctory allusions, we now move to powerful and suggestive tales. Whether the tale at hand was made up by rabbis to serve some larger systemic purpose is hardly clear. The Messiah was born when the Temple was destroyed; hence, God prepared for Israel a better fate than had appeared.

A more concrete matter—the identification of the Messiah with a known historical personality—was associated with the name of Aqiba. He is said to have claimed that Bar Kokhba, leader of the second-century revolt, was the Messiah. The important aspect of the story, however, is the rejection of Aqiba's view. The discredited messiah figure (if Bar Kokhba actually was such in his own day) finds no apologists in the later rabbinical canon. What is striking in what follows, moreover, is that we really have two stories. At G, Aqiba is said to have believed that Bar Kokhba was a disappointment. At H–I, he is said to have identified Bar Kokhba with the King-Messiah. Both cannot be true, so what we have is simply two separate opinions of Aqiba's judgment of Bar Kokhba/Bar Kozebah.

Y. TAANIT 4:5

[X G] R. Simeon b. Yohai taught, "Aqiba, my master, would interpret the following verse: 'A *star (kokhab) shall come forth out of Jacob*' [Num. 24:17] 'A disappointment (Kozeba) shall come forth out of Jacob.'"
[H] R. Aqiba, when he saw Bar Kozeba, said, "This is the King Messiah."
[I] R. Yohanan ben Toreta said to him, "Aqiba! Grass will grow on your cheeks before the Messiah will come!"

The important point is not only that Aqiba had been proved wrong. It is that the very verse of Scripture adduced in behalf of his viewpoint could be treated more generally and made to refer to righteous people in general, not to *the* Messiah in particular.

Y. NEDARIM 3:8

[I F] R. Gershom in the name of R. Aha: "'*[I see him, but not now; I behold him, but not nigh;] a star shall come out of Jacob [and a scepter shall rise out of Israel]*' [Num. 24:17]. From whom will a star come out? From him who is destined to arise from Jacob."
[G] R. Aha in the name of R. Huna, "Esau, the evil one, is destined to put on his cloak and to dwell with the righteous in the Garden of Eden in the age to come. But the Holy One, blessed be he, will drag and throw him out of there."
[H] What is the scriptural basis for this statement?
[I] "*Though you soar aloft like the eagle, though your nest is set among the stars, thence I will bring you down,*" says the Lord [Obadiah 4].
[J] And "stars" refers only to the righteous, as you say, "*[And those who are wise shall shine like the brightness of the firmament;] and those who turn many to righteousness, like the stars for ever and ever*" [Dan. 12:3].

The evidence of the Talmud of the Land of Israel thus far has suggested that, in the two centuries beyond the closure of the Mishnah, the generally familiar notion of *the* Messiah who would raise the dead and resolve the problems of Israel's destiny had entered the rabbinic canon. Among authorities who contributed to the Mishnah, this same conventional viewpoint surely circulated, even though the Mishnah itself presents a different and more limited conception of the end.

In fact, however, the Talmud of the Land of Israel contains units of discourse in the Mishnah's own, rather reticent, conception. That is, the familiar mishnaic eschatology, lacking all use for a Messiah figure and resolving matters quite differently, makes its appearance here too. The end time will be brought about by the conduct of Israel. The issue of supernatural intervention *without* regard for Israel's own condition plays no role in discourse like the following:

Y. TAANIT 1:1

[VII H] R. Eliezer says, "If the Israelites do not repent, they will not be redeemed forever, since it is said, *'For thus said the Lord God, the Holy One of Israel, "In returning and rest you shall be saved; in quietness and in trust shall be your strength." And you would not'"* [Isa. 30:15].

[I] R. Joshua said to him, "And is it so that if Israel should stand and not repent, they will not be redeemed forever?"

[J] R. Eliezer said to him, "The Holy One, blessed be he, will appoint over them a king as harsh as Haman, and forthwith they will repent and so will be redeemed."

[K] What is the scriptural basis for this view?

[L] *"Alas! that day is so great there is none like it; it is a time of distress for Jacob; yet he shall be saved out of it"* [Jer. 30:7].

[M] R. Joshua said to him, "And lo, it is written, *'For thus says the Lord, "You were sold for nothing, and you shall be redeemed without money"'* [Isa. 52:3]. [Redemption is without preconditions.]"

[N] How does R. Eliezer deal with the cited verse?

[O] It presupposes repentance, as Scripture has said, *"He took a bag of money with him"* [Prov. 7:20].

[P] R. Joshua said to him, "And lo, it is written, *'I am the Lord; in its time I will hasten it'"* [Isa. 60:22].

[Q] How does R. Eliezer deal with this verse?

[R] It speaks of repentance, as it says, *"And now, Israel, what does the Lord your God require of you, but to fear the Lord your God, to walk in all his ways, to love him, to serve the Lord your God with all your heart and with all your soul"* [Deut. 10:12].

[S] R. Aha in the name of R. Joshua b. Levi: "If you have merit, I shall hasten it, and if not, it will come only in its time."

While a little ingenuity would easily resolve the apparent contradiction between an eschatology focused upon miraculous intervention by the Messiah and a teleology centered upon Israel's moral condition, to us such harmonization is unimportant. Indeed, it proves our point, for we seek to differentiate two clearly distinct ideas. The appearance of two separate streams of thought on a given question requires description and interpretation, rather than (mere) harmonization. Since the Mishnah, the document upon which the Yerushalmi is supposed to comment, contains only one of these ideas, it would appear that the other—the messianic idea—flows from some source other than the inherited document. That thesis, as noted at the outset, gains strength from the literary context in which the Messiah myth made its appearance. On the basis of the literary setting alone, we must say that the Messiah myth derived from reflection upon something other than the propositions of the Mishnah. True, the figure of the Messiah rapidly gained full naturalization as a rabbi. The myth, once received, underwent the natural processes of absorption into the larger rabbinic framework. But the messianic eschatology hardly fit into the Mishnah's system.

The question of place of the mishnaic figure in the framework of rabbinic Judaism, alas, cannot find a ready solution, for the Messiah myth carries its own meanings. These prove to be integral and definitive in its character. Unless drained of all its antecedent meaning, the Messiah myth not only stands separate from the eschatological theory of the Mishnah, but also contradicts the very character of the Mishnah's entire system. The reason is that one cannot address and describe both a world in stasis, one awaiting sanctification at the magical moment of perfection, and also a society in transit, which moves toward salvation at the end of time. One cannot speak at one and the same moment of sanctification and salvation. These categories represent essentially distinct judgments of the critical issue, Israel's destiny. At the heart of it all, we may speak of *being* or we may talk of *becoming*, but we cannot stand still in classic perfection and at the same time move toward an age of resolution. The images collide. The symbols do not fit. The very condition upon which we focus exhibits deep asymmetry. We may confront either structure or history, either condition or destiny, but not both. To revert to mythic language, Israel is saved either by repentance *or* by the Messiah. But stories about the one at this point do not intersect, let alone harmonize, with tales about the other. Rabbinizing the Messiah hardly matters. The Messiah remains a salvific figure, out of place in a realm of consecration unto perfection.

In speaking of the myth of the Messiah, we also confront a range of deeper issues, captured and presented in the sources at hand within the Messiah myth. These deeper questions concern precisely the issue of the meaning and end of Israel's history: whether history matters, indeed, constitutes a critical dimension of Israel's existence, and if it does, how it is to be explained. The Mishnah, its apology in Abot, and its closest associate the Tosefta are all three wholly consistent on this point. As a sequence of one-time events, each bearing a distinctive message and pointing in a given direction, history presents no significant testimony. True, events must be taken seriously, but Israel copes with them by discovering what makes them uneventful—their shared taxonomic traits, their susceptibility to the power of orderly classification. That is how the Mishnah absorbs events into its system. How the Talmud of the Land of Israel treats these same questions is the next step in our search.

THE USES AND MEANING OF HISTORY
IN THE TALMUD OF THE
LAND OF ISRAEL

Disorderly historical events entered the system of the Mishnah and found their place within the larger framework of the Mishnah's orderly world. But to claim that the Mishnah's framers merely ignored what was happening would be incorrect. They worked out their own way of dealing with historical events, the disruptive power of which they not only conceded but freely recognized. Further, the Mishnah's authors did not intend to compose a history book or a work of prophecy or apocalypse. Even if they had wanted to narrate the course of events, they could hardly have done so through the medium of the Mishnah. Yet the Mishnah presents its philosophy in full awareness of the issues of historical calamity confronting the

Jewish nation. So far as the philosophy of the document confronts the totality of Israel's existence, the Mishnah by definition *also* presents a philosophy of history.

The Mishnah's subordination of historical events contradicts the emphasis of a thousand years of Israelite thought. The biblical histories, the ancient prophets, the apocalyptic visionaries all had testified that events themselves were important. Events carried the message of the living God. Events constituted history, pointed toward, and so explained, Israel's destiny. An essentially ahistorical system of timeless sanctification, worked out through construction of an eternal rhythm which centered on the movement of the moon and stars and seasons, represented a life chosen by few outside of the priesthood. Furthermore, the pretense that what *happens* matters less than what *is* testified against palpable and memorable reality. Israel had suffered enormous loss of life. As we shall see, the Talmud of the Land of Israel takes these events seriously and treats them as unique and remarkable. The memories proved real. The hopes evoked by the Mishnah's promise of sanctification of a world in static perfection did not. For they had to compete with the grief of an entire century of mourning.

Y. TAANIT 4:5

[X B] Rabbi would derive by exegesis twenty-four tragic events from the verse, *"The Lord has destroyed without mercy all the habitations of Jacob; in his wrath he has broken down the strongholds of the daughter of Judah; he has brought down to the ground in dishonor the kingdom and its rulers"* [Lam. 2:2].
[C] R. Yohanan derived sixty from the same verse.
[D] Did R. Yohanan then find more than Rabbi did in the same verse?
[E] But because Rabbi lived nearer to the destruction of the Temple, there were in the audience old men who remembered what had happened, and when he gave his exegesis, they would weep and fall silent and get up and leave.

We do not know whether things happened as the storyteller says. But the fact remains that the framers of the Yerushalmi preserved the observation that, in Rabbi's time, memory of world-shaking events continued to shape Israel's mind and imagination. For people like those portrayed here, the Mishnah's classification of tragedy cannot have solved many problems.

Accordingly, we should not be surprised to observe that the Talmud of the Land of Israel contains evidence pointing toward substantial steps taken in rabbinical circles away from the position of the Mishnah. We find materials that fall entirely outside the framework of historical doctrine as established within the Mishnah. These are, first, an interest in the periodization of history and, second, a willingness to include events of far greater diversity than those in the Mishnah. So the Yerushalmi contains an expanded view of the range of human life encompassed by the conception of history.

Let us take the second point first. Things happen that demand attention and constitute "events"; within the Mishnah these fall into two classifications, biblical history and events involving the Temple. A glance at the catalogue, cited above (p. 34) from M. Ta. 4:6, tells us what kind of happening constitutes an "event," a historical datum demanding attention and interpretation. In this Talmud, by contrast, we find, in addition to Temple events, two other sorts of *Geschichten*: Torah events, that is, important stories about the legal and supernatural doings of rabbis, and also political events.

These events, moreover, involve people not considered in the Mishnah: Gentiles as much as Jews, Rome as much as Israel. The Mishnah's history, such as it is, knows only Israel. The Talmud greatly expands the range of historical interest when it develops a theory of Rome's relationship to Israel, and, of necessity also, Israel's relationship to Rome.

Only by taking account of the world at large can the Talmud's theory of history yield a philosophy of history worthy of the name, that is, an account of who Israel is, the meaning of what happens to Israel, and the destiny of Israel in this world and at the end of time. Israel by itself—as the priests had claimed—lived in eternity, beyond time. Israel and Rome together struggled in historical time—an age with a beginning, a middle, and an end. That is the importance of the expanded range of historical topics found in the present Talmud. When, in the Babylonian Talmud, we find a still broader interest, in Iran as much as Rome and in the sequence of world empires past and present, we see how such a rich and encompassing theory of historical events begins with a simple step toward a universal perspective. It was a step that I think the scribes and priests represented by the Mishnah, unlike the ancient prophets and apocalyptists, were incapable of taking.

The concept of periodization—the raw material of historical thought—hardly presents surprises, since apocalyptic writers began their work by differentiating one age from another. When the Mishnah includes a statement of the "periods" into which time is divided, however, it speaks only of stages of the cult: Shiloh, Nob, Jerusalem. One age is differentiated from the next not by reference to world-historical changes but only by the location of sacrifice and the eating of the victim. The rules governing each locale impose taxa upon otherwise undifferentiated time. So periodization constitutes a function of the larger system of sanctification through sacrifice. The contrast between "this world" and "the world to come," which is not a narrowly historical conception in the Mishnah, now finds a counterpart in the Talmud's contrast between "this age" and the age in which the Temple stood. That distinction is very much an act of this-worldly historical differentiation. It not only yields apocalyptic speculation, but also generates sober and worldly reflection on the movement of events and the meaning of history in the prophetic-apocalyptic tradition. Accordingly, the Talmud of the Land of Israel presents both the expected amplification of the established concepts familiar from the Mishnah and a separate set of ideas, perhaps rooted in prior times but still independent of what the Mishnah in particular had encompassed.

Let us first survey what is new and striking. From the viewpoint of the Mishnah, as I have suggested, the single most unlikely development is interest in the history of a nation other than Israel. For the Mishnah views the world beyond the sacred Land as unclean, tainted in particular with corpse-uncleanness. Outside the holy lies the realm of death. The faces of that world are painted in the monotonous white of the grave. Only within the range of the sacred do things happen. There, events may be classified and arranged, all in relationship to the Temple and its cult. By standing majestically unchanged by the vicissitudes of time, the cult rises above history. Now ancient Israelite interest in the history of the great empires of the world—perceived, to be sure, in relationship to the history of Israel—reemerges within the framework of the documents that succeeded the Mishnah. Naturally, in the Land of Israel only one empire mattered; this is Rome, which, in the Yerushalmi, is viewed solely as the counterpart to Israel. The world then consists of two nations: Israel, the weaker, and Rome, the stronger. Jews enjoy a sense of vastly enhanced importance when they contemplate such a world, containing as it does only two peoples that matter, of whom one is Israel. But from our perspective, its utility for the morale of the defeated people holds no interest. What strikes us is the evidence of the formation of a second and separate system of historical interpretation, beyond that of the Mishnah.

History and doctrine merge, with history being made to yield doctrine. What is stunning is the perception of Rome as an autonomous actor, that is, as an entity with a point of origin (just as Israel has a point of origin) and a tradition of wisdom (just as Israel has such a tradition). These are the two points at which the large-scale conception of historical Israel finds a counterpart in the present literary composition. This sense of poised opposites, Israel and Rome, comes to expression in two ways.

First, as we shall now see, it is Israel's own history that calls into being its counterpoint, the anti-history of Rome. Without Israel, there would be no Rome—a wonderful consolation to the defeated nation. For if Israel's sin created Rome's power, then Israel's repentance would bring Rome's downfall. Here is the way in which the Talmud presents the match:

Y. ABODAH ZARAH 1:2

[IV E] *Saturnalia* means "hidden hatred" [*sina'ah temunah*]: The Lord hates, takes vengeance, and punishes.

[F] This is in accord with the following verse: *"Now Esau hated Jacob"* [Gen. 27:41].

[G] R. Isaac b. R. Eleazar said, "In Rome they call it Esau's Saturnalia."

[H] *Kratesis*: It is on the day on which the Romans seized power.

[K] Said R. Levi, "It is the day on which Solomon intermarried with the family of Pharaoh Neccho, King of Egypt. On that day Michael came down and thrust a reed into the sea, and pulled up muddy alluvium, and this was turned into a huge pot, and this was the great city of Rome. On the day on which Jeroboam set up the two golden calves, Remus and Romulus came and built two huts in the city of Rome. On the day on which Elijah disappeared, a king was appointed in Rome: *"There was no king in Edom; a deputy was king"* [1 Kings 22:47].

The important point is that Solomon's sin provoked heaven's founding of Rome.

Quite naturally, the conception of history and anti-history will assign to the actors in the anti-history—the Romans—motives explicable in terms of history, that is, the history of Israel. The entire world and what happens in it enter into the framework of meaning established by Israel's Torah. So what the Romans do, their historical actions, can be explained in terms of Israel's conception of the world. A striking example of the tendency to explain Rome's deeds through Israel's logic is the reason given for Trajan's war against the Jews.

Y. SUKKAH 5:1

[VII   A] In the time of Tronianus the evil one, a son was born to him on the ninth of Ab, and the Israelites were fasting.

[B] His daughter died on Hanukkah, and the Israelites lit candles.

[C] His wife sent a message to him, saying, "Instead of going out to conquer the barbarians, come and conquer the Jews, who have rebelled against you."

[D] He thought that the trip would take ten days, but he arrived in five.

[E] He came and found the Israelites occupied in study of the Light of Torah, with the following verse: "*The Lord will bring a nation against you from afar, from the end of the earth, as swift as the eagle flies, a nation whose language you do not understand*" [Deut. 28:49].

[F] He said to them, "With what are you occupied?"

[G] They said to him, "With thus-and-so."

[H] He said to them, "That man [I] thought that it would take ten days to make the trip but arrived in five days." His legions surrounded them and killed them.

[I] He said to the women, "Obey my legions and I shall not kill you."

[J] They said to him, "What you did to the ones who have fallen do also to us who are yet standing."

[K] He mingled their blood with the blood of their men, until the blood flowed into the ocean as far as Cyprus.

[L] At that moment the horn of Israel was cut off, and it is not destined to return to its place until the son of David will come.

What is important here is the source of what we might call "historical explanation," deriving, as it does, from the larger framework of the sages' conviction. Trajan had done nothing except with God's help and by God's design. Here is another example:

103

Y. GITTIN 5:7

[I A] In the beginning the Romans decreed oppression against Judah, for they had a tradition in their hands from their forefathers that Judah had slain Esau, for it is written, *"Your hand shall be on the neck of your enemies"* [Gen. 49:8].

This means, again, that things make sense wholly in the categories of Torah. The world retains its logic, and Israel knows (and can manipulate) that logic.

At the foundations is the tension between Israel's God and the pagan gods. That is, historical explanation here invokes the familiar polemic of Scripture. Accordingly, the development of an interest in Roman history—of a willingness to take as important events in the history of some nation other than Israel—flows from an established (and rather wooden) notion of the world in which God and gods ("idols") compete. Israel's history of subjugation testifies, not to the weakness of Israel's God, but to his strength. The present prosperity of idolaters, involving the subjugation of Israel, attests only to God's remarkable patience, God's love for the world he made. This conception, familiar to be sure in the Mishnah itself, now gets absorbed into historical categories of "now" and "then." That is to say, the notion of competition between God and no-gods, Israel and Rome, is set within the framework of differentiation between "this age" and "the time to come." Since that notion marks a stop beyond the way in which the same theme had come to expression in the Mishnah and Tosefta, we had best review the development of the same passage in its literary—hence canonical—sequences. (The citation of the Mishnah is given in italics, the citation of the subsequent Tosefta in boldface type, and the Yerushalmi's contribution in ordinary type.)

Y. ABODAH ZARAH 4:7

[A] *They asked the sages in Rome, "If God is not in favor of idolatry why does he not wipe it out?"*

[B] *They said to them, "If people worshiped something of which the world has no need, and leave something that the world needs!"*

[C] *"But lo, people worship the sun, moon, stars, and planets.*

[D] *"Now do you think he is going to wipe out his world because of idiots?"*

[E] *They said to them, "If so, let them destroy something of which the*

world has no need, and leave something that the world needs!"
[F] *They said to them, "Then we should strengthen the hands of those who worship these, which would not be destroyed, for then they would say, 'Now you know full well that they are gods, for lo, they were not wiped out!'"*
[I A] *Philosophers asked the sages in Rome, "If God is not in favor of idolatry, why does he not wipe it out?" They said to them, "If people worshiped something of which the world had no need, he certainly would wipe it out. But lo, people worship the sun, moon, and stars. Now do you think he is going to wipe out his world because of idiots?"* [M. 4:7A–D].
[B] "But let the world be in accord with its accustomed way, and the idiots who behave ruinously will ultimately come and give a full account of themselves. If one has stolen seeds for planting, are they not ultimately going to sprout? If one has had sexual relations with a married woman, will she not ultimately give birth? But let the world follow its accustomed way, and the idiots who behave ruinously will ultimately come and give a full account of themselves" [T. A.Z. 6:7].
[II A] Said R. Zeira, "If it were written, 'Those who worship them are like them,' there would be a problem. Are those who worship the sun like the sun, those who worship the moon like the moon? But this is what is written: 'Those who make them are like them; so are all who trust in them' [Ps. 115:8]."
[B] Said R. Mana, "If it were written, 'Those who worship them are like them,' it would pose no problem whatsoever. For it also is written, 'Then the moon will be confounded, and the sun ashamed' [Isa. 24:23]."
[C] R. Nahman in the name of R. Mana, "Idolatry is destined in the end to come and spit in the face of those that worship idols, and it will bring them to shame and cause them to be nullified from the world."
[D] Now what is the scriptural basis for that statement?
[E] "All the worshipers of images will be put to shame, who make their boast in worthless idols" [Ps. 97:7].
[F] R. Nahman in the name of R. Mana, "Idolatry is destined in time to come to bow down before the Holy One, blessed be He, and then be nullified from the world."
[G] What is the scriptural basis for that statement?
[H] "All worshipers of images will be put to shame . . . ; all gods bow down before him" [Ps. 97:7].

The important point comes at II C–H, at which the Talmud's sages present a temporal differentiation absent in the Mishnah.

105

The problem of the Mishnah is a philosophical one. The Tosefta's anonymous authorities make that point explicit. There is a certain logic, an inevitability, upon which Israel may rely. True, idolatry prospers. But idolaters, will be called to account. Now that essentially atemporal notion, which can sustain the interpretation of a last judgment for individuals, moves into a temporal-historical framework at the third stage. Not merely the idolater, as an individual, will come to account. The *age* of idolatry itself will come to an end. We differentiate between this age, which is bad, and another age, a period in time, which will be good. The notion of temporal sequences upon which historical thinking rests in no way serves the framers of the Mishnah passage. By contrast, it is essential to the thought, concerning idolatry, of the authorities cited in the Talmud.

The concept of two histories, balanced opposite one another, comes to particular expression, within the Yerushalmi, in the balance of Israelite sage and Roman emperor. Just as Israel and Rome, God and no-gods, compete (with a foreordained conclusion), so do sage and emperor. In this age, it appears that the emperor has the power, as do Rome and the pagan gods with their temples in full glory. God's Temple, by contrast, lies in ruins. But just as sages overcome the emperor through their inherent supernatural power, so too will Israel and Israel's God in the coming age control the course of events.

Y. TERUMOT 8:10
(TRANSLATED BY ALAN AVERY-PECK)

[IV A] As to Diocles the swineherd, the students of R. Yudan the Patriarch would make fun of him.

[B] He [Diocletian] became emperor and moved to Paneas.

[C] He sent letters to the rabbis, [saying], "You must be here [to see] me immediately after the end of the [coming] Sabbath."

[D] He instructed the messenger [who was to deliver these orders], "Do not give them the letters until the eve [of Sabbath], just as the sun is setting." [Diocletian hoped to force the rabbis to miss the appointment, for they would not travel on the Sabbath. Then he could have revenge on them because of their cavalier treatment of him (A).]

[E] The messenger came to them on the eve [of Sabbath] as the sun was setting.

[F] [After receiving the message] R. Yudan the Patriarch and R. Samuel bar Nahman were sitting in the public baths in Tiberias. Antigris, [a certain spirit, appeared and] came to their side.

[G] R. Yudan the Patriarch wished to rebuke him [and chase him away].

[H] R. Samuel bar Nahman said to him [Yudan], "Leave him be. He appears as a messenger of salvation."

[I] [Antigris] said to them, "What is troubling the rabbis?"

[J] They told him the story [and] he said to them, "[Finish] bathing [in honor of the Sabbath]. For your creator is going to perform miracles [for you]."

[K] At the end of the Sabbath [Antigris] took them and placed them [in Paneas].

[L] They told [the emperor], "Lo, the rabbis are outside!"

[M] He said, "They shall not see my face until they have bathed."

[N] [Diocletian] had the bath heated for seven days and nights [so that the rabbis could not stand the heat].

[O] [To make it possible for them to enter, Antigris] went in before them and overpowered the heat.

[P] [Afterwards] they went and stood before [the king].

[Q] He said to them, "Is it because your creator performs miracles for you that you despise the [Roman] Empire?"

[R] They said to him, "Diocles the swineherd did we despise. But Diocletian the emperor we do not despise."

[S] Diocletian said to them, "Even so, you should not rebuke [anyone], neither a young Roman, nor a young associate [of the rabbis, for you never know what greatness that individual will attain]."

The this-worldly, practical wisdom contained at the end should not blind us to the importance of the story within the larger theory of history presented in the Yerushalmi. The Mishnah finds ample place for debates between "philosophers" and rabbis. But in the Mishnah the high priest in the Temple and the king upon his throne do not weigh in the balance, or stand poised against, equal and opposite powers, the pagan priest in his temple, the Roman emperor on his throne. The very conception is inconceivable within the context of the Mishnah.

For the Yerushalmi, by contrast, two stunning innovations appear: first, the notion of emperor and sage in mortal struggle; second, the idea of an age of idolatry and an age beyond idolatry. The world had to move into a new orbit indeed for Rome to enter into the historical context formerly defined wholly by what happened to Israel.

To our secular eyes these developments seem perfectly natural.

After all, the Jews really had been conquered. Their Temple really had been destroyed. So why should they not have taken an interest in the history of the conqueror and tried to place into relationship with their own history the things that happened to him? We find self-evident, moreover, the comfort to be derived from the explanations consequent upon the inclusion of Roman history, in the Yerushalmi's doctrine of the world. But Israel had been defeated many times before the composition of the Mishnah, and the Temple had lain in ruins for nearly a century and a half when Judah the Patriarch promulgated the Mishnah as Israel's code of law. So the circumstances in which the Talmud's materials were composed hardly differed materially from the conditions in which, from Bar Kokhba onward, sages selected from what lay at hand and composed the Mishnah.

The Scripture that, after all, was present offered testimony to the centrality of history as a sequence of meaningful events. Biblical writings amply testified to the message and uses of history as a source of teleology for any Israelite system. Prophecy and apocalyptic had long coped quite well with defeat and dislocation. Yet, in the Mishnah, Israel's deeds found no counterpart in Roman history, while, in the Palestinian Talmud, they did. In the Mishnah, time is differentiated quite apart from national and historical categories. For, as in Abot, "this world" is when one is alive, "the world to come" when a person dies. True, we find also "this world" and "the time of the Messiah," but detailed differentiation among the ages of "this world" or "this age" hardly generates problems in mishnaic thought. Indeed, no such differentiation appears. Accordingly, the developments briefly outlined up to this point constitute a significant shift in the course of intellectual events, to which the sources at hand—the Mishnah, Tosefta, and Talmud of the Land of Israel—amply testify.

Differentiation between the time in which the Temple stood and the present age, of course, hardly will have surprised the authors of the Mishnah. It was a natural outcome of the Mishnah's own division of ages. We recall how time was divided by the location of the altar, and how the divisions were explained by reference to what was done in that regard. Now we find a specification of the exact years involved. Not surprisingly, however, since the Mishnah, unlike the Tosefta, does not speculate on when the Temple will be rebuilt so here the framers of the passage in Yerushalmi do not specify the year in which they think the Temple will be rebuilt. The Messiah's coming plays no role at all.

Y. MEGILLAH 1:12

[XI O] So with the tent of meeting: it spent forty years less one in Gilgal. In Gilgal it spent fourteen years, seven when they were conquering the land and seven when they were dividing it.

[P] In Shilo it spent three hundred and sixty-nine years.

[Q] In Nob and Gibeon it spent fifty-seven years, thirteen in Nob and forty-four in Gibeon.

[R] In Jerusalem in the time of the first building it was there for four hundred and ten years.

[S] In the time of the second building it was four hundred ten years. This was meant to fulfill the statement of Scripture: *"The latter splendor of this house shall be greater than the former, says the Lord of hosts; and in this place I will give prosperity, says the Lord of hosts"* [Hag. 2:9].

Strikingly absent is any prediction as to *when* the third temple would be rebuilt. In due course many would take up the work of speculation and calculation. But, in his exegesis of the Mishnah, the author of this passage does not do so.

The principal point of differentiation between one age and another remained the destruction of the Temple, which, in the spirit of M. Sot. 9:15 (cited above, p. 26), marked the turn of the age. Rules held applicable to Temple times were reexamined to see whether they continued to apply. For example, "What is the law as to tearing one's garments *at this time* upon hearing God cursed in euphemisms?" (Y. San. 7:8 VII C). But the important point is the least obvious. Not everything bad in the current age was to be blamed on the destruction. The explanation of contention in discussions of the law, for instance, involved *not* the differentiation between historical periods, but the (timeless) failure of the disciples. "In the beginning there was no contention; but ill-prepared disciples caused it" (Y. Hag. 2:I C). But the end of the matter still turns upon history: "The Torah is not going to be restored to its wholeness until the son of David comes" (ibid., E). In context, the meaning is "a long time from now." The step seems a small one. "This age" and "the other age" shifted at 70. Now, as soon as some other point of differentiation enters which is not based upon the destruction of the

Temple, a new possibility emerges. Specifically, the potentiality for a theory of Israel's life which was not spun out of the cult and that for a theory of its history begins to move toward realization. This much we can deduce from the slight evidence at hand.

A further mark of the development in differentiating among historical periods is found in the commemoration of important events. When one day is differentiated from another because of what happened on that same date a long time ago, so also goes the Mishnah's principal criterion for distinguishing the passage of time. The framers of the Mishnah, following the priestly tradition, knew that one day differed from another because of the passage of the moon through fixed stars in heaven (e.g., Passover falls on the first full moon after the vernal equinox) and because of the consequent revision of the cultic offerings on earth (as at Numbers 28—29). As we noted, sages also absorbed into their system one-time historical events, such as the seventeenth of Tammuz and the ninth of Ab. But those events proved incidental to the construction of a larger system, with Mishnah's tractates named for festivals of the natural year and focused upon Temple rites for those days. When, therefore, we discover units of discourse devoted to specific historical events and their meaning, we find ourselves in a new situation, because events we regard as historical, as distinct from those we see as natural or supernatural, also have now come to be taken seriously. One day differs from another not by virtue of the criterion of creation, but on account of a political or other historical event. The only such historical, non-natural event absorbed into the Mishnah's system involved the Temple. Accordingly, in what follows, we deal with a different approach to time from the one characteristic of the Mishnaic system.

Let me explain. Having evidently inherited from former times a calendar of important celebrations in Israel's history which were marked by the prohibition against fasting, the Yerushalmi's sages pursued the issue. In the following unit of discourse we find attention to the traits of commemorative days, consonant with the interest in historical periodization noted earlier.

Y. MEGILLAH 1:4

[IX B] On the twelfth of that month [of Adar] is Tirion's day? [That day on which the decrees of Trajan were annulled is a holiday and it is

forbidden to fast on that day, contrary to Meir's view of acceptable behavior on the twelfth of Adar, in line with M. Meg. 1:4G.]
[C] And R. Jacob bar Aha said, "Tirion's day has been annulled, for it
is the day on which Lulianos and Pappos were killed."
[D] The thirteenth of that month of Adar is Nicanor's Day.
[E] What is Nicanor's Day? The ruler of the Kingdom of Greece was
passing by the Land of Israel en route to Alexandria. He saw Jerusalem and broke out into cursing and execration, saying, "When I come
back in peace, I shall break down that tower." The members of the
Hasmonean household went forth and did battle with his troops and
killed them until they came to see those nearest the king. When they
reached the troops nearest the king, they cut off the hand of the king
and chopped off his head and stuck them on a pole, and wrote underneath them, "Here is the mouth that spoke shamefully and the hand
that stretched out arrogantly." These he set up on a pike in sight of
Jerusalem.

The importance of this passage is that attention focuses upon the
meaning of days distinguished because of the specific events that
took place then. There is no further taxonomic interest. The events
are of a clearly historical character—that is, in no way related to the
cult or the natural course of the moon in the heavens—and bear no
claim that what happens matters only if the Temple is directly affected. True, in the background the Temple always is an issue. Further, the days under discussion, when it is forbidden to mourn, appear on the so-called Fasting Scroll; hence all the events fall into a
single taxon. Yet the Mishnah's treatment of that matter neglects the
very thing the Yerushalmi's authorities take up: the specifics of what
happened, the exegesis, in its own terms, of the Scroll and the
events to which it refers. And that is the main point. The framers of
the passage at hand move out beyond the limits of the Mishnah's
system when they narrate events essentially independent of happenings in the cult. Such events, moreover, are distinguished from one
another and are in no way forced into a uniform taxon. In this step,
as in others we have reviewed, we see how the authors represented
in the Yerushalmi move into a framework of thought in which Israel's being is described and interpreted in historical-eschatological
terms, not in natural-supernatural ones.

Still, the Temple's destruction would always mark the caesura of time. Important political events were to be dated in relation to that date. Israel lost the right to judge capital cases "forty years before the Temple was destroyed" (Y. San. 7:2 III A). So, too, forty years before the destruction, ominous signs of the coming end began to appear:

Y. SOTAH 6:3

[IV A] Forty years before the destruction of the Temple the western light went out, the crimson thread remained crimson, and the lot for the Lord always came up in the left hand.
[B] They would close the gates of the Temple by night and get up in the morning and find them wide open.
[C] Said Rabban Yohanan ben Zakkai to the Temple, "O Temple, why do you frighten us? We know that you will end up destroyed.
[D] "For it has been said, 'Open your doors, O Lebanon, that the fire may devour your cedars!'" [Zech. 11:1].

Reference to the destruction of the Temple as a principal landmark in the division of history is hardly surprising. The framers of the Mishnah surely will not have been surprised, since, for them, as M. Sot. 9:15 shows, with the destruction, the old age had turned into the new and darkening one. What was important to them was to find the counterpart in the life of the sages, since the holy life of the Temple and the holy life of the Torah circles matched one another. So, in all, the Temple continued to provide the principal and generative paradigm—whether historical or cultic.

But as I have emphasized, the definition of significant, hence historical, events now expanded to encompass things that happened beyond the Temple walls, yet still in connection with the Temple's destruction. The main point is that, in the Talmud at hand, the established symmetry was shattered. The Temple's destruction had been made the counterpoise to the decline in the generations of sages. But now the Temple's destruction stood for much more and testified, so to speak, in a wider variety of cases to the decline of the supernatural world, whether priestly or scribal (to use our terms, not theirs). The message of M. Sot. 9:15 was one thing, the message of the tales at hand a larger and more encompassing *other* story. That, then, is the turning point, the transformation of the Temple's destruction into an event bearing consequences in many other ways.

The most important change is the shift in historical thinking adumbrated in the pages of the Yerushalmi, a shift from focus upon the Temple and its supernatural history to close attention to the people Israel and its natural, this-worldly history. Once Israel, holy Israel, had come to form the counterpart to the Temple and its supernatural life, that other history—Israel's—would stand at the center of things. Accordingly, a new sort of memorable event came to the fore in the Talmud of the Land of Israel. Let me give this new history appropriate emphasis: *it was the story of Israel's suffering, remembrance of that suffering, on the one side, and an effort to explain events of such tragedy, on the other.* So a composite "history" constructed out of the Yerushalmi's units of discourse which were pertinent to consequential events would contain long chapters on what happened to Israel, the Jewish people, and not only, or mainly, what had earlier occurred in the Temple.

This expansion in the range of historical interest and theme forms the counterpart to the emphasis, throughout the law, upon the enduring sanctity of Israel, the people, which paralleled the sanctity of the Temple in its time. What is striking in the Yerushalmi's materials on Israel's suffering (as we saw above, p. 103) is the sages' interest in finding a motive for what the Romans had done. That motive derived specifically from the repertoire of explanations already available in Israelite thought. In adducing scriptural reasons for the Roman policy, as we saw, sages extended to the world at large that same principle of intelligibility, in terms of Israel's own Scripture and logic that, in the law itself, made everything sensible and reliable. So the labor of writing history (or at least, telling stories about historical events) went together with the work of making laws. The whole formed a single explanation of things that had happened—it created a historical explanation. True, one enterprise involved historical events, the other, legal constructions. But the outcome was one and the same.

The components of the historical theory of Israel's sufferings were manifold. First and foremost, history taught moral lessons. Historical events entered into the construction of a teleology for the Yerushalmi's system of Judaism as a whole. What the law demanded reflected the consequences of wrongful action on the part of Israel. So, again, Israel's own deeds defined the events of history. Rome's role, like Assyria's and Babylonia's, depended upon Israel's provoking divine wrath as it was executed by the great empire. This mode of thought comes to simple expression in what follows.

Y. ERUBIN 3:9

[IV   B] R. Ba, R. Hiyya in the name of R. Yohanan: "*Do not gaze at me because I am swarthy, because the sun has scorched me. My mother's sons were angry with me, they made me keeper of the vineyards; but, my own vineyard, I have not kept!'* [Song 1:6]. What made me guard the vineyards? It is because of not keeping my own vineyard.
[C] "What made me keep two festival days in Syria? It is because I did not keep the proper festival day in the Holy Land.
[D] "I imagined that I would receive a reward for the two days, but I received a reward only for one of them.
[E] "Who made it necessary that I should have to separate two pieces of dough-offering from grain grown in Syria? It is because I did not separate a single piece of dough-offering in the Land of Israel."

Israel had to learn the lesson of its history to also take command of its own destiny.

But this notion of determining one's own destiny should not be misunderstood. The framers of the Talmud of the Land of Israel were not telling the Jews to please God by doing commandments in order that they should thereby gain control of their own destiny. To the contrary, the paradox of the Yerushalmi's system lies in the fact that Israel can free itself of control by other nations *only* by humbly agreeing to accept God's rule. The nations—Rome, in the present instance—rest on one side of the balance, while God rests on the other. Israel must then choose between them. There is no such thing for Israel as freedom from both God and the nations, total autonomy and independence. There is only a choice of masters, a ruler on earth or a ruler in heaven.

With propositions such as these, the framers of the Mishnah will certainly have concurred. And why not? For the fundamental affirmations of the Mishnah about the centrality of Israel's perfection in stasis—sanctification—readily prove congruent to the attitudes at hand. Once the Messiah's coming had become dependent upon Israel's condition and not upon Israel's actions in historical time, then the Mishnah's system will have imposed *its* fundamental and definitive character upon the Messiah myth. An eschatological teleology framed through that myth then would prove wholly appropriate to the method of the larger system of the Mishnah. When this fact has been fully and completely spelled out in the final chapter, we shall then have grasped the distinctive history of the myth of the Messiah in the formative history of Judaism.

What, after all, makes a messiah a false messiah? In this Talmud, it is not his claim to save Israel, but his claim to save Israel without the help of God. The meaning of the true Messiah is Israel's total submission, through the Messiah's gentle rule, to God's yoke and service. So God is not to be manipulated through Israel's humoring heaven in rite and cult. The notion of keeping the commandments so as to please heaven and get God to do what Israel wants is totally incongruent to the text at hand. Keeping the commandments as a mark of submission, loyalty, humility before God is the rabbinic system of salvation. So Israel does not "save itself." Israel never controls its own destiny, either on earth or in heaven. The only choice is whether to cast one's fate into the hands of cruel, deceitful men, or to trust in the living God of mercy and love. We shall now see how this critical position is spelled out in the setting of discourse about the Messiah in the Talmud of the Land of Israel.

Bar Kokhba, above all, exemplifies arrogance against God. He lost the war because of that arrogance. In particular, he ignored the authority of sages:

Y. TAANIT 4:5

[X J] Said R. Yohanan, "Upon orders of Caesar Hadrian, they killed eight hundred thousand in Betar."

[K] Said R. Yohanan, "There were eighty thousand pairs of trumpeteers surrounding Betar. Each one was in charge of a number of troops. Ben Kozeba was there and he had two hundred thousand troops who, as a sign of loyalty, had cut off their little fingers.

[L] "Sages sent word to him, 'How long are you going to turn Israel into a maimed people?'

[M] "He said to them, 'How otherwise is it possible to test them?'

[N] "They replied to him, 'Whoever cannot uproot a cedar of Lebanon while riding on his horse will not be inscribed on your military rolls.'

[O] "So there were two hundred thousand who qualified in one way, and another two hundred thousand who qualified in another way."

115

[P] When he would go forth to battle, he would say, "Lord of the world! Do not help and do not hinder us! *'Hast thou not rejected us, O God? Thou dost not go forth, O God, with our armies'*" [Ps. 60:10].

[Q] Three and a half years did Hadrian besiege Betar.

[R] R. Eleazar of Modiin would sit on sackcloth and ashes and pray every day, saying "Lord of the ages! Do not judge in accord with strict judgment this day! Do not judge in accord with strict judgment this day!"

[S] Hadrian wanted to go to him. A Samaritan said to him, "Do not go to him until I see what he is doing, and so hand over the city [of Betar] to you. [Make peace . . . for you.]"

[T] He got into the city through a drain pipe. He went and found R. Eleazar of Modiin standing and praying. He pretended to whisper something into his ear.

[U] The townspeople saw [the Samaritan] do this and brought him to Ben Kozeba. They told him, "We saw this man having dealings with your friend."

[V] [Bar Kokhba] said to him, "What did you say to him, and what did he say to you?"

[W] He said to [the Samaritan], "If I tell you, then the king will kill me, and if I do not tell you, then you will kill me. It is better that the king kill me, and not you.

[X] "[Eleazar] said to me, 'I should hand over my city.' ['I shall make peace . . . .']"

[Y] He turned to R. Eleazar of Modiin. He said to him, "What did this Samaritan say to you?"

[Z] He replied, "Nothing."

[AA] He said to him, "What did you say to him?"

[BB] He said to him, "Nothing."

[CC] [Ben Kozeba] gave [Eleazar] one good kick and killed him.

[DD] Forthwith an echo came forth and proclaimed the following verse:

[EE] *"Woe to my worthless shepherd, who deserts the flock! May the sword smite his arm and his right eye! Let his arm be wholly withered, his right eye utterly blinded!* [Zech. 11:17].

[FF] "You have murdered R. Eleazar of Modiin, the right arm of all Israel, and their right eye. Therefore may the right arm of that man wither, may his right eye be utterly blinded!"

[GG] Forthwith Betar was taken, and Ben Kozeba was killed.

We notice two complementary themes. First, Bar Kokhba treats heaven with arrogance, asking God merely to keep out of the way.

Second, he treats an especially revered sage with a parallel arrogance. The sage had the power to preserve Israel. Bar Kokhba destroyed Israel's one protection. The result was inevitable.

Now in noticing the remarkable polemic in the story, in favor of sages' rule over that of Israelite strongmen, we should not lose sight of the importance of the tale for our present argument about the Messiah and history. First, the passage quite simply demonstrates an interest in narrating other events than those involving the Temple or the sages in court. This story and numerous others not quoted here testify to the emergence of a new category of history (or re-emergence of an old one), namely, the history not of the supernatural cult but of Israel the people. It indicates that, for the framers of those units of Yerushalmi which are not concerned with Mishnah exegesis, and for the editors who selected materials for the final document, the history of Israel the people had now attained importance and demanded its rightful place. Once Israel's history thus reached center stage, a rich heritage of historical thought would be invoked. Second, the Messiah, the centerpiece of salvation history and hero of the tale, would emerge as a critical figure. The historical theory of this Yerushalmi passage is stated very simply. In their view Israel had to choose between wars, either the war fought by Bar Kokhba or the "war for Torah." "Why had they been punished? It was because of the weight of the war, for they had not wanted to engage in the struggles over the meaning of the Torah" (Y. Ta. 3:9 XVI I). Those struggles, which were ritual arguments about ritual matters, promised the only victory worth winning. Then Israel's history would be written in terms of wars over the meaning of the Torah and the decision of the law.

True, the skins are new, but the wine is very old. For while we speak of sages and learning, the message is the familiar one. It is Israel's history that works out and expresses Israel's relationship with God. The critical dimension of Israel's life, therefore, is salvation, the definitive trait, a movement in time from now to then. It follows that the paramount and organizing category is history and its lessons. As I suggested at the outset, in the Yerushalmi we witness, among the Mishnah's heirs, a striking reversion to biblical convictions about the centrality of history in the definition of Israel's reality. The heavy weight of prophecy, apocalyptic, and biblical historiography, with their emphasis upon salvation and on history as the indicator of Israel's salvation, stood against the Mishnah's quite separate thesis of what truly mattered. What, from their viewpoint, demanded description and analysis and required interpretation? It was the category of sanctification, for eternity. The true issue framed by history and apocalypse was how to move toward the foreordained end of salvation, how to act *in time* to reach salvation *at the end of time*. The Mishnah's teleology beyond time and its capacity to posit an eschatology without a place for a historical Messiah take a position beyond that of the entire antecedent sacred literature of Israel. Only one strand, the priestly one, had ever taken so extreme a position on the centrality of sanctification and the peripheral nature of salvation. Wisdom had stood in between, with its own concerns, drawing attention both to what happened and to what endured. But to Wisdom what finally mattered was not nature or supernature, but rather abiding relationships in historical time.

The Talmud's reversion to Scripture's paramount motifs, with Israel's history and destiny foremost among them, forms a complement to the Yerushalmi's principal judgment upon Mishnah itself. An important exegetical initiative of the Yerushalmi was to provide, for statements of the Mishnah, prooftexts deriving from Scripture. Whereas the framers of the Mishnah did not think their statements required evidential support, the authors of the Talmud's exegetical units on the Mishnah took prooftexts which were drawn from Scripture to be the prime necessity. Accordingly, there is yet another testimony to the effort, among third- and fourth-century heirs of the Mishnah, to draw that document back within the orbit of Scripture, to "biblicize" what the Mishnah's authors had sent forth as a freestanding and "non-biblical" Torah.

The single most interesting indicator of the Talmud's reversion to Scripture lies in the effort to go beyond systematizing biblical events to show their taxonomic status. Now they proposed to draw lessons from biblical history. True, the framers of the Mishnah would not have been surprised at their heirs' effort to find in ancient Israel's writings lessons for the new day. They had done the same within the pages of the Mishnah itself. A glance, for example, at the homiletical materials at M. Ta. 2:1–4 shows how routinely they invoked biblical events, parallels, and analogies. But the Mishnah contains no counterpart to vast stretches of the Yerushalmi's treatment of Scripture, specifically in its amplification of biblical stories to rewrite the repertoire of ancient Israel's history. Evidence of that tendency has already been given, for example, in the rabbinization of the Messiah (above, pp. 94–98). So now a single (if lengthy) example may suffice to make the point: amplification of the narrative about a major event in ancient Israel's history.

Y. ABODAH ZARAH 1:1

[I V] Said R. Yudan, father of R. Mattenaiah, "The intention of a verse of Scripture [such as is cited below] was only to make mention of the evil traits of Israel.

[W] "'On the day of our king when Jeroboam was made king the princes became sick with the heat of wine; he stretched out his hand with mockers' [Hos. 7:5].

[X] "On the day on which Jeroboam began to reign over Israel, all Israel came to him at dusk, saying to him, 'Rise up and make an idol.'

[Y] "He said to them, 'It is already dusk. I am partly drunk and partly sober, and the whole people is drunk. But if you want, go and come back in the morning.'

[Z] "This is the meaning of the following Scripture, 'For like an oven their hearts burn with intrigue; all night their anger smolders; in the morning it blazes like a flaming fire' [Hos. 7:6]."

[AA] "'All night their anger smolders.'

[BB] "'In the morning it blazes like a flaming fire.'

[CC] "In the morning they came to him. Thus did he say to them, 'I know what you want. But I am afraid of your sanhedrin, lest it come and kill me.'

[DD] "They said to him, 'We shall kill them.'

[EE] "That is the meaning of the following verse: 'All of them are hot as an oven, and they devour their rulers' [Hos. 7:7]."

. . .

[KK] When he would see an honorable man, he would set up against him two mockers, who would say to him, "Now what generation do you think is the most cherished of all generations?"

[LL] He would answer them, "It was the generation of the wilderness which received the Torah."

[MM] They would say to him, "Now did they themselves not worship an idol?"

[NN] And he would answer them, "Now do you think that, because they were cherished, they were not punished for their deed?"

[OO] And they would say to him, "Shut up! The king wants to do exactly the same thing. Not only so, but [the generation of the wilderness] only made one [calf], while [the king] wants to make two."

[PP] *"[So the king took counsel and made two calves of gold] and he set up one in Bethel, and the other he put in Dan* [1 Kings 12:29]."

[QQ] The arrogance of Jeroboam is what condemned him decisively.

[RR] Said R. Yose bar Jacob, "It was at the conclusion of a sabbatical year that Jeroboam began to rule over Israel. That is the meaning of the following verse: *'[And Moses commanded them.] At the end of every seven years, at the set time of the year of release, at the feast of booths, when all Israel comes to appear before the Lord your God at the place which he will choose, you shall read this law before all Israel in their hearing'* [Deut. 31:10–11].

[SS] "[Jeroboam] said, 'I shall be called upon to read [the Torah, as Scripture requires]. If I get up and read first, they will say to me, 'The king of the place [in which the gathering takes place, namely, Jerusalem] comes first.' And if I read second, it is disrespectful to me. And if I do not read at all, it is a humiliation for me. And, finally, if I let the people go up, they will abandon me and go over to the side of Rehoboam, the son of Solomon.'

[TT] "That is the meaning of the following verse of Scripture: *[And Jeroboam said in his heart, 'Now the kingdom will turn back to the house of David;] if this people go up to offer sacrifices in the house of the Lord at Jerusalem, then the heart of this people will turn again to their Lord, to Rehoboam, king of Judah, and they will kill me and return to Rehoboam, king of Judah'* [1 Kings 12:27–28].

[UU] "What then did he do? *'He made two calves of gold'* [1 Kings 12:28], and he inscribed on their heart, '. . . lest they kill you' [as counsel to his successors].

[VV] "He said, 'Let every king who succeeds me look upon them.'"

Familiar motifs such as the danger of arrogance occur here, just as in passages in which sages explain events of their own day. The main point, however, is not to be missed. The extensive recounting of biblical tales and the interest in making points through the narrative of historical events mark a break from the Mishnah's approach. The framers of the Mishnah rarely found a use for the historical materials of Scripture. It is highly unusual to find in the Mishnah passages like this. Interest in expanding biblical history, apart from the salvific focus imposed by that history, testifies to the process: the renewal, in the Yerushalmi, of an age-old homiletic practice of retelling biblical tales. The earlier document contains slight signs of such interest; its successor is rich in such evidence.

The reversion to the prophetic notion of learning history's lessons carried in its wake a reengagement with the Messiah myth. The climax comes in an explicit statement that the conduct required by the Torah will bring the coming Messiah. That explanation of the holy way of life, as it is focused now upon the end of time and the advent of the Messiah, must strike us as surprising in light of the facts surveyed in an earlier chapter.

The framers of the Mishnah had found it possible to construct a complete and encompassing teleology for their system with scarcely a single word about the Messiah's coming at that time when the system would be perfectly achieved. So with their interest in explaining events and accounting for history, the third- and fourth-century sages represented in these units of discourse invoked what their predecessors had at best found to be of peripheral consequence to their system. The following contains the most striking expression of this viewpoint.

Y. TAANIT 1:1

[X J] *"The oracle concerning Dumah. One is calling to me from Seir, 'Watchman, what of the night? Watchman, what of the night?'* [Isa. 21:11]."

[K] The Israelites said to Isaiah, "O our Rabbi, Isaiah, what will come for us out of this night?"

[L] He said to them, "Wait for me, until I can present the question."

[M] Once he had asked the question, he came back to them.

[N] They said to him, "Watchman, what of the night? What did the Guardian of the ages tell you?"

[O] He said to them, "The watchman says: *'Morning comes; and also the night. If you will inquire, inquire; come back again'* [Isa. 21:12]."

[P] They said to him, "Also the night?"

[Q] He said to them, "It is not what you are thinking. But there will be morning for the righteous, and night for the wicked, morning for Israel, and night for idolaters."

[R] They said to him, "When?"

[S] He said to them, "Whenever you want, He too wants [it to be]—if you want it, he wants it."

[T] They said to him, "What is standing in the way?"

[U] He said to them, "Repentance: *'Come back again'* [Isa. 21:12]."

[V] R. Aha in the name of R. Tanhum b. R. Hiyya, "If Israel repents for one day, forthwith the son of David will come.

[W] "What is the scriptural basis? *'O that today you would hearken to his voice!'* [Ps. 95:7]."

[X] Said R. Levi, "If Israel would keep a single sabbath in the proper way, forthwith the son of David will come.

[Y] "What is the scriptural basis for this view? *'Moses said, "Eat it today, for today is a sabbath to the Lord; today you will not find it in the field"'* [Exod. 16:25].

[Z] *"And it says, 'For thus said the Lord God, the Holy One of Israel, "In returning and rest you shall be saved; in quietness and in trust shall be your strength." And you would not'* [Isa. 30:15]."

A discussion of the power of repentance would hardly have surprised a Mishnah sage. What is new is at V–Z, the explicit linkage of keeping the law with achieving the end of time and the coming of the Messiah. That motif stands separate from the notions of righteousness and repentance, which surely do not require it. So the condition of "all Israel," a social category in historical time, comes under consideration, and not only the status of individual Israelites in life and in death. The latter had formed the arena for the Mishnah's demonstration of its system's meaning. Now history as an operative category, drawing in its wake Israel as a social entity, comes once more on the scene. But, except for the Mishnah's sages, it had never left the stage.

We must not lose sight of the importance of this passage, with its emphasis on repentance, on the one side, and the power of Israel to reform itself, on the other. The Messiah will come any day that Israel makes it possible. If all Israel will keep a single sabbath in the proper (rabbinic) way, the Messiah will come. If all Israel will repent for one day, the Messiah will come. "Whenever you want . . . ," the Messiah will come.

Now, two things are happening here. First, the system of religious observance, including study of Torah, is explicitly invoked as having salvific power. Second, the persistent hope of the people for the coming of the Messiah is linked to the system of rabbinic observance and belief. In this way, the austere program of the Mishnah develops in a different direction, with no trace of a promise that the

Messiah will come if and when the system is fully realized. Here a teleology lacking all eschatological dimension gives way to an explicitly messianic statement that the purpose of the law is to attain Israel's salvation: "If you want it, God wants it too." The one thing Israel commands is its own heart; the power it yet exercises is the power to repent. These suffice. The entire history of humanity will respond to Israel's will, to what happens in Israel's heart and soul. With the Temple in ruins, repentance can take place only within the heart and mind.

A SIDE TRIP: THE FATHERS
ACCORDING TO RABBI NATHAN

While not part of the Talmud of the Land of Israel, the *Fathers According to Rabbi Nathan*, a secondary expansion of Abot, should come under brief consideration at this point. The work came to closure, Saldarini holds, in the third century. Most of its materials belong in the classification of Yerushalmi's units of discourse that interpret or expand a passage of the Mishnah. Since the tractate remains close to Abot, it also falls well within the framework of the Mishnah's view of the questions at hand. When the authors speak of "anointing oil" and "anointing," they mean consecration of the priesthood (ARN 1). A reference to "the Messiah" occurs quite in passing:

THE FATHERS ACCORDING TO RABBI NATHAN
(TRANSLATED BY JUDAH GOLDIN, PP. 137–38)

. . . "*These are the two anointed ones, that stand by the Lord of the whole earth*" [Zech. 4:14]. This is a reference to Aaron and the Messiah, but I cannot tell which is the more beloved. However, from the verse, "*The Lord has sworn, and will not repent: 'You are a priest for ever after the manner of Melchizedek'*" [Ps. 110:4], one can tell that the King-Messiah is more beloved than the righteous priest.

For our purposes, the importance of this passage lies in the notion that there are various messiahs, serving diverse purposes. The conception of *the* Messiah as distinct from messiahs is hardly developed.

The tractate provides a great many stories about sages, including sages' relationships with the emperor. Yohanan ben Zakkai's escape from Jerusalem and colloquy with Vespasian (which makes the point that the sage and the emperor weigh equally in the balance) occurs in a classic formulation. But the *Fathers According to Rabbi Nathan* contains no better articulated theory of Israel's history and destiny than does the Mishnah tractate that it serves to amplify. The framers do include a statement that makes explicit the familiar notion that the Temple is the nexus between the supernatural and the natural world: "So long as the Temple service is maintained, the world is a blessing to its inhabitants and the rains come down in season . . . but when the Temple service is not maintained, the world is not a blessing to its inhabitants and the rains do not come down in season" (ARN 4). But this does not express the redactors' principal point of interest, which is with sages, their teachings and example.

In all, the tractate repeats the pattern already noted. That is, where units of discourse framed in the Land of Israel's circles of masters and disciples discuss statements of the Mishnah, they remain entirely within the circle of issues defined by the Mishnah's authors: nature and supernature, sage, priest, and sanctification, all within the enduring life of Israel. Within such a setting, there is little room for protracted interest in history or eschatology. Consequently, the Messiah myth proves of slight interest.

FROM SANCTIFICATION TO SALVATION

The framers of the Yerushalmi took over a document portraying a system which was centered upon sanctifying Israel through the creation of a world in stasis, that is, wholly perfect within itself. They left behind them a document in which that original goal of sanctification in stasis competed with another, for within the pages of the Talmud of the Land of Israel we find a second theory of what matters in Israel's life: a system centered on the salvation of Israel in a world moving toward a goal, a world to be perfected only at the conclusion of the journey through time. So the bridge formed by the Talmud of the Land of Israel leads from a world in which nothing happens but sanctification, to one in which everything happens en route to salvation at the end.

To understand these choices, let us turn to the points of contrast and tension and the specification of opposites. These indicate the range of permissible choices, hence the boundaries of the reality posited by a given discourse. If we were to administer a psychological test to the storytellers asking them to state the opposite of a given word, the results would not be in doubt. If we say "this world," the storytellers who speak of kings and wars would answer "the world to come," or "this age" and "the age to come." If, by contrast, we presented to storytellers who relate tales of sages a given symbol of the natural world, they would reply with a counterpart, a symbol of the supernatural world. As we shall see in a moment, when (supernatural) rabbis die, for example, the (natural) world responds with miracles. In this sense, therefore, we confront two separate constructions of the world—polar possibilities. The one involves a historical-messianic explanation of historical events, the other, a supernatural explanation of natural ones. True, prayer may speak of either kind of occurrence, but at the climactic moment on the Day of Atonement, the prayer of the high priest turns to the natural world:

Y. YOMA 5:2

[II   B] This was the prayer of the high priest on the Day of Atonement, when he left the Holy Place whole and in one piece: "May it be pleasing before you, Lord, our God and God of our fathers, that [a decree of] exile not be issued against us, not this day or this year, but if a decree of exile should be issued against us, then let it be exile to a place of Torah.

[C] "May it be pleasing before you, Lord, our God and God of our fathers, that a decree of want not be issued against us, not this day of this year, but if a decree of want should be issued against us, then let it be a want of [the performance of] religious duties.

[D] "May it be pleasing before you, Lord, our God and God of our fathers, that this year be a year of cheap food, full bellies, good business; a year in which the earth forms clods, then is parched so as to form scabs, and then moistened with dew,

[E] "so that your people, Israel, will not be in need of the help of one another.

[F] "And do not heed the prayer of travelers [that it not rain]."

The high priest's prayer by itself obviously does not prove that, in all circumstances or contexts of sanctification, nature and supernature are alone. But it does at least illustrate the (to the Mishnah) self-evident association proposed at the outset. And the principal

125

point must not be missed. One could speak of the ultimate resolution of Israel's circumstances without invoking the name of the Messiah or the concept of events leading to a foreordained climax and conclusion with his coming at the end of time. Just as M. Sot. 9:15's author could refer to the resurrection of the dead without in the same breath speaking of the coming of the Messiah, so too it remained possible to do this in the pages of the Yerushalmi.

The main point is that, for the framers of the Mishnah, one could speculate about the meaning and end of the holy way of life of the holy people without any reference to the coming of the Messiah. For them and their heirs in the Talmud of the Land of Israel, the conception of redemption did not invariably invoke the salvific myth of the Messiah. Other units of discourse in the Yerushalmi carry forward this same treatment of the matter, as in the following:

Y. YOMA 3:2

[III A] One time R. Hiyya the Elder and R. Simeon b. Halapta were talking in the valley of Arabel at daybreak. They saw that the light of the morning star was breaking forth. Said R. Hiyya the Elder to R. Simeon b. Halapta, "Son of my master, this is what the redemption of Israel is like—at first, little by little, but in the end it will go along and burst into light.

[B] "What is the scriptural basis for this view? 'Rejoice not over me, O my enemy; when I fall, I shall rise; when I sit in darkness, the Lord will be a light to me' [Mic. 7:8]."

How then does the Judaism of sanctification, as represented in the Yerushalmi, take up events we should regard as historical? That is, how is Israel to dispose of the events of the day, if not through fervent prayer for the intervention of the Messiah? Bar Kokhba's way, sages maintained, was arrogant. What alternative did they offer? The answer is that within the framework of sanctification, as in the Mishnah, so in the Yerushalmi, world-shaking events were treated as trivial, with history converted into a symptom of the condition of private life, and great events turned into epiphenomena within the framework of everyday reality. Accordingly, within this system, as the Yerushalmi expresses it, historical events play a decidedly subordinated role. Among the deeds that make history, mainly personal and private actions come to the fore, not those that bear (to us) self-evident political and social importance. Accordingly, historical events need not take a leading role in the salvation of Israel—even when salvation is at issue. The "harsh decree" may be averted through piety, charity, a right attitude—surely not very consequential deeds in the larger historical scheme of things.

Y. TAANIT 2:1

[IX A] Said R. Eleazar, "Three acts nullify the harsh decree, and these are they: prayer, charity, and repentance."
[B] And all three of them are to be derived from a single verse of Scripture:
[C] "If my people who are called by my name humble themselves, and pray and seek my face, and turn from their wicked ways, then I will hear from heaven, and will forgive their sin and heal their land" [2 Chron. 7:14].
[D] "Pray"—this refers to prayer.
[E] "And seek my face"—this refers to charity,
[F] as you say, "As for me, I shall behold thy face in righteousness; when I awake, I shall be satisfied with beholding thy form" [Ps. 17:15].
[G] "And turn from their wicked ways"—this refers to repentance.
[H] Now if they do these things, what is written concerning them?
[I] "Then I will hear from heaven and will forgive their sin and heal their land."

Forgiveness of sin draws in its wake prosperity, represented by the "healing of the land." These references therefore cannot apply solely to what happens to the individual. They deal with the fate of the whole of society. True, the harsh decree may come from the state; but the outcome is the same. Through repentance and its associated actions Israel can make its own history. In a statement like this, the issue of the coming of the Messiah simply plays no role. The historical-salvific-messianic does not merge with the timeless-sanctificatory-sagacious in materials of this kind; so far as I can see, within the pages of the Yerushalmi, no such union appears.

In Israel there were holy men who bore within themselves the power to save Israel. In this framework, the notion of the Messiah loses all pertinence. Every sage, if sufficiently holy, could effect miracles for Israel. Whether salvation is at issue remains in doubt. For, in context, we deal with supernatural, not this-worldly, events: a

127

miracle in nature, effected by a holy man, rather than a once-for-all historical resolution of Israel's situation, that is, "salvation" in the ordinary sense. The power of the holy or righteous man to save Israel is made explicit in the following:

Y. YOMA 1:1

[V   D] Said R. Hiyya bar Ba, "The sons of Aaron died on the first day of Nisan. And why is their death called to mind in connection with the Day of Atonement?

[E] "It is to indicate to you that just as the Day of Atonement effects expiation for Israel, so the death of the righteous effects atonement for Israel."

[F] Said R. Ba bar Binah, "Why did the Scripture place the story of the death of Miriam side by side with the story of the burning of the red cow?

[G] "It is to teach you that, just as the dirt of the red cow [mixed with water] effects atonement for Israel, so the death of the righteous effects atonement for Israel."

The supernatural power associated with the death of the righteous person—in this context, the sage—appears in miracles marking the event.

Y. ABODAH ZARAH 3:1

[II   A] When R. Aha died, a star appeared at noon.

[B] When R. Hanan died, the statues bowed low.

[C] When R. Yohanan died, the icons bowed down.

[D] They said that [this was to indicate] there were no icons like him [so beautiful as Yohanan himself].

[E] When R. Hanina of Bet Hauran died, the Sea of Tiberias split open.

[F] They said that [this was to commemorate the miracle that took place] when he went up to intercalate the year, and the sea split open before him.

[G] When R. Hoshaiah died, the palm of Tiberias fell down.

[H] When R. Isaac b. Eliasheb died, seventy [infirm] thresholds of houses in Galilee were shaken down.

[I] They said that [this was to commemorate the fact that] they [were shaky and] had depended on his merit [for the miracle that permitted them to continue to stand].

[J] When R. Samuel bar R. Isaac died, cedars of the land of Israel were uprooted.

[K] They said that [this was to take note of the fact that] he would take a branch [of a cedar] and [dance, so] praising a bride [at her wedding, and thereby giving happiness to the bride].

[L] The rabbis would ridicule him [for lowering himself by doing so]. Said to them R. Zeira, "Leave him be. Does the old man not know what he is doing?"

[M] When he died, a flame came forth from heaven and intervened between his bier and the congregation. For three hours there were voices and thunderings in the world: "Come and see what a sprig of cedar has done for this old man!"

[N] [Further] an echo came forth and said, "Woe that Samuel b. R. Isaac has died, the doer of merciful deeds."

[O] When R. Yose bar Halputa died, the gutters ran with blood in Laodicea.

[P] They said [that the reason was] that he had given his life for the rite of circumcision.

The (natural) death of a sage invokes (supernatural) miracles, and so the sage enters into his eternal life. Not *the* Messiah alone, but *any* sufficiently holy and meritorious sage will mark in such a way the shift from one world to the next. But the worlds that are exchanged vary according to the system. We do not find here the social history of Israel marked by the coming of the Messiah, but rather, the individual life of a sage commemorated in nature through supernature. This type of story therefore calls into question the concept of only *one* Messiah presiding over a unique event at the end of a sequence of happenings all pointing toward that one-time eschatological climax. Either Israel is *saved* through the Messiah who resurrects the dead, or Israel is *sanctified* through the presence, in life and in death, of the righteous. We cannot demonstrate that these statements speak of different things to different people. We can only show, as I have here, that when a unit of discourse deals with the one, it rarely, if ever, mentions the symbols or issues of the other.

But these sets of opposites — time vs. eternity, life vs. death, nature vs. supernature, on the one side, and history vs. the end of time, this world vs. the time of the Messiah, death vs. resurrection, on the other — need not persist as separate and contradictory. The sage as holy man does his work now and does it mainly through ongoing nature and unchanging supernature. *The* Messiah—as distinct from *a* (any) sage—does his work at the end of time. He does it once. In the resurrection of the dead, he carries out a single, one-time action, by its nature one that need not be repeated. He is a single and therefore unique figure, a kind of holy man to be sure, but one of a kind, who performs a single, unique deed. Once *a* messiah, in the sense of a high priest appointed for a given task to be repeated many times, gives way to *the* Messiah, meaning a man designed to do a single task never to be repeated, we leave the framework of the Mishnah altogether.

This does not mean that people faced or even recognized a choice between one teleology and another. It means that the eschatology beyond history, the teleology beyond time, worked out in the Mishnah, stands essentially asymmetrical to the parallel theories spelled out in the second and third sections of this chapter. They may be harmonized. They may sit side by side without colliding. But they may not be represented as one and the same thing. They never meet. And, in the canonical literature of Judaism examined up to now, the two theories of where things are heading scarcely intersect in a single pericope. The supernatural sage with his power over individual life and the natural world, and the eschatological Messiah—both within the model of the rabbi, in the image of God—never meet, except when King David is perceived as Rabbi David. In any event Rabbi David is mostly a rabbi, and only rarely a messiah or the Messiah. If we did not know that David was the prototype of the Messiah, the Yerushalmi would not have made us think so. In all, the eschatological Messiah is difficult to locate. "Messiah" defines a category of holy man.

3

The Messiah
in the Compositions
of Scriptural Exegesis

THE DOCUMENTS

Compositions of scriptural exegesis emerged almost as soon as books of Scripture had reached closure, whether or not in the status of a canon, that is, of official and authoritative statements. (Scribalism is a gloss-tradition, with or without a canon.) The most striking early exegesis is that of Chronicles on Samuel and Kings. From that time onward, in various forms and for diverse purposes, Israelite thinkers framed their ideas in the form of citation and exegesis (eisegesis) of verses, chapters, and occasionally even whole books of canonical Scripture. Within the distinctive framework of formative Judaism beginning with the Mishnah, however, it was only out of the matrix of mishnaic exegesis, as represented in the pages of the Talmud of the Land of Israel, that aggregates of systematic compositions of scriptural exegesis began to take shape. That fact, demonstrated in my *Midrash in Context*, explains why we rank the compositions of scriptural exegesis as we do, in sequence after the Talmud of the Land of Israel.

To state matters simply: the same fundamental categories of units of discourse constructed in the Yerushalmi as exegesis of Mishnah serve to classify those units constructed and collected in the earliest compositions of exegesis of Scripture, at about A.D. 400. What rabbis thought important to accomplish in the explanation and expansion of Mishnah, therefore, they did also in the interpretation of Scripture. Why they did so is to be explained as part of the history of mishnaic interpretation. The crisis precipitated by the authority and character of Mishnah vis-à-vis Scripture provoked a kind of literary and hermeneutic exercise for Scripture itself, the sort of collection previ-

131

ously unattested in the formation of the rabbinic canon. The results lie before us in the compositions of scriptural exegesis.

Compositions of scriptural exegesis emerge in three types within the canonical framework of formative Judaism. First are those in which exegetes undertake a line-by-line explanation of passages of Scripture. Second are those in which exegetes take up large-scale topics of Scripture and work out their ideas by citing various verses from different books of the Bible, without subjecting any one passage to a line-by-line explanation. Third are those in which we find both types of discourse side by side. Since dating compilations of biblical exegesis remains a primitive art, we have only the most tentative suggestions on when and in what sequence the various collections reached closure. Following M. D. Heer, we must agree, however, that the two extant compositions of the third type, Genesis Rabbah and Leviticus Rabbah, came into being at much the same time as the Talmud of the Land of Israel, that is, in the late fourth and early fifth centuries. Five extant compositions of the second type—those made up of wide-ranging discourse on themes—are generally thought to come from the fifth and sixth centuries. These are Lamentations Rabbah, Esther Rabbah 1, Pesiqta deRab Kahana, Song of Songs Rabbah, and Ruth Rabbah. The four extant compositions of the first type (a line-by-line exegesis) in Heer's view date from not before the end of the fourth century. These are Mekhilta of R. Ishmael, Sifra (to Leviticus), Sifré Numbers, and Sifré Deuteronomy. Accordingly, these compositions entered the canon between ca. 400 and 600, possibly beginning with works of line-by-line exegesis and probably ending with works of discursive, topical essays.

For our present purpose, we deal with the documents according to the classifications defined through relationship to Scripture: first, compositions mainly of line-by-line exegesis; second, collections of mixtures of the two types of material; third, works composed mainly of thematic exercises. The classifications seem sufficiently firm to justify treating the eleven documents evenly among these three groups. Still, I shall keep materials of one document separate from those of others within the same classification.

In the bibliography under the name of M. D. Heer the reader will find references to the articles on which rest the foregoing assessments of the dating of the several documents. Heer provides citations, moreover, to the basic scholarly literature on each item. As is clear, for the moment we rely upon the conventional consensus presented in Heer's articles. That means, to be sure, that we cannot draw conclusions that rely heavily upon that consensus.

LINE-BY-LINE EXEGESIS OF
PENTATEUCHAL BOOKS:
MEKHILTA deR. ISHMAEL, SIFRA,
SIFRÉ NUMBERS, SIFRÉ DEUTERONOMY

While the pentateuchal materials in general treat questions of social order and theology, they also provide exegetes interested in messianic motifs with ample occasion to pursue those interests. The sages' work on passages most openly demanding a messianic reading, e.g., Lev. 26 and Deut. 32, shows only how efficiently they discover references to what interests them, namely, the importance of study of Torah and of obedience to it. The large-scale reading of these passages about the future strikingly avoids any messianic angle, even where this is invited by the frame of discourse. What sages refrain from doing finds its counterpart in their treatment of the theme of the Messiah and the larger issues inherent in that myth. We find nothing more than routine rehearsal of familiar facts, e.g., about the age of the Messiah in contrast to the present age, troubles attendant upon the Messiah's coming, and the like. There is nothing that would have surprised the Mishnah's authors. References even to these matters, furthermore, turn out to be few and far between. The compositions pursue other interests entirely. So far as the Messiah myth appears, therefore, it is entirely within the framework established by the Mishnah and its documents of close continuation (including the Yerushalmi's Mishnah exegesis but excluding the Yerushalmi's autonomous units of discourse). We look in vain for a new idea or even for new importance accorded to a familiar one.

Mekhilta deR. Ishmael provides a line-by-line amplification of most of Exodus. The materials form a pastiche of diverse items lacking any common exegetical program. They occur in a wide variety of other compilations. No systematic work has been done to determine whether the present document's version of a unit of discourse which appears also in some other composition is prior or subsequent to the equivalent statement elsewhere. It follows that we can come to no reliable judgment about the time or context of the compilation. Happily, the materials pertinent to our topic are so few and discrete that this hardly matters. All we find are such commonplaces as these: the generation of the Messiah runs on for three generations (ed. Lauterbach, 2:161); prior to the coming of the Messiah, there will be a time of suffering (ibid., 2:120); "No one knows when the kingdom of David will be restored to its former position" (ibid., 2:125). These cover nearly the entire matter. One important point of contact with already familiar materials is the following (ibid., 2:120):

MEKHILTA deR. ISHMAEL, ED. LAUTERBACH 2:120

R. Eleazar of Modiin says, "If you succeed in keeping the Sabbath, the Holy One, blessed be he, will give you six good portions: The Land of Israel, the future world, the new world, the kingdom of the house of David, the priesthood, and the Levites' offices." In this sense it is said: "*Eat that today,*" etc.

R. Eliezer says, "If you succeed in keeping the Sabbath you will escape the three visitations: The day of Gog, the suffering preceding the advent of the Messiah, and the Great Judgment Day." In this sense it is said: "*Eat that today.*"

These statements embellish the simple assertions listed above, using one of the available prooftexts to say pretty much the same thing.

Mekhilta deR. Ishmael stays so close to the biblical narrative that the framers may not have found occasion to deal with more wide-ranging issues. In any event they did not seek to do so. The compilation contains no large-scale reflection on the meaning and end of Israel's history—no effort, for instance, to balance the events of the exodus from Egypt against those to come at the end of time. Nor is there any comparison, e.g., between Egypt and Rome. The martyrdom of sages is adduced as a sign that trouble was coming upon the generation in the time of Aqiba: "These two men have been taken from our midst only because it is revealed . . . that great suffering is destined to come upon our generation" (ibid., 3:142). But the martyrs' deaths are explained by reference to their individual and personal failings—in all, perfectly routine.

Providing a systematic exegesis to Leviticus, Sifra's framers stress that passages of Mishnah, normally cited verbatim, rest not upon reason alone, but upon correct exegesis of Scripture. The polemic of the document is against the view that the Mishnah, reaching conclusions through reason, enjoys autonomous standing vis-à-vis Scripture. The Mishnah, rather, rests upon the foundations of the written Torah, deriving support for its statements solely through disciplined exegesis of Scripture. In the nature of things, the composition of Leviticus exegesis remains very close to verses of Scripture, read in sequence. A detailed catalogue of Sifra's nearly one hundred references to the "messiah" (see B. Kosowsky, *Otzar Leshon Hatanna'im. Concordantiae Verborum quae in Sifra aut Torat Kohanim Reperiuntur* [Jerusalem, 1968] 3:1233f.) would serve no purpose, since *every* reference speaks of an anointed priest, such as appears in Leviticus itself, or, on one occasion, a priest anointed for war. The other usage, that of *the* Messiah, Savior at the end of days, never occurs. Furthermore, when the writers of Sifra refer to "messiah," without further qualification, they still mean only the high priest who is consecrated through application of anointing oil—and that alone.

What I find striking in Sifra is its persistent policy of avoiding reference to contemporary events, on the one side, and of interpreting Scripture wholly in terms of ancient Israel's history on the other. It is as if no one wants to say the obvious, that the curses of Lev. 26 are realized in Israel's contemporary history. For example, the verse, *"And you shall not walk according to the rules of the Gentiles"* (Lev. 18:20), is made to refer to Egypt and Canaan, not to extant nations of the day (Sifra Qedoshim Pereq 11:16). This does not imply that the exegetes distinguished their own day from times gone by in order to avoid anachronism. On the contrary, when it comes to reading into Leviticus their own contemporary concerns, sages did so without any hesitation, as the following example shows:

SIFRA BEHUQOTAI PEREQ 1:1-2

A. *"If you walk in my statutes and observe my commandments . . ."* [Lev. 26:3]: This verse teaches that the Omnipresent yearns for Israel to labor in Torah. . . .

B. *"If you walk in my statutes. . . ."* May one then suppose that reference is made [merely] to keeping the commandments [not to studying

Torah]? When Scripture states, "*And observe my commandments,*" we find clear reference to the matter of keeping the commandments.
C. Accordingly, how am I to interpret the statement, "*If you walk in my statutes*"? [It can only mean that the Israelites] should labor in [study of] Torah.

The introduction of "study of Torah," so characteristic of and distinctive to rabbinical exegetes, shows what might have been done elsewhere.

So in regard to the Messiah's coming, the exegetes who are represented here carefully ignored what was going on in their own day and concentrated their interest in a rather narrowly historical reading of both legal and historical materials. The result, as I said, is that the apocalyptic vision at Lev. 26, with blessings and curses involving punishment by a foreign enemy for Israel's failure to observe the covenant, provides the exegetes with nothing useful in the encounter with events of the third or fourth century. Perhaps sages could not bear to suggest that the events of their own time came about because of Israel's disloyalty to the covenant. The necessary conclusion may have proved too painful; Israel's Christian critics on the margins and from within, with their different conception of the ancient covenant, would then be vindicated by the condition of Israel itself. In any event, we observe time and time again a single, pronounced point: the curses were *already* realized in biblical times, long ago. This is a powerful apologetic, even if incredible in the context.

It follows that Sifra's exegetes wielded a two-edged sword. On the one side, they called for obedience to the Torah as expounded by sages; so Sifra Behuqotai Parasha 2:1, "*If you will not hearken to me*" (Lev. 26:14), means "If you will not hearken to the interpretation of sages." On the other side, the repeated dire punishments were to allude to times long past: for example, "*And you shall perish among the nations*' (Lev. 26:38). Said R. Aqiba, 'The passage refers to the ten tribes who were taken away into exile in Media.'" To be sure, in context we find reference to the tragedy in the time of Vespasian, that is, at the destruction of the Second Temple. But this allusion is forthwith assimilated into a conventional list involving Greece, Haman, and God. The main point is that only the Torah distinguishes Israel from the nations (all: ibid., Pereq 8:10). So the message proves familiar. We look in vain for a doctrine of Israel's history and destiny other than the familiar one of the Mishnah. In all, Sifra falls into the same category as Tosefta, a continuation of the Mishnah's lines of thought.

Sifré to Numbers conforms precisely to the pattern of Sifra. "Messiah" refers solely to the high priest consecrated through anointing with holy oil in approximately a dozen references (see B. Kosowsky, *Otzar Leshon Hatanna'im. Thesaurus "Sifrei" Concordantiae Verborum quae in "Sifrei" Numeri et Deuteronomium Experiuntur* [Jerusalem, 1972] 3:1267). To be sure, the established belief in a messianic age which was preceded by a time of troubles makes its appearance in Sifré Num. 40, probably a brief allusion to the exegesis of Isa. 21:12, cited above, p. 122. So too, the Messiah's origin in the house of David is known (Sifré Num. 42), as is the future war against Gog and Magog (Sifré Num. 76). These conventional facts prove incidental at best. References to "the age to come" do not in general draw in their wake allusions to the Messiah.

Sifré to Deuteronomy, for its part, does contain a number of references to *the* Messiah, that is, specifically to the one anointed by God to save Israel. But the references point mostly to "the age of the Messiah" in contrast to "this age," as in Sifré Deut. 351: "the three generations of the messianic age" (cf. also ibid. 363) and "the days of the Messiah" (ibid. 16, 104, 188, 362, 372, 398, 410). A passage on the anointing of David (1 Sam. 16:6, Sifré Deut. 17) bears no messianic doctrine or consequence. Of greater interest, when the exegetes represented in Sifré Deut. come to the Song of Moses, Deut. 32:1–43 (Sifré Deut. 306–41, Finkelstein, pp. 328–90), they fail to introduce a single reference to the Messiah as an active figure or even to the history of Israel in their own day. That enormous essay, like the parallel materials of Sifra Lev. 26, works out its themes in terms of other considerations entirely, according to the issues and values of Torah. Obedience to Torah determines Israel's fate, stated explicitly at, among other places, Sifré Deut. 309. When we remember that the whole of the exegesis refers to "the future" or to "the age to come," the absence of all reference to the Messiah is truly remarkable. The Targums present a striking parallel when taking up such passages which invite messianic comment (below, pp. 238–46).

LINE-BY-LINE EXEGESIS TOGETHER WITH
DISCURSIVE EXPOSITIONS OF THEMES:
GENESIS RABBAH AND
LEVITICUS RABBAH

Like Mekhilta, Sifra, and the two Sifrés, Genesis Rabbah works its way, verse by verse, through certain texts. But, unlike the first category of scriptural exegeses, the present type includes a second sort of material entirely—sizable expositions of topics or themes rather than line-by-line comments on a given verse. However, when we rapidly review the uses to which, in both types of discourse, the Messiah myth is put, we find no significant difference. Most of the references to the stated theme are casual and cover familiar ground. The established program in the rabbinical canon leads us to expect allusions to the Messiah and the messianic age ("days of the Messiah"). Here too, we find such allusions as, e.g., "They will return to perfection only when the son of Perez [the Messiah] comes" (Gen. R. 12:6, 98:7). There will be a great famine "in the messianic future" (Gen. R. 25:3), with reference to Amos 8:11, "*A thirst for hearing the words of the Lord.*" Finally, there are a few routine references to the "advent of the Messiah" (e.g., Gen. R. 35:2), to Israel's advantage at that time (Gen. R. 83:5), and to the certainty that God will remember his promise to redeem Israel, phrased as his "raising up the fallen tabernacle of David" (Gen. R. 88:7). But "the future world" also appears without explicit introduction of the Messiah (as at Gen. R. 97, end).

We find two noteworthy developments in Genesis Rabbah not observed in the documents considered to this point. First, there is concrete reference to the descent, from the messianic house, of a specific rabbinical figure. Alleged to be the forebear of the house of patriarchs who were the rulers of the Jewish community of the Land of Israel from the late first century through the early fifth, Hillel is now declared to derive from the house of David:

GENESIS RABBAH 98:8
(TRANSLATED BY H. FREEDMAN, P. 956)

"*Until Shiloh comes*" [Gen. 49:10]: the Rabbis debated the question, From whom was Hillel descended? R. Levi said, "A genealogical scroll was found in Jerusalem, in which it was written that Hillel was descended from David, R. Hiyya the Elder from Shephatiah the son of Abital, the house of Kalba Shabua from Caleb, the house of Zizith Hakeseth from Abner, the house of Kobshin from Ahab, the house of Yazath from Asaph, the house of Jehu from Sepphoris, the house of Jannai from Eli, R. Jose b. R. Halafta from Jonadab the son of Rechab, and R. Nehemiah from Nehemiah the Tirshathite."

This specification concerning Hillel's origin served a blatant political purpose for the patriarch and yielded no secondary developments of interest.

Second, in exactly the same context, we find reflection on what will happen in the messianic time. A particular issue is the relationship of the Torah and commandments to the coming age:

GENESIS RABBAH 98:9
(TRANSLATED BY H. FREEDMAN, PP. 957–58)

R. Hanin said, "Israel will not require the teaching of the royal Messiah in the future, for it says, *'Unto him shall the nations seek'* (Isa. 11:10), but not Israel. If so, for what purpose will the royal Messiah come, and what will he do? He will come to assemble the exiles of Israel and to give [the Gentiles] thirty precepts, as it says, *'And I said unto them: If ye think good, give me my hire; and if not, forbear. So they weighed for my hire thirty pieces of silver'* [Zech. 11:12]."

Both passages, with their fresh initiatives, occur in the interpretation of Gen. 49:10; the reference to the "scepter" that "shall not depart from Judah . . . until Shiloh comes" is understood (as in the Targums) as an explicit messianic prediction. It is not surprising, therefore, to find explicit interest in the identity of the Messiah and the character of his age. When we recall that the Talmud of the Land of Israel, composed at approximately the same time, likewise contains units of discourse on the identity of the Messiah, the first passage presents no surprises. As to the second, it is difficult to assess whether it attests the beginnings of a new sort of speculation on the Messiah myth. A single, tame reference scarcely suggests large-scale interest in rethinking the familiar Messiah myth in a systematic and creative way. We do not know the meaning of the new point.

Leviticus Rabbah presents expected and routine materials, but

also some surprising initiatives. In the former category are references to "the lamp of King Messiah" (Lev. R. 31:11), which the
priest merits because of *"causing a lamp to burn continually"* (Lev.
24:2). A hitherto unknown role for the Messiah is to have him, along
with Elijah, "record a good deed when a man does it." In former
times the prophet alone did so, but now, they both do, with God
signing beside them (Lev. R. 34:8). The Messiah serves as part of
that other system, the one exemplified in Abot and focused upon individual deeds and retribution. The passage is a singleton. Again,
reference to "this world" does not invariably trigger allusion to "the
days of the Messiah." Just as often we find "world to come" (Lev. R.
11:9). David appears as a rabbi who attends synagogues and houses
of study (Lev. R. 35:1). None of these rather casual references is
exceptional.

What does stand out in Leviticus Rabbah is a highly developed
theory of the periodization of Israel's history. An acute sense of historical time, its division and direction—for which, in the materials
reviewed heretofore, I can show no parallel—now makes an appearance. Specifically, two lengthy passages, well worth detailed attention, present a periodization of the past in terms of suffering under
one or another pagan kingdom, with a clear implication that the periods, though different from one another, form a progression toward
a foreordained conclusion. This development, moreover, is expressed in discourse on passages in which, to put it mildly, we
should scarcely have expected to find it. The interpretive approach
now becomes one of allegory, in which Scripture, which speaks
about one thing, is made to address other things entirely. The contrast between one approach to a passage, in which the plain sense of
Scripture governs the interpretation of a passage, and this other approach, just presented, will be clear when we contrast Sifra's reading with that of Leviticus Rabbah on precisely the same verse. We
see, then, a remarkably fresh way of reading the verse and an unus-
ually imaginative message derived from that reading—in all, a har-
binger of something new.

The first of the two passages treats the various unclean animals as
symbols for the conquerors of Israel, and the reference to the various beasts' processes of ingestion and digestion (*maaleh gerah*), and
to the moral traits of those nations. The exegesis is so fanciful, the

direction so clear, the messianic-historical message so blatant, that the passage must stand out. Yet whom it represents, how it was composed, and what it means cannot be answered on the basis of the passage itself. (See Lev. 11:4–6.)

LEVITICUS RABBAH 13:5
(TRANSLATED BY J. ISRAELSTAM, PP. 175–76)

"And the rock-badger" alludes to Media, "He exalts with the throat" in that it extolled the Holy One, blessed be he, as it is said, "Thus says Cyrus, king of Persia: All the kingdoms of the earth has the Lord, the God of the heavens, given me [etc.]" [Ezra 1:2]. "And the hare" alludes to Greece, "She raises with the throat" in that it extolled the Holy One, blessed be he. Alexander of Macedon, when he saw Simeon the Just, said: "Blessed be the Lord, God of Simeon the Just." "The swine" alludes to Edom [Rome], "but use not the throat," in that it does not extol the Holy One, blessed be he, and it is not content with not extolling, but reviles and blasphemes, saying, "Whom have I in heaven?" [Ps. 73:25].

Another interpretation: "The camel" alludes to Babylon, "It elevates a stranger," in that it exalted Daniel, as it is said, "Then the king made Daniel great . . . and Daniel was in the gate of the king" [Dan. 2:48f.].

"The rock-badger" alludes to Media, "It elevates a stranger," in that it exalted Mordecai, as it is said, "And Mordecai sat in the king's gate" [Esther 2:19].

"The hare" alludes to Greece, "It elevates a stranger," in that it exalted righteous men. When Alexander beheld Simeon the Just, he rose to his feet. The Cutheans said to him: "Do you stand up before a Jew?" Said he: "When I go forth to battle, I behold his likeness and I am victorious."

"The swine" alludes to Edom [Rome], "It treats not a stranger with the treatment due to a stranger," in that it does not exalt righteous men, and is not content with not exalting them, but slays them. This is alluded to in what is written, "I was angry with my people, I profaned my inheritance, and gave them into your hand; you showed them no mercy; upon the aged you very heavily laid your yoke" [Isa. 47:6]. This refers to R. Aqiba and his colleagues [who were martyred].

Another interpretation: "The camel" is an allusion to Babylon; "Which is maaleh gerah," i.e., which brought in its train (garar) another empire to follow it. "The hare" is an allusion to Media; "Which is maaleh gerah," i.e., which brought in its train (garar) another empire to follow it. "The rock-badger" is an allusion to Greece; "Which is *maaleh gerah,"* i.e., which brought in its train *(garar)* another empire to follow it. *"The swine"* is an allusion to Edom [Rome]; *"Which does not do gerah,"* i.e., which will not bring in its train *(garar)* another empire to follow it. [Afterwards the Messiah will come.] And why is the last-named called *"hazir"* [i.e., swine or boar]? Because it will yet restore *(hazar)* the crown to its [rightful] owner [Israel]. This is indicated by what is written, *"And saviors shall come up on Mount Zion to judge the mount of Esau; and the kingdom shall be the Lord's"* [Obadiah 21].

As we see, this fanciful interpretation transforms the animals of Lev. 11:4–6 into symbols of the nations, while at the same time absorbing them into the history of Israel and relating the history of the nations to important events in Israel's life. In my view this represents the first step taken in the canon to form a fully articulated historical-apocalyptic doctrine within the rabbinic system. For, whatever people may have been thinking in earlier times, here we have, canonically speaking, the earliest well-articulated effort to draw together and periodize Israel's history. The outcome is absolutely inevitable: reference to saviors on Mount Zion and to the coming kingdom.

An example of how the same passage is explained is important, in that it allows us to see how exegetes in Leviticus Rabbah and Sifra treat the same verse. We consider in close sequence Lev. 13:2 as it is dealt with in Sifra and in Leviticus Rabbah. The contrast between the two tells the entire story.

SIFRA NEGAIM PEREQ 1:4

[E] *"A rising or a scab or a bright spot"* [Lev. 13:2].

[F] *"A swelling*—this is a swelling.

[G] *"A spot"*—this is a spot.

[H] *"A scab"* [SPHT]—this is secondary [in color] to the bright spot.

[I] *"And its shade is deep"* [Lev. 13:3: *"And the shade of the plague is deep"*]—[the color of the SPHT is] secondary to that of the swelling.

[J] What is the meaning of the word "scab" [S'T]? Prominent. . . .

[N] What is the meaning of the word "scab" [SPHT]? Secondary.

[O] As it is said, *"Put me [SPHYNY], I pray you, in one of the priest's places . . ."* [1 Sam. 2:36].

We see that the exegete interprets the words of the verse in accord with the plainest meaning he can find. He is not interested in a fanciful reading of one thing into something else, that is, allegory in a simple sense. Now let us see how the exegete of the same verse in Leviticus Rabbah treats it:

LEVITICUS RABBAH 15:9
(TRANSLATED BY J. ISRAELSTAM, PP. 197–98)

"*A rising [se'eth]*" alludes to Babel, since it is said, "*You shall take up this parable against the king of Babylon, and say: How have the oppressors ceased! The exactress of gold [madhebah] ceased!*" [Isa. 14:4].

"*A scab [sappaḥath]*" alludes to Media, which reared Haman, who inflamed [*shaf*] the people [of Media] like a snake, of which it is said, "*Upon your belly you shall go*" [Gen. 3:14].

"*A bright spot [baḥereth]*" alludes to Greece [i.e., Syria] who made herself conspicuous by her decrees against Israel, saying to them: "Write on the horn of an ox that you have no share in the God of Israel." "*The plague of leprosy*" alludes to Edom [i.e., Rome], because it[s power] is derived from the strength of [the blessing of] the old man [viz. Isaac].

What for Sifra is a simple, factual statement, for Leviticus Rabbah becomes a picture of Israel's history of sickness: Babylonia, Media, Greece, Rome—all of them blotches upon the skin of Israel. The verse then bears the deep meaning that the sequence of skin ailments represents in graphic form the history of Israel under the rule of oppressor-kingdoms. It is not clear whether anyone entertained the further notion that, at the end of time, Israel would attain purity through an eschatological act of purification by the anointed Priest-King-Messiah. We have no hint of that further polemic. What we do have, however, is clear evidence of a new and fresh kind of historical thought. By itself, the appearance of these rather odd exegeses does not really testify to a growing tendency to interpret in historical and apocalyptic terms verses of Scripture which treat matters of cult or law and are normally taken at face value.

There is no significant difference between the use of the two forms of exegesis—line by line and discursive. If anything, the seemingly more familiar of the two, explaining passages verse by verse, turns out to sustain the more innovative materials. So there is no correlation between the use of a new mode of discourse and the introduction of what seems to be fresh motifs.

DISCURSIVE EXPOSITIONS OF THEMES: LAMENTATIONS RABBAH, ESTHER RABBAH 1, SONG OF SONGS RABBAH, RUTH RABBAH, AND PESIQTA deR. KAHANA

We now reach a dramatic shift in the character of the canonical discourse on the Messiah and the issues attendant upon that myth. Up to this point, and for most of the compositions surveyed in the present section, we have been on familiar ground. The figure of the Messiah plays a role only slightly larger than it did in the Talmud of the Land of Israel. The entire historical-eschatological question smolders but produces little smoke and no flame at all. We find nothing in any of the collections bearing the title "Rabbah" that would have surprised the Yerushalmi's thinkers and authors. On the contrary, truly new and important initiatives come few and far between. But when we turn to the sort of composition represented by Pesiqta deR. Kahana, we enter a wholly new world, one in which issues of Israel's history and destiny burn on every page, and where the figure of the Messiah in particular hovers throughout.

The movement is sudden and unexpected. It takes place within the hitherto unexplored territory of a new principle of redactional framework, on the one side, and (for the canon) a new interest in the life situation of synagogue liturgy, on the other. First, while the other exegetical compositions reviewed so far follow the principle of organization supplied by Scripture, and lay out ideas—whether narrowly exegetical or more broadly discursive—in accordance with the order of verses of a particular biblical book, the Pesiqta does not. Rather, it lays out its compositions according to calendrical order of the special Sabbaths and festivals throughout the year. That is a completely different principle of organization. Second, while we find nothing akin to a liturgy—not even a hymn or a prayer—in the pertinent passages of prior compositions, we uncover in the Pesiqta materials relevant to the synagogue, a place of worship, rather than to the schoolhouse, a place of study. Surely one of the most powerful of these liturgical compositions is the messianic hymn set out at the end of this section.

In all of this we follow the order of documents given by Heer. However, we have no reason to suppose that one document comes before or after some other; not all of Heer's suggestions, which place the several compositions in the fifth and sixth centuries, seem equally plausible. The temporal priority of the exegetical collections surveyed above (pp. 133–37) (which contain only names of authorities occurring also in the Mishnah and treating Exodus, Leviticus, Numbers, and Deuteronomy) seems likely, but has not been sufficiently proved. In general, as I said, the same modes of thought on the framing of exegetical units of discourse seem to have governed work on units of discourse for both the Talmud of the Land of Israel and Genesis Rabbah and Leviticus Rabbah. But to place those documents within the same period of time, perhaps from 375 to 450, is merely a guess. Likewise, placing in this same period the other exegetical collections—which deal with books of the Hebrew Scriptures used in the synagogue liturgy on special occasions, such as Lamentations for the ninth of Ab, Esther for Purim, Song of Songs Rabbah for Passover, and Ruth for Pentecost—is at best a plausible conjecture. Still, it is probable that in the present set of materials we find ourselves in the two hundred years or so which end with the Muslim conquest of the Middle East, that is, at A.D. 400–640.

Most, though not all, of the discourse in Lamentations Rabbah is composed around themes or topics rather than around verses of Scripture. Many present rather elaborate tales. But we find no new ideas, only well-developed narrative restatements of familiar themes. For instance, the story of the birth of the Messiah and his name (see above, Y. Ber. 2:4) recurs with elaborations but no major changes (Lam. R. I.16.51). So too Aqiba's view of Bar Kokhba at Y. Ta. 4:5 is reproduced (Lam. R. II.2.4). In addition to the ten "horns," e.g., of Abraham, Isaac, Joseph, Moses, and the like, is "the horn of the Messiah" with 1 Sam. 2:10 as the prooftext (Lam. R. II.2–3.6). Of greater interest is what appears to be a secondary expansion of the theme of the distinct "periods" of Israel's history. Now the periods are paired and contrasted:

LAMENTATIONS RABBAH I.14.42
(TRANSLATED BY A. COHEN, P. 123)

"They are knit together." He caused them to alternate in their behavior to me. He brought them upon me in pairs, viz., Babylon and the

Chaldeans, Media and Persia, Greece and Macedon, Edom (Rome) and Ishmael. He made them alternate in their treatment, so that Babylon was severe but Media lenient, Greece severe but Edom lenient, the Chaldeans severe but Persia lenient, Macedon severe but Ishmael lenient. Thus it is written, *"So part of the kingdom shall be strong, and part thereof broken"* [Dan. 2:42]. Through it all I did not repudiate my God, but *"they are come upon my neck,"* and twice daily I proclaimed His unity, saying, *"Hear, O Israel, the Lord our God, the Lord is one"* [Deut. 6:4].

I should have supposed the reference to "Ishmael," in contrast to Edom/Rome, meant Islamic as against Roman-Christian rule. But since Heer places the document in this period, we take account of the passage here.

The one important new initiative presents a statement of certainty that the Messiah is coming. Proof for that assumption is that the prophetic predictions of punishment of Israel have come true. It must follow that the promise of future redemption, in the rebuilding of Jerusalem, also will reach fulfillment. Whether the absence of reference to the Messiah myth in particular bears any significance is not clear. The passage is eschatological, yet contains no explicit reference to the Messiah.

LAMENTATIONS RABBAH 5:18
(TRANSLATED BY A. COHEN, PP. 242–43)

"For the mountain of Zion which is desolate" [5:18].

Long ago, as R. Gamaliel, R. Eleazar b. Azariah, R. Joshua, and R. Aqiba were on the way to Rome, they heard the noise of the crowds at Rome from Puteoli a hundred and twenty miles away. They all fell aweeping, but R. Aqiba laughed. They said to him, "Aqiba, we weep and you are merry!" He replied to them, "Wherefore are you weeping?" They answered, "These heathen peoples who worship idols and bow down to images live in safety, ease, and prosperity, whereas the 'Footstool' of our God is burnt down by fire and has become a dwelling for the beasts of the field, so should we not weep?" He said to them, "For that reason I am merry. If they that offend Him fare thus, how much better shall they fare that obey Him?"

On another occasion they were coming up to Jerusalem, and when they reached Mount Scopus they rent their garments [in mourning]. When they arrived at the Temple Mount, they saw a fox emerging from the Holy of Holies. They fell aweeping, but R. Aqiba laughed. They said to him, "Aqiba, you always surprise us. We weep and you are merry!" He replied to them, "Wherefore are you weeping?" They answered, "Shall we not weep that from a place of which it was written, *And the common man that draws nigh shall be put to death* [Num. 1:51], a fox emerges, and concerning it the verse is fulfilled, *For the mountain of Zion, which is desolate, the foxes walk upon it*?" He said to them: "For that reason am I merry. Behold it states, *And I will take unto Me faithful witnesses to record, Uriah the priest, and Zechariah the son of Jeberechiah* [Isa. 8:2]. Now what connection has Uriah with Zechariah? Uriah lived in the time of the first Temple while Zechariah lived in the time of the second Temple! But what did Uriah say? *Thus says the Lord of hosts: Zion shall be plowed as a field, and Jerusalem shall become heaps* [Jer. 26:18]. And what did Zechariah say? *There shall yet old men and old women sit in the broad places of Jerusalem, every man with his staff in his hand for very age* [Zech. 8:4]; and it continues, *And the broad places of the city shall be full of boys and girls playing in the broad places thereof* [ibid. 5]. The Holy One, blessed be He, said, *Behold I have these two witnesses, and if the words of Uriah are fulfilled, the words of Zechariah will be fulfilled; and if the words of Uriah prove vain the words of Zechariah will prove vain.* I rejoiced because the words of Uriah have been fulfilled and in the future the words of Zechariah will be fulfilled." Thereupon in these terms did they address him: "Aqiba, you have consoled us; may you be comforted by the coming of the herald [of the redemption]!"

I am not entirely certain about the conclusion to be drawn from this long passage. While the formulation is dramatic, the idea itself is commonplace. Making the tribulations of Israel serve as confirmation, also, of the coming redemption hardly represents a new conception within the rabbinic canon. Nor does the omission of any specific allusion to the Messiah prove that the Messiah myth lies only in the distant background or is entirely absent. In all, the strength of the composers of Lamentations Rabbah—their narrative power—is amply illustrated. But we also see their weakness: the absence of genuinely fresh conceptions. In narrative they reframed in new ways dogmas that were tried and true. We look in vain for much development of historical thinking, on the one side, or of the Messiah myth, on the other.

Esther Rabbah I, comprising the proems and Chapter One, develops the now familiar notion that successive periods in Israel's history exhibit their own distinctive traits. Now, however, no period appears more lenient, none more oppressive than the next.

ESTHER RABBAH I 1:2
(TRANSLATED BY M. SIMON, P. 2)

"In the morning you shall say: Would it were evening!" [Deut. 28:67]. In the morning of Babylon you will say, "Would it were the evening thereof!" In the morning of Media you will say, "Would it were the evening thereof!" In the morning of Greece you will say, "Would it were the evening thereof!" In the morning of Edom you will say, "Would it were the evening thereof!" Another explanation of "In the morning you will say: Would it were evening!": in the morning of Babylon you will say, "Would it were the evening of Media!" In the morning of Media you will say, "Would it were the evening of Greece!" In the morning of Greece you will say, "Would it were the evening of Edom!" Why? *"For the fear of your heart which you shall fear, and for the sight of your eyes which you shall see"* (ibid).

It seems to me that we remain within the frame of discourse established in Leviticus Rabbah. So far as a doctrine of Israel's history is concerned, it states simply that each age is succeeded by a worse one. The natural conclusion is that when things become totally unbearable, the Messiah will come. That conclusion is already contained within the dogma, repeated at M. Sot. 9:15, that prior to the Messiah's coming there will be an age of tribulation. Not only does logic lead from the present passage to that inexorable conclusion, but we have evidence that people in the present setting followed the logic where it led. For the sequence of oppressive periods in Israel's history now is explicitly linked to the coming of the Messiah:

ESTHER RABBAH I 1:4
(TRANSLATED BY M. SIMON, PP. 5–6)

Samuel opened with the text, *"'And yet for all that, when they are in the land of their enemies, I did [E.V. 'will'] not reject them, neither did I abhor them, to destroy them utterly, to break my covenant with them; for I am the Lord their God'* [Lev. 26:44]. *'I did not reject them,'* in Babylon; *'Neither did I abhor them'* in Media. *'To destroy them utterly'*—when subject to Greece. *'To break my covenant with them'*—when subject to the kingdom of wickedness. *'For I am the Lord their God'*—in the messianic era."

R. Hiyya taught, "*'I did not reject them'* in the days of Vespasian; *'Neither did I abhor them'* in the days of Trajan *'To destroy them utterly'*—in the days of Haman. *'To break my covenant with them'*—in the days of the Romans. *'For I am the Lord their God'*—in the days of Gog and Magog."

The interpretation attributed to Samuel explicitly places the kingdom of the Messiah at the climax of the rule of oppressive empires. So there is a pattern of contrasts, from the rule of the nations to the rule of the Messiah. The final step in the doctrine of Israel's history—tribulation then redemption, or evil rule then God's messianic dominion—provides a firm link between the Messiah myth and the larger doctrine of Israel's history and destiny. This link would never again be severed. From this point in the formation of the rabbinic canon, as soon as people speak of eschatological history, they will invoke the person of the Messiah.

Song of Songs Rabbah goes over familiar themes and motifs, e.g., references to the messianic future (Song R. I.5.1) and to the sequence of oppressive periods, "the night of Egypt and the night of Babylon" (Song R. III.1.1). The coming of the Messiah will be preceded by remarkable events. If one sees an untoward event, he should expect the Messiah. For example:

SONG OF SONGS RABBAH 8:9:3
(TRANSLATED BY M. SIMON, PP. 315–16)

R. Abba b. Kahana said, "If you see seats filled with Babylonians in the Land of Israel, look out for the coming of the Messiah. Why so? Because it says, *'He has spread a net for my feet'* [Lam. 1:13]."

R. Simeon b. Yohai taught, "If you see a Persian horse tethered to a grave in the land of Israel, look out for the coming of the Messiah. Why so? Because it says, *'And this shall be peace: when the Assyrian shall come into our land, and when he shall tread in our palaces, then shall we raise against him seven shepherds'* [Mic. 5:4]."

My sense of the passage is that the rabbis' meaning was sarcastic. These are remarkable, unlikely events, things indicative of the change of the natural order of things. It is difficult to assign much importance to these statements.

But we find two strikingly new and important initiatives. First, there is a vast expansion of the notion of tribulations prior to the coming of the Messiah:

SONG OF SONGS RABBAH 2:13:4
(TRANSLATED BY M. SIMON, PP. 126–27)

R. Yohanan said, "In the first year of the septennate in which the scion of David will come, will be fulfilled the statement of the Scripture, 'And I will cause it to rain upon one city' [Amos 4:7]. In the second year famine will assail it. In the third year there will be a great famine, from which men, women, and children will perish, and pious men and men of good deeds will become few, and the Torah will begin to be forgotten in Israel. In the fourth year there will be scarcity of a kind and plenty of a kind. In the fifth year there will be great plenty and the people will eat, drink, and be merry, and the Torah will be renewed and restored to Israel. In the sixth year there will be thunderings, in the seventh year wars. At the expiration of the seventh year the scion of David will come."

Said Abaye, "How many septennates have passed like this, and yet he has not come! He will come only in the circumstances described by Resh Laqish: 'In the generation in which the scion of David will come, the meetinghouse shall be a bawdy house and Galilee shall be laid waste and Gabalina shall be desolate and the men of Galilee shall go about from town to town and find no pity and the wisdom of the scribes shall become putrid and the God-fearing and pious shall cease and truth shall be abandoned and the generation will be brazen-faced like a dog.' How do we know that Truth will be abandoned? Because it says, 'And truth is lacking [ne-edereth], and he that departs from evil makes himself a prey' [Isa. 59:15]."

"Whither does Truth go? The School of R. Jannai said, "It will go and settle in separate groups [adarim] in the wilderness."

The Rabbis say, "In the generation in which the scion of David will come, the wise men of the generation will die, and the rest will waste away with grief, and sorrow and much trouble will come upon the community and cruel decrees will be promulgated, one coming on top of another."

R. Nehorai said, "In the generation in which the scion of David will come, the young will insult their elders and the old will rise before the young, as it says, 'The daughter rises up against her mother, the *daughter-in-law against her mother-in-law; a man's enemies are the men of his own house'* [Mic. 7:6], and a son will feel no shame before his father."

R. Nehemiah said, "Before the days of the Messiah there will be great poverty and scarcity, and the vine will cast its fruit and the wine will turn bad and the whole of the government will be converted to *minut* [heresy], and there will be no reproof."

R. Abba b. Kahana said, "The scion of David will come only in a generation which is brazen-faced like a dog."

R. Levi said, "The scion of David will come only in a generation which is full of impudence and deserves to be exterminated."

R. Jannai said, "If you see one generation after another cursing and blaspheming, look out for the coming of the Messiah, as it says, *'Wherewith thine enemies have taunted, O Lord, wherewith thine enemies have taunted the footsteps of thine anointed'* [Ps. 89:51], and immediately afterwards it is written, *'Blessed be the Lord for evermore, Amen and Amen.'"*

This passage carries forward the themes of M. Sot. 9:15, to which we notice explicit reference. If that is the case, then we must recognize an instance of "messianization." That is, we see here the introduction of the explicit Messiah myth into a passage in which it formerly was absent. The conception of the tribulations prior to the Messiah's coming, independently framed of the litany of M. Sot. 9:15, is now joined to that passage. The result is a reframing of the matter, which joins the catalogue of eschatological suffering with the Messiah myth. It does not require a long step from the one to the other, once people have taken for granted that all eschatological discourse involves the figure of the Messiah.

Second, and still more interesting, we now find the notion that Israel may do nothing to hasten the coming of the Messiah. The sign of Israel's obedience will be its acceptance of the oppressive rule of pagan powers.

SONG OF SONGS RABBAH 2:7:1
(TRANSLATED BY M. SIMON, PP. 114–15)

R. Yose b. Hanina said, "These are two adjurations, one addressed to Israel and one to the other nations. God adjured Israel not to rebel against the yoke of the Governments, and He adjured the Governments not to make their yoke too heavy on Israel, for by making their yoke too heavy on Israel they would cause the end to come before it was due."

. . . .

R. Helbo said, "Four adjurations are mentioned here. God adjured Israel that they should not rebel against the Governments, that they should not seek to hasten the end, that they should not reveal their mysteries to the other nations, and that they should not attempt to go up from the diaspora by force. For if they do, why should the King Messiah come to gather the exiles of Israel?"

R. Onia said, "He addressed to them four adjurations corresponding to the four generations who tried to hasten the end and came to grief, namely, once in the days of Amram, once in the days of Dinai, once in the days of Ben Koziba, and once in the days of Shuthelach the son of Ephraim, as it says, 'The children of Ephraim were as archers handling the bow' [Ps. 78:9]."

Some say, "Once in the days of Amram, once in the generation of the same persecution, once in the days of Ben Koziba, and once in the says of Shuthelach the son of Ephraim, as it says, 'The children of Ephraim were as archers handling the bow.'"

They reckoned [that the four hundred years of bondage began] from the time when the decree was pronounced, when God spoke with Abraham between the pieces, but it really began from when Isaac was born. What did they do? They assembled and went forth to battle, and many of them were slain. Why was this? "Because they did not believe in the Lord and did not trust in his salvation," but anticipated the end and transgressed the adjuration.

Israel's passive acceptance of the government of the Gentiles thus will induce God to respond by sending the Messiah: if Israel rebels, it is a sign that the Messiah is not wanted. The critique of Bar Kokhba implied as much. There is here, once more, an explicit joining of the Messiah myth to a larger conception of Israel's history and destiny. The conception presents a paradox. For now Israel undertakes the active task of obedient suffering as a sign of its utter and complete dependence upon God. Once Israel has wholly accepted God's rule, then God will respond and so send the Messiah to rule Israel.

The logic is clear and perfect. Accordingly, Israel's social circumstance, its historical situation, and its eschatological destiny are reworked into a single seamless web of doctrine, wholly congruent, moreover, to the dreadful and disappointing conditions of the age. The explicit reference to Bar Kokhba's war produces no surprise. It is merely the final step in the tendency already announced in the pages of the Talmud of the Land of Israel. Nonetheless, the passage at hand retains remarkable importance, for it constitutes as complete and encompassing a theory of Israel's history and destiny as has come before us. As we see, the theory resorts to the Messiah myth to attain total plausibility.

If we could show that each document deliberately took up the themes of its predecessor, we would not be surprised to find that the materials at hand appear to be expansions and amplifications of themes discerned in the foregoing collections. Once we speak of tribulations attendant upon the coming of the Messiah, the next step is to specify what these are and the order in which they will strike. When we ask about what Israel can do to hasten the coming of the Messiah, we naturally turn to the character of the tribulations themselves and contrast them with what the Messiah is supposed to bring. Thus, the contrast between oppressive rule and the Messiah's dominion draws in its wake the astonishing yet predictable doctrine that, to hasten matters, Israel should suffer patiently. We need hardly spell out the obvious fact that this doctrine accords with the social circumstances at hand: powerlessness and fatigue. The defeated people now receive the message that in acceptance of defeat, it will triumph. The reason is that God will respond to Israel's inner character. The paradox is no paradox at all. The nation surely would survive, since continued resistance was evidently perceived to be hopeless. So the formation of canonical doctrine appears, in retrospect, to have moved from theme to secondary development, on the one side, and to follow the main lines of the social circumstance in which Israel found itself, on the other.

Ruth Rabbah, dealing as it does with the progenitor of the Davidic dynasty, repeats familiar motifs, e.g., "the messianic age" (Ruth R. 3:7, 5:6). There is one original concept, the comparison of the future redeemer to the former redeemer, that is, to Moses (Ruth R. 5:6). Just as Moses was hidden for three months, so the future redeemer will be revealed and then hidden from Israel. The notion that a good deed is recorded is now restated; Elijah writes it down, the Messiah and God then seal the record (Ruth R. 5:6). In accord with the genealogical obsession in the Book of Ruth, we find a fair number of references to the line of the Messiah down to David, e.g., Ruth R. 8:1, "Said the Holy One, blessed be he, to David, 'What need did I have to record the genealogy of Perez, Hezron, Ram, Amminadab, Nashon, Salmon, Boaz, Obed, and Jesse? It was only on account of you.'" Given the purpose of the document, however, we must be surprised by the entirely conventional character of its thought on the stated theme.

Pesiqta deR. Kahana brings us into a new and amazing world. Here eschatology forms a prevailing and dominant motif of discourse. We have to take account of a sizable repertoire of passages in which, while the Messiah in particular does not appear, the diverse themes of the eschaton are played and replayed. Let us first review the passages in which the specific theme of the Messiah comes to the fore, and then briefly turn to the larger framework of the document as a whole.

Pisqa 5, which deals with the theme that Israel will be redeemed at the advent of the new moon marking the month of Nisan (in which Passover occurs at the full moon), contains most of the explicit references to the coming of the Messiah. Some of the allusions go over now familiar ground, e.g., the Messiah appeared in Israel and then disappeared (Braude, pp. 103, 104). But an entirely fresh mode of discourse is taken up as well. Specifically, since the Song of Songs, with its celebration of spring, is read in the synagogue on Passover, the exegetes introduce verses from that book and provide them with a messianic reading in conformity with the context of Nisan's redemption established in Pisqa 5. The result is both a rephrasing of familiar matters, such as the notion of the tribulations that will prefigure the coming of the Messiah, and also the introduction of essentially new modes of discourse about the Messiah.

PESIQTA deR. KAHANA PISQA 5
(TRANSLATED BY WILLIAM BRAUDE AND ISRAEL J. KAPSTEIN, PP. 108–9)

"My beloved spoke [anah] and said unto me" [Song 2:10]. R. Azariah asked, "But do not the words 'spoke' and 'said' mean the same thing? No, here the word anah means not 'spoke' but 'answered,' that is, [on Mount Carmel] he answered me at Elijah's bidding, and then through the Messiah he will say [encouraging things] to me. What will he say to me? 'Rise up, my love, my fair one, and come away [ibid.]. For lo, the winter is past' [ibid., 2:11]."

"That is," said Azariah, "the wicked kingdom which enticed mortals into a wintry way has passed on, the wicked kingdom alluded to in the verse, 'If your brother [Esau, from whom came Edom and Rome], the son of your mother [Rebekah] . . . entice you . . . saying: Let us go and serve other gods' [Deut. 13:7]."

"The rain is over and gone" [Song 2:11] refers to the enslavement [under Edom] that is over and gone. "The flowers appear on the earth" [Song 2:12], the flowers standing metaphorically, as R. Isaac said, for the craftsmen in the verse, And the Lord showed me four craftsmen [who wreak deliverance for Israel]" [Zech. 2:3].

These craftsmen are Elijah, the king Messiah, Melchizedek, and the priest who was anointed in time of war [to exhort the armies of Israel].

By the words "The time of singing is come" [Song 2:12] is meant [the season when plants are pruned or cut back—hence metaphorically speaking] the time has come for the foreskin to be cut; the time has come for the wicked to be broken and cut down: "The Lord has broken the staff of the wicked" [Isa. 14:5]; the time has come for the wicked kingdom to be rooted out of the world; the time has come for the kingdom of heaven to be revealed: "And the Lord shall be king over all the earth [etc.]" [Zech. 14:9].

"And the voice of the turtle [twr] is heard in our land" [Song 2:12], words which mean, according to R. Yohanan, that the voice of the king Messiah, the voice of the one who will lead us with great care through the final turnings [tyyr] of our journey is heard in the land: "How beautiful upon the mountains are the feet of the messenger of good tidings" [Isa. 52:7].

"The fig tree drops [as into a grave] her unripe and sickly figs" [Song 2:13]. R. Hiyya bar Abba said, "In the days of the Messiah a great pestilence will come, and the lives of the wicked will come to an end."

The diverse materials at hand proceed to attach to Song 2:13 the account, cited earlier, of what will happen in the seven years prior to the coming of the Messiah, with the entire passage repeated pretty much verbatim. If we ask what new doctrines are at hand—as distinct from powerful restatements of familiar ideas—it is difficult to point to any at all. Rather, we see a filigree of verses of Song of Songs woven into messianic themes. It does not seem a long step from the notions reviewed in earlier compositions to the idea that the wicked kingdom will be uprooted. The passage as a whole, however, does appear fresh and original, because of its aesthetic force, its capacity to make use of new figures for old concepts.

A further noteworthy passage again reverts to M. Sot. 9:15, introducing the explicit reference to the Messiah:

PESIQTA deR. KAHANA PISQA 5
(TRANSLATED BY BRAUDE AND KAPSTEIN, P. 111)

R. Abba bar Kahana said, "The son of David will not come except in a generation whose every member deserves extermination." R. Yannai said, "The son of David will not come except in a base, a dog-faced generation."

The passage then goes over the ground of Levi's citation of Ps. 89:52–53. In the messianic age the King-Messiah will try cases in Jerusalem (Pisqa 18, Braude, p. 321).

Supplement 6, serving Isa. 61:10, read on the New Moon, presents the following stunning hymn to the Messiah:

PESIQTA deR. KAHANA SUPPLEMENT 6
(TRANSLATED BY BRAUDE AND KAPSTEIN, P. 488)

The words, *"For he has clothed me with the garments of salvation"* [Isa. 61:10] refer to the seven garments which, according to Scripture, the Holy One will have put on successively from the time the world was created until the time he requites wicked Edom. When he created the world, he put on glory and majesty, as is said, *"Thou art clothed with glory and majesty"* [Ps. 104:1]. When he appeared over the Red Sea, he put on haughtiness, as is said, *"The Lord reigns; he is clothed in haughtiness"* [Ps. 93:1]. When he gave the Torah, he put on strength, as is said, *"The Lord puts on strength for the sake of his people"* [Ps. 29:11]. When he forgives the iniquities of Israel, he will put on a white garment, as is said, *"his raiment was as white snow"* [Dan. 7:9]. When he requites the peoples of the world, he will put on garments of vengeance, as is said, *"And he put on garments of vengeance for clothing"* [Isa. 59:17]. When the Messiah appears, God will put on the sixth garment: he will be clothed in righteousness, as is said, *"he put on righteousness as a coat of mail, and a helmet of salvation upon his head"* (ibid.). When he requites Edom, he will put on the seventh garment: he will put on red apparel, as is said, *"Wherefore is thine apparel red?"* [Isa. 63:2]. The splendor of the garment he puts on the Messiah will stream forth from world's end to world's end, as implied by the words, *"As a bridegroom puts on a priestly diadem"* [Isa. 61:10].

Israel will live in his radiance and say, "Blessed is the hour in which the Messiah was created! Blessed is the womb whence he came! Blessed is the generation whose eyes behold him! Blessed is the eye which has been given the privilege of seeing him whose lips open with blessing and peace, whose diction is pure delight, whose garments are glory and majesty, who is confident and serene in his speech, the utterance of whose tongue is pardon and forgiveness, whose prayer is a sweet savor, whose supplication during his study of Torah is purity and holiness. Blessed are Israel. How much is laid up for them! As is said, *'Oh how abundant is thy goodness which thou hast laid up for them that fear thee'* [Ps. 31:20]."

This passage stands all by itself. As I said at the outset, we find ourselves in the synagogue and at prayer, rather than at the schoolhouse in study. The exegesis of Scripture falls away; the utilization of prooftexts becomes still more incidental to the main point. In Pesiqta deR. Kahana, the formative canonical literature reaches a climax in messianic fervor. Established themes recur, but, as we now see, a wholly new mood comes to expression, a powerful yearning for the fall of Edom (Rome) and for the coming of the Messiah.

From these specific passages, let us now attend to the larger context of the composition as a whole. For even the remarkable hymn above does not convey the entire eschatological flavor of the discourse of Pesiqta deR. Kahana. For the present purpose, we are best served simply by Braude and Kapstein's summary of the pertinent sections, those that deal with the ninth of Ab, Pisqas 16–22:

Further discourse in connection with the Fast of the Ninth of Ab is pursued in Pisqas 16–22. These Pisqas are based on the *haftarahs*, the readings from the Prophets devoted to the seven Sabbaths of Consolation which follow the Fast. In Pisqa 16, treating Isa. 40:1, God assures Israel that Isaiah and other Prophets will bring true comfort and consolation to Israel and Zion. Zion is not to despair, Pisqa 17, accompanying Isa. 49:14, says again and again: God is still the merciful and gracious protector of Israel; even the punishment he inflicts upon Israel is for beneficent ends. Israel has had to suffer, continues Pisqa 18, accompanying Isa. 54:11, because of her lack of knowledge of Torah and her lack of good deeds and righteous men; but vindication and comfort will come to Israel and Jerusalem. In the meantime, however great the suffering, says Pisqa 19, based on Isa. 51:12, Israel is to remember that study of Torah, deeds of kindness, and offerings to God for ever qualify her as God's own people. Accordingly, declares Pisqa 20, accompanying Isa. 54:1, when Zion is restored, the boundaries of Jerusalem will rise up to the very throne of glory. Indeed, continues Pisqa 21, commenting on Isa. 60:1, the glory of Zion's restoration will surpass the glory of the revelation on Sinai. Israel's greatest joy, however, concludes Pisqa 22, accompanying Isa. 61:10, will be that God their King will have come back to Zion [pp. xii–xiii].

Braude and Kapstein thus provide us with a statement of the doctrine of Israel's history and destiny expressed in the document at hand. As we see, it is not only with reference to Passover that the messianic theme comes to dominate. When the ninth of Ab presents the occasion, the entire range of historical-eschatological symbols—the restoration of Zion, the mercy of God, the ultimate benevolence of God even when he punishes Israel, the explanation of the present condition of Israel and Jerusalem, the coming glory of Israel in Zion—all make their appearance. Accordingly, we see, even where the Messiah in particular plays no role, the larger eschatological framework now will demand his presence and take it for granted.

THE OVERALL STATE OF OPINION IN FIFTH- AND SIXTH-CENTURY COMPOSITIONS OF SCRIPTURAL EXEGESIS: (I) THE MESSIAH

Before surveying as a whole what we do find in the exegetical compilations, let us begin with a backward glance at what we do not find. No matter where we turn, from Genesis Rabbah to Pesiqta deRab Kahana, we uncover no systematic or overriding interest in reading a messianic motif into those verses of Scripture which, to begin with, do not exhibit it. For the rabbinical exegetes' Christian counterparts—that is, the entire cohort of Church fathers, who wrote in Latin, Greek or Syriac—matters were quite otherwise. Christ formed the ever-present consideration, the exegetical fulcrum, in particular when reading the Old Testament. The issue of the meaning of every passage under the aspect of the Messiah therefore predominated. Deep messianic meaning was to be found even in the law about lepers, the forms of the disease and the inspection by the high priest (Tertullian against Marcion in *The Five Books against Marcion*, Alexander Roberts and James Donaldson, eds., Peter Holmes, trans., *The Ante-Nicene Fathers* [repr. Grand Rapids, 1957] 3:407). That deep meaning, quite naturally, awaited discovery in the relationship of Leviticus 13 and 14 to Christ's healing of the leper. This one very minor instance shows the paramount, and predictable, exegetical principle utilized by those for whom the figure of the Messiah defined the correct interpretation of all Scripture. If we ask for its counterpart in rabbinic compilations, this can be only the figure of Israel: the suffering people, God's first and last love. To the context and condition of Israel, the Messiah served as ancillary and auxiliary. He was never the focus, never the centerpiece. A glance at Leviticus 13 in Lev. R. cited above shows the matter clearly.

Yet even when we identify "Israel" as the exegetical fulcrum of all rabbinical collections of biblical interpretation, we scarcely advance the argument, for the work of differentiating one composition from the next is not developed very far. We do have Braude and Kapstein's striking statement, part of which I quoted just now, on what they conceive to be the polemical purpose of the compilation they translated. But the document, in the terms in which they describe its overview and message, scarcely differs from any other rabbinic document. Anywhere we look, one way or the other we should discern pretty much the same message. That is to say, the definitive elements remain constant, much as Christ forms the dominant motif in any patristic essay. How could we expect otherwise? Yet to say, for this reason, that we cannot differentiate, let us say, Tertullian's writings from Augustine's, would be obtuse. Whether, along these same lines, we may differentiate the "Israel" of one document from that of another, or distinguish the fundamental viewpoint and polemic of one composition of exegesis from those of another, remains to be seen. No one has tried to do so. Accordingly, the survey of exegetical compositions just now concluded represents a first, and very primitive, step. If we propose to survey a given topic or theme as treated in an entire and vast literature, we err by treating as essentially homogeneous (except in the detail under consideration) an enormous set of quite varied books. The labor of differentiation, which must precede the work of restoration (and perhaps of harmonization), has yet to begin.

With that important, indeed nearly paralyzing, qualification, we turn to the figure of the Messiah in the books we have briefly encountered.

If we could demonstrate that the system of classification within which we have worked—treating wholly exegetical compilations first, wholly discursive ones last—has conformed to the temporal order in which the compositions reached closure, then the picture would be unambiguous. We should be able to state that the earliest collections tend to treat only casually the topic of the Messiah, while the latest ones find the myth a matter for urgent consideration. As it is, we have the same facts at hand. But the way in which we describe and interpret them changes. The simple fact is that we find a correlation between the character of a composition and the contents and use of the Messiah myth in that composition. But how should we interpret that fact? Let us first review, and then interpret, the data.

The line-by-line exegesis of pentateuchal books, from Exodus through Deuteronomy, leaves us in closest contact with the Mishnah's views. The Messiah myth clearly is known. Facts concerning the Messiah—his coming and the preceding age, what he will do—prove to be commonplace repetitions. When, for instance, the priestly documents refer to the anointed priest, the exegetical compositions know as "messiah" only that same priest. Sifra and Sifré Numbers in this regard stand within the circle of the Mishnah. Where we observe the opportunity—indeed, the open invitation—to introduce the Messiah myth, the exegetes ignore it. Instead, they impose the category of Torah study. True, Sifré Deut. speaks of the "days of the Messiah." But the Messiah as a force in history and pivot of eschatology attracts scant interest. What has been said to this point applies without variation to Genesis Rabbah and Leviticus Rabbah. To be sure, we note the appearance of some details not found in compilations previously examined. We find no more importance accorded to the Messiah myth in the larger hermeneutical framework of Genesis Rabbah and Leviticus Rabbah than in that of Sifra, Sifré Numbers, or Sifré Deuteronomy.

The line-by-line, discursive exegetical compositions on biblical books used in synagogue liturgy on special Sabbaths and festivals do not vastly change the established picture of the Messiah and of the importance accorded to him. Familiar ideas recur, such as the tribulations coming on the eve of the Messiah's advent. True, the Messiah plays a part in the forgiveness of sin, but this is merely in conjunction with Elijah and God.

Only when we reach Pesiqta deR. Kahana, as I have emphasized, do we enter a new world. Now familiar themes play and replay, but the Messiah, among other powerful eschatological motifs, takes on an enormous presence. Indeed, we may state simply that, if Torah study forms the recurrent leitmotif of earlier compositions, the eschatological hope of Israel, with the Messiah at the center, constitutes the recurrent and definitive theme of the last document reviewed.

How shall we describe and interpret these facts? When exegetes in the life situation of the schoolhouse remain close to the text of Scripture, organizing their ideas around the sequences of biblical verses and tying at least some of those ideas to the verses themselves, then the Messiah myth proves peripheral. True, we notice a tendency to introduce the figure of the Messiah into passages in which, in the Mishnah in particular, that figure is strikingly ignored. But the instances are few, the contexts unimpressive. On the other hand, when we enter the frame of discussion carried on in the synagogue and organized in terms of its calendar (hence no longer the framework of scriptural exegesis as the organizing principle), the situation changes completely. Then, as we have seen, the figure of the Messiah becomes vivid; discourse on the messianic themes as critical to eschatology becomes lively and engaged. The very anomalous character of Pesiqta deR. Kahana, which is not a compilation of scriptural exegesis at all (at least as the Rabbah collections constitute compilations of exegesis), therefore seems to me to point to the heart of the matter.

How shall we explain that fact, and what does it mean? We know too little about the social context in which both the collections of exegesis, on the one side, and also the remarkable composition of Scripture into constructions pertinent to special Sabbaths and festivals, on the other, came to expression and reached closure. Accordingly, when people systematically explained passages of Mishnah and verses of Scripture and compiled the explanations into compositions of mishnaic explanation and of exegesis following the order and structure of the Mishnah and Scripture respectively, we cannot say why they did things one way. When, on the other hand, they found

themselves free of the discipline of an established document of revelation—Mishnah or Scripture—we cannot say why they did things
some other way. We simply do not know whether this fact finds its
explanation in the history of literature, in the social setting, in the
political context, in the theological circumstances, in that of the rabbinical estate, or (in the matter of Pesiqta deRab Kahana, for example) in the totally different setting of the (popular) synagogue as distinct from the (elitist) master-disciple circle. In the present
framework, it is not possible even to hazard a guess.

THE OVERALL STATE OF OPINION IN
FIFTH- AND SIXTH-CENTURY COMPOSITIONS
OF SCRIPTURAL EXEGESIS:
(II) ISRAEL'S HISTORY AND DESTINY

While compositions of close exegesis of scriptural verses present
little evidence of interest in the Messiah myth, these same passages
testify to rich speculation on the meaning of Israel's history and destiny. Furthermore, a systematic rethinking of that matter apparently
was under way. When the process of reconsideration reached completion, the Messiah myth gained critical importance in the larger
theory of the place of Israel in the history of humanity—what was to
be demanded of the people Israel if it was to reach the climax of its
history.

Specifically, the view that Bar Kokhba and others had acted arrogantly against God, joined with a certain reserve about the Messiah
myth altogether, shifted the discourse in a sequence of well-defined
steps. Rabbis presented matters in this way: the known messianic
pretenders, represented by Bar Kokhba, had asked God to allow
them to do their own work. The opposite conception was that Israel
must do nothing to force God's hand. The arrogance of former generations had led to the defeat and suffering of Israel in the present
age. The process had to be reversed. Israel had to accept defeat and
suffering. Why? As proof that the former arrogance had turned to
humility and complete acceptance of God's rule. Once Israel accepted God's rule, God would indeed rule. Then what? Then the
Messiah, representing God's rule, would come. We see, therefore, a
sequence of propositions and their corollaries, each involving a
statement of a historical event, its consequences, and its meaning. If

policy x had yielded consequence y, then the converse of policy x would yield the opposite of consequence y. This kind of analogical-contrastive thinking may be seen to underlie the historical doctrines of Israel's destiny as worked out in the present part of the canon in formation.

Standing outside the system, we observe the Messiah myth now changing from a powerful motivation for historical and political action into an equally powerful incentive to passivity and self-resignation to Israel's historical and political condition. That is the story which emerges from the sources we have just reviewed. The literature that tells that story, moreover, forms the bridge from exegetical to discursive passages. For the one point of contact, indeed intersection, lies in the movement from the periodization of Israel's history, fully framed in line-by-line exegesis of Scripture, to the messianization of Israel's eschatology, expressed mostly in discursive, broad-ranging passages that are not constrained by Scripture's sequence.

Scripture is rich in reflection on the meaning of Israel's history, the explanation of its destiny. Indeed, Scripture taken as a whole serves best to answer the question. But, since the Mishnah, in the interim, had addressed other issues in other ways, reversion to the historical and eschatological focus in context still marked an important initiative. Such symbols as the war of Gog and Magog, the suffering preceding the advent of the Messiah, the judgment day, the lost ten tribes, and the like, were of little use to the framers of the Mishnah's system. They remain part of an undifferentiated background of ideas which was occasionally introduced. As for the authors of Mekhilta, Sifra, and the two Sifrés, these same matters appeared hardly more suggestive to them than to the sages of the Mishnah. Only when we reach Leviticus Rabbah do the symbols of historical and eschatological theory come to the fore.

The first major step in our review is the restatement of a systematic periodization of Israel's history, presented, on the one side, by the allegory of forbidden animals (Lev. R. 13:5) and on the other by the allegory of skin ailments. Both passages take up the conquerors of Israel—Babylonia, Media, Greece, Rome—and set them into relationship with another known entity, the denizens of the animal world and specifications of skin diseases. We can hardly invoke at this point the notion that rabbis here founded an apocalyptic-eschatological tradition in the pattern of Daniel. That is hardly the case. But without a clear delineation of periods, no one could have proceeded toward further speculation on the sequence of events or on the meaning of Israel's history as adumbrated in that sequence. The passages, tied as they are to the exegesis of specific verses, retain the literary character of line-by-line exegetical collections. But they point toward important conceptual initiatives revealed only in discursive compositions.

It seems to me that the recognition of historical periods must stand logically prior to the assignment of characteristics or qualities to those periods. Furthermore, before sequences of periods were specified, it is unlikely that people could have imagined how to arrange events in a pattern pointing toward the end and climax of such a sequence. Accordingly, I am inclined to suppose that the contrasts drawn at Lam. R. I 14:42, between the severe and the lenient periods of pagan rule, became possible only after the several periods had been identified and brought to full definition. The contrasting judgment at Esther R. I 2, in which each period is represented as a trial, changes nothing. Indeed, it appears to be a negative response to the original proposal of a pattern of harsh, then gentle, rulers. Finally, the specification of an end to it all—"*For I am the Lord their God*'—in the messianic era" [Esther R. 1:4]) marks a considerable step forward. Earlier formulations, after all, discerned distinct historical periods, without specifying where they were leading or what the sequence meant. But this is a step in a simple progression of ideas, beginning with the recognition that, first, there are periods; second, they stand in some sort of meaningful sequence and relationship to one another; and ending, third, with the knowledge that things are heading in a certain direction.

If the first of the two truly stunning intellectual achievements of the exegetical compositions—periodization, with the Messiah introduced at the end—shows us how Israel's history emerged as a well-conceived construction, the second, and still more important, turns attention to the deep meaning of that historical pattern. The conception that Israel's history yields redemptive lessons is hardly the invention of fifth- and sixth-century exegetical theologians. But how that conception emerges and the way in which it comes to expression tell us what was new. I see two stages in the formation of the truly distinctive idea of the age, that Israel's history demanded its acceptance of suffering, in consequence of which Israel, having accepted God's sovereignty, would be ruled by God through the Messiah.

First came the principle, put into Aqiba's mouth, that just as the prophetic predictions of Israel's future suffering have come true, so the prophetic predictions of Israel's coming consolation would surely come true. In this way, attention must come to rest upon what to ordinary folk must have proved the critical issue facing all of Israel's thinkers, namely, the present appalling condition of God's first love, the people of the covenant.

Second was the statement that Israel must await God's action rather than act on its own. That notion, contained in the Yerushalmi's tales of the sages' criticism of Bar Kokhba, comes to more general expression in the simple and logical question: If the exiles attempt by force to return to the homeland, then "why should the King Messiah come to gather the exiles of Israel?" (Song R. 2:7:1). If Israel hopes for the Messiah, then the people must accept with complete resignation the destiny meted out to them by God.

The meaning of Israel's history, therefore, must emerge from the response of Israel to its history: humility and acquiescence must prevail in the rule of the nations, as God's imposed test and penalty. I am inclined to see as not wholly new the statement in the exegetical composition at hand, since a very specific expression of the same viewpoint emerged in the Yerushalmi's units of discourse dealing with Bar Kokhba. But there what had appeared particular and unique now came forth as general and universal. Among others, Bar Kokhba served as a paradigm for the lessons Israel must learn from its history.

We need hardly dwell on the simple logic of the matter: God will rule (through the Messiah) when Israel truly accepts God's rule. Nor is it possible to square the astonishing principles at hand with the opposing view that the Messiah will come only to a generation deserving utter extermination. That view, itself a restatement in messianic terms of the eschatological conviction announced at M. Sot. 9:15, carried its own theory of the meaning of Israel's history. Of the two positions, the former clearly elicited more imaginative force: "Blessed are Israel. How much is laid up in store for them!"

4

The Messiah in the Documents of Exegesis and Expansion: The Talmud of Babylonia and Other Extant Writings

THE TALMUD OF BABYLONIA

The Talmud of Babylonia, the second and more important systematic exegesis of the Mishnah, reached closure between 500 and 600. That, at any rate, is the conventional date. If it is sound, then we deal with a document later than the earlier compilations of scriptural exegesis and contemporary with the later ones. For that reason we place the second Talmud at the end of this survey of the unfolding canonical consensus.

Comparing this Talmud with its predecessor requires results of scholarly inquiries which have not yet been undertaken. Specifically, while we have a clear picture of the types of discourse, organized in freestanding and cogent units, exhibited by the Talmud of the Land of Israel, we have no equivalent taxonomy for the Talmud of Babylonia. True, a rapid bird's-eye view of the latter leaves little in obscurity. We are able to see that the Talmud of Babylonia overall appears to be constructed of three kinds of discourse: (1) units closely or expansively exegetical of the Mishnah; (2) autonomous, wide-ranging essays on themes at best intersecting with those of a passage of the Mishnah, just as in the other Talmud; (3) scriptural-exegetical discourses, cast as either verse-by-verse comments or discursive thematic constructions. Whether there are other taxa I do not know. Not surprisingly, all units of discourse relevant to the problem are of the second or third (or other) type; in no passage of Mishnaic exegesis do we find the Babylonian Talmud introducing the Messiah theme into any explanation of a passage of the Mishnah lacking that theme.

Babylonian rabbis carried forward the three types of literary constructions available in their time, the first two learned from the Talmud of the Land of Israel and the third familiar from the exegetical compilations. If I had to point to the single exegetical composition most like the sort we find, in the aggregate, in the Talmud of Babylonia, it would be Leviticus Rabbah. That is to say, we seem to have a rough balance of the two sorts of exegetical units of discourse into which we can divide all such constructions. But this is only an impression. A further impression is that the Talmud of Babylonia exhibits traits familiar from the Talmud of the Land of Israel. Many of the generalizations offered above seem to me equally applicable to the second of the two Talmuds. But, as I said, the necessary taxonomical analysis has yet to begin, so I can offer only these few shaky efforts at generalization.

Once more we take up our two principal themes, exploring the data both for the reappearance of the known and also for the development of fresh initiatives and new perspectives. Coming at the end of nearly half a millennium of reflection, the Talmud of Babylonia served as an encyclopedia and reprise. But it exhibited familiar ideas in new ways as well.

We first survey the data in the first two sections below, and then in the fifth part we undertake an analysis to compare the data of the Babylonian Talmud with the entire antecedent corpus of information about the Messiah and thought about Israel's history and destiny.

THE MESSIAH

As in the Talmud of the Land of Israel, so here, when the Mishnah establishes a usage, the talmudic exegetes preserve it. For example, the anointed priest appears (B. Ta. 31a). But what makes the Talmud of Babylonia distinctive in its larger context is the power of its framers to construct sustained and fairly compendious discussions on a given theme. These discussions draw upon a wide variety of materials, which are rearranged, and probably reshaped as well, for the purposes governing the work as a whole. The compositors then provide an encyclopedic account of the subject, carefully encompassing each of its pertinent components. In that way they treat the matter whole and complete, assembling information to present a picture transcending the parts.

Rather than disassemble this construction as it treats our topic, we treat it whole, then proceed to survey the constituent elements of the Babylonian Talmud's largest and most compendious repertoire of units of discourse on the Messiah. I have abbreviated the essay, however, to signal the main themes while lightening the burden of detail (most prooftexts, for example), and I have altogether omitted materials clearly extraneous to the main topic.

B. SANHEDRIN 96b–99a (PASS.)
(TRANSLATED BY H. FREEDMAN, PP. 654–70)

[1] R. Nahman said to R. Isaac, "Have you heard when Bar Naflé will come?" "Who is Bar Naflé?" he asked. "Messiah," he rejoined, "as it is written, '*In that day I will raise up the tabernacle of David* (ha-nofeleth) *[that is fallen]*' [Amos 9:11]." He replied, "Thus has R. Yohanan said, 'In the generation when the son of David [i.e., Messiah] will come, scholars will be few in number, and as for the rest, their eyes will fail through sorrow and grief. Multitudes of trouble and evil decrees will be promulgated anew, each new evil coming with haste before the other has ended.'"

[2] Our rabbis taught: In the seven year cycle at the end of which the son of David will come—in the first year, this verse will be fulfilled: "*And I will cause it to rain upon one city and cause it not to rain upon another city*" [Amos 4:7]; in the second, the arrows of hunger will be sent forth; in the third, a great famine, in the course of which men, women, and children, pious men and saints will die, and the Torah will be forgotten by its students; in the fourth, partial plenty; in the fifth, great plenty, when men will eat, drink and rejoice, and the Torah will return to its disciples; in the sixth, [heavenly] sounds; in the seventh, wars; and at the conclusion of the septennate the son of David will come. R. Joseph demurred, "But so many septennates have passed, yet has he not come!"—Abaye retorted: "Were there then [heavenly] sounds in the sixth and wars in the seventh! Moreover, have they [the troubles] been in this order!"

[3] "*[Wherewith thine enemies have reproached, O Lord; wherewith they have reproached the footsteps of thine anointed]*" [Ps. 89:52]. It has been taught, R. Judah said, "In the generation when the son of David comes, the house of assembly will be for harlots. Galilee in ruins, Gablan lie desolate, the border inhabitants wander from city to city, receiving no hospitality, the wisdom of scribes in disfavor, God-

fearing men despised, people be dog-faced, and truth entirely lacking, as it is written, 'Yea, truth fails, and he that departs from evil makes himself a prey' [Isa. 59:15].'"

[4] It has been taught: R. Nehorai said, "In the generation when Messiah comes, young men will insult the old, and old men will stand before the young [to give them honor]; daughters will rise up against their mothers, and daughters-in-law against their mothers-in-law. The people shall be dog-faced, and a son will not be abashed in his father's presence."

[5] It has been taught, R. Nehemiah said, "In the generation of Messiah's coming impudence will increase, esteem be perverted, the vine yield its fruit, yet shall wine be dear, and the kingdom will be converted to heresy with none to rebuke them. This supports R. Isaac, who said: 'The son of David will not come until the whole world is converted to the belief of the heretics.'" Raba said, "What verse [proves this]? 'It is all turned white: he is clean' [Lev. 13:13]."

[6] Our rabbis taught: "For the Lord shall judge his people, and repent himself of his servants, when he sees that their power is gone, and there is none shut up, or left" [Deut. 32:36], the son of David will not come until denunciators are in abundance. Another interpretation [of "their power is gone"]: until scholars are few. Another interpretation: until the [last] perutah has gone from the purse. Yet another interpretation: until the redemption is despaired of. Israel had neither Supporter nor Helper. Even as R. Zera, who, whenever he chanced upon scholars engaged thereon [i.e., in calculating the time of the Messiah's coming], would say to them, "I beg of you, do not postpone it, for it has been taught: Three come unawares: Messiah, a found article and a scorpion."

[7] R. Kattina said, "Six thousand years shall the world exist, and one [thousand, the seventh], it shall be desolate. . . ." Abaye said, "It will be desolate two [thousand]. . . ."

[8] The Tanna debe Eliyyahu teaches: "The world is to exist six thousand years. In the first two thousand there was desolation, two thousand years the Torah flourished; and the next two thousand years is the messianic era, but through our many iniquities all these years have been lost."

[9] Elijah said to Rab Judah, the brother of R. Salla the Pious, "The world shall exist not less than eighty-five jubilees, and in the last jubilee the son of David will come." He asked him, "At the beginning or at the end?" He replied, "I do not know." "Shall [this period] be completed or not?" "I do not know," he answered. R. Ashi said, "He spoke

thus to him, 'Before that, do not expect him; afterwards you may await him.'"

[10] R. Hanan b. Tahlifa sent [word] to R. Joseph, "I once met a man who possessed a scroll written in Hebrew in Assyrian characters. I said to him, 'Whence has this come to you?' He replied, 'I hired myself as a mercenary in the Roman army, and found it amongst the Roman archives. In it is stated that four thousand two hundred and thirty-one years after the creation, the world will be orphaned. [As to the years following,] some of them will be spent in the war of the great sea monsters, and some in the war of Gog and Magog, and the remaining [period] will be the messianic era, while the Holy One, blessed be he, will renew his world only after seven thousand years.'"

[11] It has been taught: R. Nathan said, "This verse pierces and descends to the very abyss: '*For the vision is yet for an appointed time, but at the end it shall speak, and not lie: though he tarry, wait for him; because it will surely come, it will not tarry*' [Hab. 2:3]." Not as our Masters, who interpreted the verse, "*until a time and times and the dividing of time*" [Dan. 7:25]; nor as R. Simlai who expounded, "*Thou hast fed them with the bread of tears, and given them tears to drink a third time*" [Ps. 80:6]; nor as R. Aqiba who expounded, "'*Yet once, it is a little while, and I will shake the heavens, and the earth*' [Hag. 2:6]: but the first dynasty [the Hasmonean] shall last seventy years, the second [the Herodian] fifty-two, and the reign of Bar Koziba two and a half years."

[12] What is meant by, "*but at the end it shall speak [we-yafeah]* and *not lie*"? R. Samuel b. Nahmani said in the name of R. Jonathan, "Blasted be the bones of those who calculate the end. For they would say, since the predetermined time has arrived, and yet he has not come, he will never come. But [even so], wait for him, as it is written, 'Though he tarry, wait for him.' Should you say, *We* look forward [to his coming] but *he* does not: therefore Scripture says: '*And therefore will the Lord wait, that he may be gracious unto you, and therefore will he be exalted, that he may have mercy upon you*' [Isa. 30:18]. But since *we* look forward to it, and *he* does likewise, what delays [his coming]? The Attribute of Justice delays it. But since the Attribute of Justice delays it, why do we await it? To be rewarded [for hoping], as it is written, 'blessed are all they that wait for him.'"

[13] Rab said, "All of the predestined dates [for redemption] have passed, and the matter [now] depends only on repentance and good deeds." But Samuel maintained, "It is sufficient for a mourner to keep his [period of] mourning." This matter is disputed by Tannaim: R.

Eliezer said, "If Israel repent, they will be redeemed; if not, they will not be redeemed." R. Joshua said to him, "If they do not repent, will they not be redeemed! But the Holy One, blessed be he, will set up a king over them, whose decrees shall be as cruel as Haman's, whereby Israel shall engage in repentance, and he will thus bring them back to the right path."

[14] R. Hanina said, "The son of David will not come until a fish is sought for an invalid and cannot be procured. . . ."

[15] R. Hama b. Hanina said, "The son of David will not come until even the pettiest kingdom ceases [to have power] over Israel. . . ."

[16] Zeiri said in R. Hanina's name, "The son of David will not come until there are no conceited men in Israel. . . ."

[17] R. Simlai said in the name of R. Eleazar, son of R. Simeon, "The son of David will not come until all judges and officers are gone from Israel. . . ."

[18] Ulla said, "Jerusalem shall be redeemed only by righteousness. . . ."

[19] R. Papa said, "When the haughty cease to exist [in Israel] the magi shall cease [among the Persians]; when the judges cease to exist [in Israel], the *chiliarchs* shall cease likewise. . . ."

[20] R. Yohanan said, "When you see a generation ever dwindling, hope for him [the Messiah]. . . ." R. Yohanan said: "When you see a generation overwhelmed by many troubles as by a river, await him. . . ."

[21] R. Yohanan said, "The son of David will come only in a generation that is either altogether righteous or altogether wicked. . . ."

[22] R. Alexandri said: R. Joshua b. Levi pointed out a contradiction, "It is written, '*in its time [will the Messiah come]*,' while it is also written, '*I [the Lord] will hasten it!*' [Isa. 60:22]. If they are worthy, I will hasten it: if not, [he will come] at the due time."

[23] R. Joshua b. Levi met Elijah standing by the entrance of R. Simeon b. Yohai's tomb. He asked him, "Have I a portion in the world to come?" He replied, "If this Master desires it." R. Joshua b. Levi said, "I saw two, but heard the voice of a third." He then asked him, "When will the Messiah come?" "Go and ask him himself," was his reply. "Where is he sitting?" "At the entrance." "And by what sign may I recognize him?" "He is sitting among the poor lepers: all of them untie [them] all at once, and rebandage them together, whereas he unties and rebandages each separately, [before treating the next] thinking, should I be wanted, [it being time for my appearance as the Messiah] I must not be delayed [through having to bandage a number of sores]." So he went to him and greeted him, saying, "Peace upon thee, Master

and Teacher." "Peace upon thee, O son of Levi," he replied. "When will thou come, Master?" asked he. "Today," was his answer. On his returning to Elijah, the latter enquired, "What did he say to you?" "'Peace upon thee, O son of Levi,'" he answered. Thereupon he [Elijah] observed, "He thereby assured you and your father of [a portion in] the world to come." "He spoke falsely to me," he rejoined, "stating that he would come today, but has not." He [Elijah] answered him, "This is what he said to you, 'Today, if you will hear his voice' [Ps. 95:7]."

[24] The disciples of R. Yose b. Kisma asked him, "When will the Messiah come?" He answered, "I fear lest you demand a sign of me [that my answer is correct]." They assured him, "We will demand no sign of you." So he answered them, "When this gate falls down, is rebuilt, falls again, and is again rebuilt, and then falls a third time, before it can be rebuilt the son of David will come." They said to him, "Master, give us a sign." He protested, "Did you not assure me that you would not demand a sign?" They replied, "Even so, [we desire one]." He said to them, "If so, let the waters of the grotto of Paneas turn into blood"; and they turned into blood. When he lay dying he said to them, "Place my coffin deep [in the earth], for there is not one palm tree in Babylon to which a Persian horse will not be tethered, nor one coffin in Palestine out of which a Median horse will not eat straw."

[25] Rab said, "The son of David will not come until the [Roman] power enfolds Israel for nine months. . . ."

[26] Ulla said, "Let him [the Messiah] come, but let me not see him." Rabbah said likewise: "Let him come, but let me not see him."

[27] R. Joseph said, "Let him come, and may I be worthy of sitting in the shadow of his ass's saddle." Abaye enquired of Rabbah, "What is your reason [for not wishing to see him]? Shall we say, because of the birth pangs [preceding the advent] of the Messiah? But it has been taught, R. Eleazar's disciples asked him: 'What must a man do to be spared the pangs of the Messiah?' [He answered,] 'Let him engage in study and benevolence'; and you Master do both." He replied: "[I fear] lest sin cause it. . . ."

[28] R. Yohanan said likewise, "Let him come, and let me not see him. . . ."

[29] R. Giddal said in Rab's name, "The Jews are destined to eat [their fill] in the days of the Messiah." R. Joseph demurred, "Is this not obvious; who else then should eat!" This was said in opposition to R. Hillel, who maintained that there will be no Messiah for Israel, since they have already enjoyed him during the reign of Hezekiah.

173

[30] Rab said: "The world was created only on David's account." Samuel said, "On Moses' account"; R. Yohanan said, "For the sake of the Messiah. What is his [the Messiah's] name?"—The School of R. Shila said, "His name is Shiloh, for it is written, 'until Shiloh come' [Gen. 49:10]." The School of R. Yannai said, "His name is Yinnon, for it is written, 'His name shall endure for ever: e'er the sun was, his name is Yinnon' [Ps. 72:17]." The School of R. Haninah maintained, "His name is Haninah, as it is written, 'Where I will not give you Haninah' [Jer. 16:13]. . . ."

[31] R. Nahman said, "If he [the Messiah] is of those living [today], it might be one like myself, as it is written, 'And their nobles shall be of themselves, and their governors shall proceed from the midst of them' [Jer. 30:21]." Rab said, "If he is of the living, it would be our holy Master; if of the dead, it would have been Daniel the most desirable man." Rab Judah said in Rab's name, "The Holy One, blessed be he, will raise up another David for us. . . ."

[32] R. Simlai expounded, "What is meant by, 'Woe unto you, that desire the day of the Lord! To what end is it for you? The day of the Lord is darkness, and not light?' [Amos 5:18]. This may be compared to a cock and a bat who were hopefully waiting for the light [i.e., dawn]. The cock said to the bat, 'I look forward to the light, because I have sight; but of what use is the light to you?" And thus a Min said to R. Abbahu: "When will the Messiah come?" He replied, "When darkness covers those people." "You curse me," he exclaimed. He retorted, "It is but a verse: 'For, behold, the darkness shall cover the earth, and gross darkness the people: but the Lord shall shine upon you, and his glory shall be seen upon you' [Isa. 60:2]."

[33] It has been taught: R. Eliezer said, "The days of the Messiah will last forty years. . . ." R. Eleazar b. Azariah said, "Seventy years. . . ." Rabbi said, "Three generations. . . ."

[34] R. Hillel said, "There shall be no Messiah for Israel, because they have already enjoyed him in the days of Hezekiah." R. Joseph said, "May God forgive him [for saying so]. Now, when did Hezekiah flourish? During the first Temple. Yet Zechariah, prophesying in the days of the second, proclaimed, 'Rejoice greatly, O daughter of Zion; shout, O daughter of Jerusalem; behold, your king comes to you! He is just, and having salvation; lowly, and riding upon an ass, and upon a colt the foal of an ass' [Zech. 9:9]."

[35] Another [Baraitha] taught: R. Eliezer said, "The days of the Messiah will be forty years. . . ." R. Dosa said, "Four hundred years. . . ." Rabbi said, "Three hundred and sixty-five years, even as the days of the solar year. . . ." Abimi the son of R. Abbahu learned, "The days of

Israel's Messiah shall be seven thousand years. . . ." Rab Judah said in Samuel's name, "The days of the Messiah shall endure as long as from the Creation until now. . . ." R. Nahman b. Isaac said, "As long as from Noah's days until our own. . . ."

[36] R. Hiyya b. Abba said in R. Yohanan's name, "All the prophets prophesied [all the good things] only in respect of the messianic era; but as for the world to come, '*the eye has not seen, O Lord, beside thee, what he has prepared for him that waits for him*' [Isa. 64:3]." Now, he disagrees with Samuel, who said, "This world differs from [that of] the days of the Messiah only in respect of servitude to [foreign] powers."

The framers of this lengthy construction clearly wished to present a generally harmonious picture of doctrine on the coming of the Messiah, conditions attendant upon his arrival, his name, the character of the age in which he would reign, and related questions. True, the authors underline points of disagreement. But these testify to an underlying consensus on the main issues. If we outline the main themes and points of firm doctrine, they are these:

1. The coming of the Messiah will be heralded by a time of trouble (paragraphs 1, 2, 3, 4, 5, 6, 14, 20, 21, 25, 26, 27, 28, 32).
2. People may calculate the time of the Messiah's coming, though it is not advisable to do so, lest the calculations err, and disappointment follow (paragraphs 9, 10, 11, 12, 13, 22, 24).
3. The history of the world is divided into three parts, the third of which is the time of the Messiah (paragraphs 7, 8, 33, 35).
4. God will intervene and send the Messiah to a generation that is worthy of it. That generation will repent of its sins, either because of its righteousness or because the lamentable conditions prevailing make repentance unavoidable. In any event it is the condition of Israel that determines when the Messiah will come (paragraphs 11, 13, 15, 16, 17, 18, 19, 21, 22, 23, 29, 34, 36).
5. The Messiah will come from the house of David (paragraphs 30, 31, and pass.)

On these points, so far as I can discern, all parties are in essential agreement. If so, we do not locate a single doctrine that would have surprised the framers of the exegetical compositions reviewed in the preceding chapters. While, in a general way, the framers of the Talmud of the Land of Israel also would have concurred, at a number of specific points there are marks of not only difference but development. But these are not blatant, and perhaps it is our eyesight, not what we see, that calls them to the surface.

We might be tempted to observe a certain urgency in the composition before us, pressure that the Messiah come soon. But that judgment, subjective to begin with, at best tells us only about the character of the opinion gathered here, that is, editors' choices. We know nothing of popular opinion, let alone attitudes and feelings prevalent in the entirety of the schools or master-disciple circles, of which the rabbinic estate was composed and from which the Talmuds of both countries emerged. Accordingly, we must not mislead ourselves into thinking that, because the general impression conveyed by these paragraphs is one of urgency and impatience, the Jewish nation in Babylonia waited at the edge for salvation. Perhaps it did. But what is at hand does not prove it.

More certain is that, when the authorities who were responsible for the collection of these materials did their work, they laid enormous emphasis upon the sin of Israel and the capacity of Israel through repentance both to overcome sin and to bring the Messiah. "The attribute of justice" delays the Messiah's coming. The Messiah will come this very day, if Israel deserves. The Messiah will come when there are no more arrogant ("conceited") Israelites, when judges and officers disappear, when the haughty and judges cease to exist, "Today, if you will obey" (Ps. 95:7). What alternatives are excluded? First, no one maintains the Messiah will come when the Israelites successfully rebel against Iran or Rome. Second, few express eagerness to live through the coming of the Messiah, the time of troubles marking the event, with the catastrophes, both social and national, that lie in wait. The contrast between this age and the messianic age, moreover, is drawn in some measure in narrowly political terms: servitude to foreign powers will come to an end. That view proves entirely consistent with opinion, familiar from some of the exegetical collections, that Israel must accept the government of the pagans and that the pagans must not excessively oppress Israel.

In all, we must ask ourselves whether the messianic myth, in all its protean power and dimensions, is presented so as to make Israel rebel against its present state or accept it. The answer, of course, is as clear here as it was in the preceding chapter. In the hands of the framers of the norm-setting literature of Judaism, the Messiah serves to keep things pretty much as they were, while at the same time promising dramatic change. The condition of that dramatic change is not richly instantiated. It is given in the most general terms. But it is not difficult to define. Israel must keep God's will, expressed in the Torah and the observance of the rites described therein. So Israel will demonstrate its acceptance of God's rule. Accordingly, the net effect of this essay is to reinforce that larger system of the Judaism of Torah study and the doing of religious duties expressed partially in the Talmuds of the Land of Israel and of Babylonia, with their exegesis of the Mishnah, and partially in the various exegetical compositions organized around the order and program of some of the books of Scripture.

Formative Judaism thus drew into its sphere that weighty conception embodied in the Messiah myth and thereby gained force and stability for that movement itself. Yet, in all, the matter of the Messiah remained subordinated: "*If you do this or that*, the Messiah will come." Thus the Messiah myth supplied the uniform apodosis of diverse protases, the fixed teleology for the variety of ineluctable demands of the system as a whole.

In this literature what is important is the life of ritual learning and doing. Attaching the promise of the coming of the Messiah reinforced the demands that truly mattered to the framers of the documents under study. If Israel at large yearned for the redemption and the end, then telling them to attain that goal by doing what rabbis wanted would vastly strengthen the rabbinic system. Perhaps we may say, upon reviewing a passage such as the one at hand, that the charismatic Messiah myth served as the engine to draw the train of fixed practices and patterns down the "routinized" tracks of the law. Absorbed with a system essentially antithetical to the activist mode defined at the time when the Messiah myth had previously governed, the impatient expectation expressed therein now served the cause of modified hope and skeptical anticipation. In all, the Messiah myth here entered a system meant to endure but ready, to be sure, to reach climax and conclusion at any moment.

Having seen how the redactors of the Talmud of Babylonia defined and organized a large-scale discussion of the Messiah myth, let us now examine the components, with attention to materials not represented in the passages just now reviewed or in the Talmud of the Land of Israel and the exegetical compositions. We follow the rough order established above.

The Coming of the Messiah;
The Time of Troubles

Occasional references to the "pangs of the Messiah" encompass some secondary refinements of the basic notion. The verse "*Not unto us, O Lord . . .*" (Ps. 115:1) speaks of the pangs of the Messiah (B. Pes. 118a). Accordingly, whenever that psalm is recited, people turn out to beseech God to spare them the anguish attendant upon the Messiah's coming. There are things one can do to be spared the travails of the Messiah, for instance, eating three meals on the Sabbath in observance of the happiness of that day (B. Shab. 118a). A Babylonian master maintained that the Jews of Babylonia would not witness sufferings before the Messiah arrived (Abbaye, B. Ket. 111a). Disciples of sages will be persecuted in the generation in which David's son comes (B. Ket. 112b).

The Time of the Messiah's Coming;
Signs of the Times

Unusual events signal the coming of the Messiah. If, for example, a certain kind of bird perches on the ground and hisses, "the Messiah will come at once" (B. Hul. 63a). If a person sees a choice vine in a dream, "he may look forward to seeing the Messiah" (B. Ber. 57a). But, in general, it was taken for granted that the Messiah would come in the remote future. Just as we noted above, if one person said to another, "Until the dead revive and the Messiah, son of David, comes," it is understood that he meant, "a long time from now."

There were three separate, yet not disharmonious, traditions on the date of the coming of the Messiah. As we saw earlier, people believed he would come in the seventh year of the seven-year cycle, on which account, in the order of petitionary blessings, the messianic prayer is placed seventh (B. Meg. 17b). Second, the Messiah will come in Nisan, corresponding to the time at which Israel was redeemed in Egypt (B. R.H. 11a). Third, the Messiah will come on a weekday but not on a Sabbath or festival day (B. Er. 43a–b).

On the one hand, among the seven things hidden from human beings is the date at which the Davidic dynasty will return and the wicked kingdom will come to an end (B. Pes. 54b). On the other hand, the date of the coming of the Messiah is foretold in the Aramaic translation of the Hagiographa (B. Meg. 3a), but it is forbidden to reveal that date. The one firm conviction is that the reign of the Messiah will come about through ending the rule of Rome and Iran (B. A.Z. 2b).

At the same time, the Messiah must not be brought "before his time":

B. BABA MESIA 85b
(TRANSLATED BY H. FREEDMAN, P. 492)

Elijah used to frequent Rabbi's academy. One day—it was New Moon—he was waiting for him, but he failed to come. Said he to him the next day, "Why did you delay?" He replied, "[I had to wait] until I awoke Abraham, washed his hands, and he prayed and I put him to rest again; likewise to Isaac and Jacob." "But why not awake them together?" "I feared that they would wax strong in prayer and bring the Messiah before his time."

One authority, however, maintained that the Messiah would come in a specific year, 468, that is, precisely four hundred years after the destruction of the Temple.

B. ABODAH ZARAH 9b
(TRANSLATED BY A. MISHCON, PP. 46–47)

Said R. Hanina, "From the year 400 after the destruction onwards, if one says unto you, 'Buy a field that is worth one thousand *denarii* for one *denar*,' do not buy it." In a *Baraitha* it is taught: From the year four thousand two hundred and thirty-one of the Creation of the World onward, if one says unto you, "Buy for yourself a field that is worth a thousand *denarii* for one *denar*," do not buy it. What difference is there between these two [given periods]? There is a difference of three years between them, the one of the *Baraitha* being three years longer.

The mélange of opinion on when the Messiah would come is not to be stirred into a uniform mass. Clearly, opinion on when the Messiah would come was shaped by diverse motives and derived from quite distinct sources. On the one side, people looked to the cyclical division of years in the seven-year cycle. On the second, they reflected upon the time of the redemption from Egypt and sought to use that event as an analogy for what was coming. And again, the notion that the time of the Messiah's coming was hidden in obscurity had to be balanced against the conception that, within Scripture, all things were to be uncovered. None of these convictions need contradict the deep-set principle that there is a fixed time, an appropriate time, for the Messiah's coming. It would upset the world's order for the Messiah to appear before the fixed date.

Only the specification of a fixed year (468) for the Messiah's coming sounds a jarring note. The logic of Hanina's calculation is not difficult to spot. The Israelites had suffered in Egypt for four hundred thirty years, then were redeemed. Perhaps the calculation was that there had been thirty good years or that it would take those additional thirty years for the Messiah to accomplish his work. In any event, the main point is that Hanina looked into the history of Israel for an analogy in the timing of the redemption, yet another time, for which Israel waited. From the notion that redemption would come in Nisan to match the redemption from Egypt, to the conception of calculating the time in line with the earlier subjugation, one does not have to take a very long step. But for the generality of opinion in this document, that step was not encouraged and was not to be taken.

This Age and the Messianic Age:
Similarities and Differences

The history of the world is divided into three ages: this age, the days of the Messiah, and the world to come (after the days of the Messiah). Yohanan maintained, for example, that the prophets spoke of the days of the Messiah, but "as for the world to come, 'Eye has not seen, Oh God, beside thee' [Isa. 64:3]" (B. Ber. 34b). Along these same lines, we have the following interpretation of Deut. 33:12:

B. ZEBAHIM 118b
(TRANSLATED BY H. FREEDMAN, P. 585)

"He covers him" [Deut. 33:12] alludes to the first Temple; "all the day," to the second Temple; "And He dwells between his shoulders," to the days of the Messiah. Rabbi said, "'He covers him,' alludes to this world; *'all the day,'* to the days of the Messiah; *'and He dwells between his shoulders,'* to the World to Come."

The same tripartite division of time is treated as routine doctrine at B. Shab. 113b. There we find a reference to this world, the days of the Messiah, and the world to come. The periodization represented by the tripartite construction, with the Messiah at the center of history, constitutes only one such theory of history. Others, more interested in that first period of two thousand years, come before us in the next section.

It was entirely feasible to construct a theory of the differences in time periods involving this world and the world to come, with diverse ages of this world ending with the coming of the Messiah, and variations thereof. For all efforts at differentiating one age from another may readily be harmonized without yielding important revisions of any one of them; they are interchangeable so far as the main point is concerned. That point is the emphasis on the difference between time and time, or age and age, on the one side, and the standing of the Messiah in the signification of difference, on the other. Unlike the thinking of the Mishnah's framers on this subject, the bulk of theories takes for granted a significant symbolic position for the figure of the Messiah.

There can be no doubt that the Messiah was expected to fulfill a political task, specifically, to replace the pagan rulers of Israel and to institute his own just government. Indeed, to Samuel was attributed the opinion that the sole point of difference between the present age and the Messiah's time was that the Israelites would no longer live in the Exile and be subject to pagan rule (B. San. 91b, B. Shab. 63a, B. Shab. 151b, B. Pes. 68a). The time of the Messiah, moreover, would be marked by peace, so that weapons would no longer be needed, *"Nation shall not lift up sword against nation"* (Isa. 2:4). The certainty that the Messiah would carry out a political task, replacing pagan kings, is familiar from the warning that people should be sure to go out to see pagan kings, so that, if the Messiah should come in their time, they would know the difference between Israelite and pagan rulers (B. Ber. 19b). In the messianic era kings would rise and princes prostrate themselves before Israel (B. Ta. 14b).

The Talmud's framers, in the following passage, explained the sequence of events that would take place when the Messiah comes. Hence they provided a coherent account of the messianic age. They did so simply by citing the available petitionary prayer, the so-called Eighteen Benedictions, and then specifying relevant verses of Scripture to explain and prove what was to happen in a sequence of steps marked by the coming of the Messiah. In so doing, the authors of the passage provided a systematic picture of the hoped-for sequence of events.

B. MEGILLAH 17b
(TRANSLATED BY MAURICE SIMON, PP. 107–8)

What was their reason for mentioning [in the Eighteen Benedictions] the gathering of the exiles after the blessing of the years? Because it is written, "But ye, O mountains of Israel, ye shall shoot forth your branches and yield your fruit to my people Israel, for they are at hand to come" [Ezek. 36:8].

And when the exiles are assembled, judgment will be visited on the wicked, as it says, "And I will turn my hand upon you and purge away your dross as with lye" [Isa. 1:25], and it is written further, "And I will restore your judges as at the first" [Isa. 1:26].

And when judgment is visited on the wicked, transgressors cease, and presumptuous sinners are included with them, as it is written, "But the destruction of the transgressors and of the sinners shall be together, and they that forsake the Lord shall be consumed" [Isa. 1:28].

And when the transgressors have disappeared, the horn of the righteous is exalted, as it is written, "All the horns of the wicked also will I cut off, but the horns of the righteous shall be lifted up" [Ps. 75:11].

And "proselytes of righteousness" are included with the righteous, as it says, "you shall rise up before the hoary head and honor the face of the old man" [Lev. 19:32], and the text goes on, "And if a stranger sojourn with you."

And where is the horn of the righteous exalted? In Jerusalem, as it says, "Pray for the peace of Jerusalem, may they prosper that love thee" [Ps. 72:6].

And when Jerusalem is built, David will come, as it says, "Afterwards shall the children of Israel return and seek the Lord their God, and David their king" [Hos. 3:5].

And when David comes, prayer will come, as it says, "Even them will I bring to my holy mountain, and make them joyful in my house of prayer" [Isa. 56:7].

And when prayer has come, the Temple service will come, as it says, *"Their burnt-offerings and their sacrifices shall be acceptable upon mine altar"* [Isa. 56:7].

We see, therefore, that the principal petitionary element of the liturgy, the Eighteen Benedictions, provides a program of the events of the messianic age. First comes the gathering of the exiles, then the provision of a righteous government of judges and the punishment of the sinners. Then the righteous exalt in Jerusalem, the city having been rebuilt. David, the Messiah, will at that point return to the rebuilt Jerusalem, an event followed by the hearing of prayer and the restoration of the Temple cult. It follows that the several independent themes—political, cultic, historical, and redemptive—here are sorted out and organized into a coherent scheme in relationship to one another. In this same context, other differences between this world and the world to come, or the messianic world, will fall into place. Jerusalem of the present time will be changed; in the world to come, only those who are invited may go up (B. B.B. 75b). That same program of Temple restoration accounted for continued interest in laws at the time in desuetude. For example, people should study the laws governing cultic sacrifices, even though they will apply only when the Messiah comes (B. San. 51b). They now gain the merit accruing to the act of study; later on, the practical value will become evident as well.

We note, finally, that the framers of the passage take for granted that people of their own standing, that is, rabbis, bear responsibility for the liturgy. Moreover, the mode of thought bringing the liturgy into its present condition, exegesis of Scripture and provision of appropriate prooftexts, allegedly governed the formation of the liturgy. To be sure, this is an *ex post facto* judgment. But the datum at hand is that the order of petitions stands as much for sage as for ordinary folk; no distinction based on divergent aspirations or conceptions—or even points of emphasis—is to be drawn.

We may cite briefly other points of difference between this age and the time of the Messiah or the world to come; these are miscellaneous and not coherent. As above, in the time of the Messiah, the harp of the sanctuary will have eight cords, and the one in the time of the world to come will have ten (B. Ar. 13b). There will be no bad news when the Messiah comes (B. Pes. 50a). In the "time to come" wild trees will bear fruit (B. Ket. 112b). When the Messiah comes,

all the Gentiles will be eager to serve Israelites (B. Er. 43b). Therefore no proselytes will be accepted, since Israel will be so well off
that proselytes will be attracted only by worldly considerations (B.
Yeb. 24b). The righting of the wrongs of the natural and political
worlds will come about. In line with the notion that the nations will
want to serve Israel, we have the view that they will bring gifts to
the Messiah (B. Pes. 118b). The other animals will rebuke the
snake.

B. TAANIT 8a
(TRANSLATED BY J. RABBINOWITZ, P. 32)

Resh Lakish said, "What is the meaning of the verse, '*If the serpent
bite before it is charmed, then the charmer has no advantage?*' [Qoh.
10:11]. In the messianic age all animals will assemble and come to the
serpent and say to him, 'The lion claws [his victim] and devours him,
the wolf tears him and devours him, but as for you what benefit do
you derive?' His reply will be, 'The charmer has no advantage.'"

A passage such as the foregoing carries us away from concrete and
this-worldly discourse on the messianic age and its politics and public life. For now the messianic age stands for something other than a
revision in the worldly standing of Israel alone. It is broadened to
encompass radical changes in the natural world. Here the messianic
age signifies a setting in which to put right any matter deemed un-
natural or out of place. So, on the one side, the differences between
this age and the messianic age may prove limited and narrowly con-
strued. On the other side, whatever anomalies people observe may
be cited as instances of things to be put right in "time to come."
Whether that time is messianic or post-messianic scarcely matters.

The Conditions that Will Lead to the
Coming of the Messiah;
What People Must Do, or Must Not Do,
to Hasten His Coming;
The Condition of Israel and the
Coming of the Messiah

If we find a single repeated message in the rabbinic system as a
whole, it is that Israel bears ultimate responsibility for its own condition. Israel therefore has the power, also, to revise and reshape its

destiny. Blaming one's own sins for what has happened carries a powerful message of hope: just as we did it to ourselves, so we can save ourselves. Indeed, this sense of mastery of one's own destiny through the conduct of the moral life and the sense of guilt for having brought about the present unenviable situation form a single message of comfort. As we observe over and over again, the talmudic part of the system introduces a significant warning, again demanding emphasis: *Israel has the power to save itself by giving up its arrogant claim to be able to do anything to save itself.* By rephrasing the message as they do, the sages take the commonplace and turn it into a paradox.

First we review how the Talmud of Babylonia framed the paramount theme: Israel ruined itself and Israel can save itself. Israel's history is made not by the nations, but by Israel. Israel's destiny is in the hand not of Iran or Rome, but of Israel. Later, we shall see the sharp and decisive qualification of what it means for Israel to save itself. This is, as is clear, to submit utterly and in complete humility to God's rule.

Israel's character and conduct now prevent the Messiah's coming, just as the deed of Israel to begin with led to its present lamentable condition. That fundamental conviction is expressed in diverse sayings, all of the same kind. For example, Elijah to Rab Judah, brother of R. Sila the Pious, "You have asked, 'Why has the Messiah not come?' Lo, this is the Day of Atonement, and yet how many virgins have been embraced in Nehardea?" (B. Yoma 19b). Along these same lines we find the converse of the claim that if Israel keeps the Sabbath one time, the Messiah will come. Turning that conviction on its head, Rab draws the consequences for the present disaster:

B. SHABBAT 118b
(TRANSLATED BY H. FREEDMAN, P. 582)

Rab Judah said in Rab's name, "Had Israel kept the first Sabbath, no nation or tongue would have enjoyed dominion over them, for it is said, 'And it came to pass on the seventh day, that there went out some of the people for to gather' [Exod. 16:27], which is followed by, 'Then came Amalek' [Exod. 17:8]."

R. Yohanan said in the name of R. Simeon b. Yohai, "If Israel were to keep two Sabbaths according to the laws thereof, they would be redeemed immediately, for it is said, *'Thus says the Lord of the eunuchs that keep my Sabbaths'* [Isa. 56:4], which is followed by, *'even them I will bring to my holy mountain'* etc. [Isa. 56:7]."

Israelite behavior, furthermore, still prevents the Messiah from coming: "Proselytes and those who play with children delay the coming of the Messiah" (B. Nid. 13b). The duty of procreation also is tied to the matter: "The son of David will not come until all the souls in *Guf* [the region in which the souls of the unborn are stored] have been disposed of" (B. Nid. 13b, B. Yeb. 62a, 63b).

In syntax, what we have is the counterpart to statements about bringing the Messiah. "If Israel will do such and such"—whatever a given teacher thought important—"the Messiah will come." Here is the opposite: "Because Israel does (or did) thus and so"—whatever someone opposes—"the Messiah has not yet come." The variable is what the distinctive system contributes. The constant—the promise of bringing the Messiah, or the threat against his coming—derives from that shared world of symbols familiar in all forms of Judaism prior to this one.

But there was an important qualification to all this, a contribution quite distinctive to the rabbinic system, not solely in its Babylonian talmudic expression. The principal condition, encompassing the specifications of various laws which must be kept in order to bring the Messiah, was that Israel was not to bring the Messiah before his time, on the one hand, and that Israel was to accept the burden of suffering and pagan rule, whether in the Exile or in the Land, on the other. This familiar notion was restated in the Talmud of Babylonia to encompass the conditions of the Exile, as was to be expected under that Talmud's circumstances. Israel must not go up to the Holy Land all together. People may emigrate to the Holy Land only as individuals. Doing so en masse, by contrast, would indicate that the nation wished to force God's hand in sending the Messiah. The Israelites must not rebel against the nations of the world, and the nations may not oppress Israel "too much" (B. Ket. 111a). To Hiyya's sons was assigned the saying, "The son of David cannot appear before the two ruling houses in Israel come to an end, that is, the Exilarch's rule in Babylonia and the Patriarch's rule in the Land of Israel" (B. San. 38a). Within the logic of the system, even without reference to the everyday politics of the Jewish nation, the saying formed a natural component.

The Identification and Origin of the Messiah

Diverse facts, deriving from ancient Israelite writings or other traditions, circulated about the figure of the Messiah. These facts surface here and there, commonly as singletons, playing no important systemic role in the Babylonian Talmud's larger framework. Some-one says, for instance, that there will be two Messiahs, one of the house of Joseph, the other of the house of David; someone else says the Messiah's name was created before creation; and a third party contributes a further random fact, that the several messiahs —Joseph and David—and Elijah bear certain supernatural tasks. Some of these allegations then provoke a successful search for prooftexts; others stand on their own. I am unable to see how the various assertions draw together into a single picture, whether syncretic or composite. Nor is it clear that most of the facts about the Messiah bear important implications for the larger worldview of the rabbis of formative Judaism at its final canonical expression in the Babylonian Talmud.

One inherited view maintained that there would be multiple messiahs—without reference to the messianic or anointed priest—and not only the Messiah of the house of David. We find an allusion to "the slaying of Messiah, the son of Joseph," for which a prooftext is Zech. 12:10, 12. The statement of Zechariah, *And the land should mourn . . . the family of the house of David apart . . . ,*" is understood to refer to the Davidites' mourning of the slain Messiah of the house of Joseph (B. Suk. 52a). The following, moreover, expresses the same view:

B. SUKKAH 52a
(TRANSLATED BY W. SLOTKI, P. 247)

Our Rabbis taught: The Holy One, blessed be he, will say to the Messiah, the son of David (may he reveal himself speedily in our days!), "Ask of me anything, and I will give it to you," as it is said, *"I will tell of the decree [etc.], 'this day have I begotten you, ask of me and I will give the nations for your inheritance'* [Ps. 2:7–8]." But when he will see that the Messiah the son of Joseph is slain, he will say to him, "Lord of the Universe, I ask of thee only the gift of life." "As to life," he would answer him, "Your father David has already prophesied this concerning you, as it is said, 'He asked life of thee, thou gavest it him [even length of days for ever and ever]' [Ps. 21:5]."

Along these same lines, the "four craftsmen" shown to Zechariah (Zech. 2:3) by the Lord are the Messiah, son of David; Messiah, son of Joseph; Elijah, and righteous priest (Melchizedek) (B. Suk. 52b). The same passage alludes to a whole crew of salvific, but non-messianic, figures: Adam, Seth, Methuselah on the right; David in the middle; Abraham, Jacob, Moses, on the left; then, a separate catalogue (all with reference to Mic. 5:4), Jesse, Saul, Samuel, Amos, Zephaniah, Zedekiah, the Messiah, and Elijah. Accordingly, "the Messiah" stands as one among many.

The Messiah (unspecified) also may bear the name of the Holy One, as may "the righteous" and Jerusalem. The prooftext for the first of the three is Jer. 23:6, "And this is the name whereby he shall be called, 'The Lord is our righteousness'" (B. B.B. 75b). The name of the Messiah was one of seven things created before the world was made, along with the Torah, repentance, the Garden of Eden, Gehenna, the Throne of Glory, and the Temple (B. Ned. 39b, B. Pes. 5a, 54a).

The Messiah of the house of David derived, of course, from the marriage of Ruth and Boaz (B. San. 93a, B. Yeb. 76b). A play on the name of Ruth yielded the explanation that she was called "Ruth," connected to the verb, "to be abundant," because "from her issued David, who saturated the Holy One, blessed be he, with songs and hymns" (B. B.B. 14b, B. Ber. 7b). The Davidic Messiah is described as follows:

B. SANHEDRIN 93b
(TRANSLATED BY H. FREEDMAN, PP. 626–27)

"And the spirit of the Lord shall rest upon him, the spirit of wisdom and understanding, the spirit of counsel and might, the spirit of knowledge of the fear of the Lord. And shall make him of quick understanding [wa-hariho] in the fear of the Lord" [Isa. 11:2–3]. R. Alexandri said, "This teaches that he loaded him with good deeds and suffering as a mill [is laden]."

Raba said, "He smells [a man] and judges, as it is written, *'and he shall not judge after the sight of his eyes, neither reprove after the hearing of his ears, yet with righteousness shall he judge the poor'* [Isa. 11:3]."

Bar Koziba reigned two and a half years, and then said to the Rabbis, "I am the Messiah." They answered, "Of Messiah it is written that he smells and judges: let us see whether he [Bar Koziba] can do so." When they saw that he was unable to judge by the scent, they slew him.

At the same time, David enjoyed the status of a rabbi. No one perceived tension between his messianic and rabbinical standing. David studied Torah through the night (B. San. 16a). He gave decisions as would a rabbinical judge:

B. BERAKHOT 4a
(TRANSLATED BY MAURICE SIMON, P. 11)

"*A prayer of David . . . Keep my soul, for I am pious*" [Ps. 86:1–2]. Levi and R. Isaac: The one says, "Thus spoke David before the Holy One, blessed be he: 'Master of the world, am I not pious? All the kings of the East and the West sleep to the third hour [of the day], but I, *'at midnight I rise to give thanks unto Thee'* [Ps. 119:62]."

The other one says, "Thus spoke David before the Holy One, blessed be He: 'Master of the world, am I not pious? All the kings of the East and the West sit with all their pomp among their company, whereas my hands are soiled with the blood [of menstruation], with the foetus and the placenta, in order to declare a woman clean for her husband. And what is more, in all that I do I consult my teacher, Mephibosheth, and I say to him: My teacher Mephibosheth, is my decision right? Did I correctly convict, correctly acquit, correctly declare clean, correctly declare unclean? And I am not ashamed [to ask].'"

He furthermore behaved in a humble way in the presence of the great rabbis.

B. MOED QATAN 16b
(TRANSLATED BY H. M. LAZARUS, PP. 104–5)

When David sat at the College Session he was not seated on cushions and coverlets but on the [bare] ground. For all the time that his Master, Ira the Jairite, was alive he taught the rabbis while being himself seated on cushions and coverlets; when his soul found rest, David used to teach the rabbis being himself seated on the ground. Said they [the rabbis] to him: "Sit, sit on the cushions and coverlets"; but he would not accede to their request.

"*Tahchemoni*" [2 Sam. 23:8]: Rab explained, "The Holy One, blessed be He, said to him [to David], 'Since you have humbled yourself you shall be like Me [that is], that I make a decree and you [may] annul it.'"

"*Chief of the Captains*" [2 Sam. 23:8], [that is,] you be chief next to the three Fathers.

"*He is Adino the Eznite,*" [that is,] when he was sitting engaged in the [study of] Torah he rendered himself pliant as a worm, but when he went marching out to [wage] war he hardened himself like a lance.

These passages show how the Babylonian Talmud represents David, ancestor of the Messiah, as a rabbi in the wholly familiar pattern defined by the Babylonian rabbinical estate itself. The obvious conclusion is that the Davidic Messiah would emerge from the rabbinical group. If people saw a conflict between the active power of the Messiah and the passivity fostered within the rabbinic circles, with their firm opposition to bringing the Messiah before God was ready and their insistence upon conformity to the law as the condition of the Messiah's coming, that conflict scarcely comes to the surface here.

Yet another proposal for the identification of the Messiah, also of the house of David to be sure, fixed upon Hezekiah of Isaiah's times. But God himself—rabbis asserted—had rejected that possibility. Since Christian critics of Judaism claimed that the prophetic promises of redemption had all been kept in the times of ancient Israel, so that Israel now awaited nothing at all, it was important to reject the claim that Hezekiah had been the Messiah (cf., for example, "Aphrahat's Nineteenth Demonstration," in my *Aphrahat and Judaism* [Leiden, 1971], pp. 84–96).

B. SANHEDRIN 94a
(TRANSLATED BY H. FREEDMAN, P. 630)

"*Of the increase of his government and peace there shall be no end*" [Isa. 9:6]: R. Tanhum said Bar Kappara expounded in Sepphoris, "Why is every *mem* in the middle of a word open, while this is closed?

The Holy One, blessed be he, wished to appoint Hezekiah as the Messiah, and Sennacherib as Gog and Magog; whereupon the Attribute of Justice said before the Holy One, blessed be he: 'Sovereign of the Universe! If Thou didst not make David the Messiah, who uttered so many hymns and psalms before thee, wilt thou appoint Hezekiah as such, who did not hymn thee in spite of all these miracles which thou wroughtest for him?' Therefore it [the *mem*] was closed."

Clearly, when people spoke about the name, family, or mission of the Messiah, they expressed judgments on pressing contemporary questions. But these judgments appear, in retrospect, to be both discrete and formed for the occasion. They do not seem to come from a rich vein of systematic thought, in which, reflecting on perennial issues of their world, rabbis paid attention, also, to the Messiah myth. When we contrast how the Torah myth absorbed within itself the whole messianic system and structure, from the figure of David to the least detail of Sabbath observance and trivial etiquette in the marketplace, we see the difference. Within the document at hand, as within the larger canon of which it forms the climax and conclusion, the matter of the Messiah served purposes quite beyond its own agenda. That is why the facts reviewed just now remain just that, isolated facts, expressive of little beyond themselves.

ISRAEL'S HISTORY AND DESTINY

While the Jews in the Land of Israel found it necessary to explain the hegemony of Rome in the context of Israel's life, the Jews of Babylonia had a second task. Aware that Rome ruled in the Holy Land, they faced the further question of coping with Iranian rule, on the one side, and fitting Iran ("Persia") into the larger scheme of Israelite history already encompassing Rome as well. So, while for the Jews in the Land of Israel, "Persia" meant the Iran of the Achaemenids, for those of Babylonia and Mesopotamia, there was a more problematic "Persia" with which to deal, contemporary, Sasanian Iran. In a land to which they laid no claim or right of possession, moreover, the Jews of the Iranian empire may well have developed a more acute sense than those in the Land of Israel of themselves as different and so as "Israel," therefore needing all the more to explain their difference from others as divine destiny. But the sources permit no meaningful comparison between the frame of mind prevailing in the two centers of rabbinic estate and government. Accordingly, it is at best a reasonable surmise, lying beyond the range of demonstration, that a more acute self-consciousness, hence a better developed historical consciousness, characterized the rabbis of Babylonia.

To begin with, noteworthy events generated the effort to explain what happened and so to nurture the idea of pattern and history. Accordingly, we first ask what events captured the attention of the Jews represented by the Babylonian Talmud. The answer is that we find few substantial references, in the form of well-constructed narratives, to world-shaking events in Iranian Babylonia, or, indeed, to contemporary events—of the third through the sixth centuries—in the Near and Middle East. Just as the Talmud of the Land of Israel bypasses the immense occasion of Constantine's conversion and the rise of Christianity to imperial power, so the Talmud of Babylonia has little to say about corresponding moments in the East. The Parthian dynasty gave way to the Sasanian one, with its devotion to Mithra and Anahita and its zeal for the faith of Mazda and his fire temples. But the Babylonian Talmud refers to such matters within its scarcely differentiated category, "paganism." The great Shapur I in the middle of the third century conquered the Roman East and came to the Land of Israel itself. The Babylonian Talmud tells no substantial stories about this earthquake in the West, making only casual reference to the matter. Emperor Julian, called by Christians "apostate," a century later promised to rebuild the Temple of Jerusalem and, in the same extraordinary year, invaded Iran and even took some Jewish villages. From the narrative powers of the sages who gave us this Talmud, these events drew slight attention. They might as well have happened in China, for the great narrative capacities revealed in the Talmud of Babylonia serve mainly to tell the story of far-away places, long-ago times, things that happened where what happens matters. They could not be in Babylonia, nor could they happen to people anyone knew. As in some of the compositions of exegesis, so in the Talmud at hand, insofar as there were events to narrate and to preserve for future study and reflection, they happened to the Temple, and, in particular, in connection with its destruction. That was the event, par excellence, that interested those storytellers who created the raw materials of Israel's history.

The dividing point in the history of Israel, therefore, was the destruction of the Temple. The two periods in Israel's history, the one in which the Temple stood and the one beginning after 70, encompassed the sequence of pagan empires to which Israel was subjugated, in the Land and, all the more so, in the Exile. These must be seen, then, as two immense grids of historical interpretation, one superimposed upon the other, but the two essentially in harmony. The first mode of reading history, the one focused upon the Temple, generated the writing of narratives, while the second, involving the sequence of empires and periods, did not. That is, we have stories about the destruction—but mostly allusions, not flesh-and-blood narratives—of the "four kingdoms" that successively ruled Israel. The narratives of the Temple, moreover, served as a principal vehicle for reflection upon the history and destiny of Israel. The later—the pagan—periods tended to provide less occasion for systematic thought. Accordingly, we turn first to the Babylonian Talmud's treatment of the decisive moment in Israel's history, the destruction of the Temple.

That historical event marks a decisive turning point in the relationship between God and Israel. Accordingly, explanation of what had happened would occupy much attention. To begin with, let us specify the issue, namely, what exactly had come to an end. It is made explicit in the following:

B. BERAKHOT 32a–b
(TRANSLATED BY MAURICE SIMON, PP. 199–200)

R. Eleazar said, "From the day on which the Temple was destroyed the gates of prayer have been closed, as it says, *Yea, when I cry and call for help he shuts out my prayer*' [Lam. 3:8]. . . ."

R. Eleazar also said, "Since the day that the Temple was destroyed, a wall of iron has intervened between Israel and their Father in Heaven. . . ."

The age beginning with the destruction of the Temple was differentiated from the former time. For example, prophecy was taken from prophets and handed over to sages (B. B.B. 12a). Or it was given to fools and children (B. B.B. 12b). As at M. Sot. 9:15, dew brings no blessing; so too the end of keeping purity laws removed taste and fragrance from fruits; the end of tithing removed fatness of grain (B. Sot. 49a).

Now these assertions ignore one striking fact: Israel continued to pray and otherwise to worship and serve God. The simple truth is that what actually ended in August of A.D. 70 was one thing only: the sacrificial cult. But in marking out the difference between one age and the other, sages referred to all manner of transcendent and trivial matters—to whatever was bothering them—without expressing much regret that cows, sheep, and goats no longer died so that parts of their innards might be burned up in a bonfire. True, restoration of the sacrificial cult constituted one plank in the platform of restoration; it hardly could have been omitted. But discourse on the catastrophe rarely centered upon how much people missed such specific things as animal sacrifices and blood rites. Emphasis lay upon the rather more general differences between the good old days and the difficult present. So the destruction of the Temple became a symbol essentially emptied of the concrete content the Temple itself had provided. While prayer for the restoration of the cult would go forward, philosophizing on the historical questions could pursue a quite abstract course of its own. Just as the "coming of the Messiah" would be used to denote any change that people wished to see, so the "destruction of the Temple" signified any alteration in Israel's condition that people could not bear. In that sense, the one formed the counterpart to the other—symbols lacking all concrete content.

The destruction of the Temple had been predicted by Israel's priests and sages. Yohanan ben Zakkai, for example, found in prophecy (Zech. 11:1) that the destruction had been foreordained (B. Yoma 39b). More interesting, a sequence of differentiated historical periods marked the final age of the Temple. Rome kept faith with Israel for a time before destroying the building.

B. ABODAH ZARAH 8b–9a
(TRANSLATED BY A. MISHCON, PP. 40–42)

The Romans sent word to the Greeks as follows: "Hitherto we have been fighting matters out, now let us argue them out, 'Of a pearl and a precious stone which shall form a setting for which?'" They sent the reply, "The pearl for the precious stone." "And of a precious stone and an onyx which shall form a setting to the other?" "The precious stone to the onyx," was the reply. "And of an onyx and the Book of the Law which shall serve as the setting for the other?" "The onyx for the Book of the Law," they replied. The Romans then sent word, "In that case,

the Book of the Law is in our possession, for Israel is with us." Thereupon the Greeks gave in.

For twenty-six years did the Romans keep faith with Israel, thereafter they subdued them. . . .

Whence can it be proved that Rome kept faith with Israel for
twenty-six years? [From the following:] For R. Kahana said, "When R.
Ishmael b. Yose was ill they sent word to him: 'Rabbi, tell us the two
or three things which you have told us in your father's name.' He then
told them, 'One hundred and eighty years before the Temple was destroyed did Rome cast her rule over Israel; eighty years before the destruction of the Temple it was decreed that neighboring countries of
Palestine were to be regarded as ritually unclean, and likewise all glass
vessels. Forty years before the Temple was destroyed the Sanhedrin
abandoned [the Temple] and held its sittings in Hanuth. . . .'"

[Now, it was mentioned above that Rome cast her rule over Israel]
180 years prior to the destruction. Is not the period longer? For R.
Yose b. Rabbi taught, "Persian rule lasted thirty-four years after the
building of the Temple, Greece ruled 180 years during the existence
of the Temple, the Hasmonean rule lasted 103 years during the Temple times, the House of Herod ruled 103 years. Thence onward, one
should go on counting the years as from the destruction of the Temple." Hence we see that it was 206 years, yet you say 180 years! But
for 26 years the Romans kept faith with Israel and did not subdue
them, and therefore those years are not reckoned in the period during
which Rome cast her dominion over Israel.

We see here a rather substantial effort to bring into relationship
with one another the various kingdoms that had ruled in the Land of
Israel, as well as the various events that marked the decline, down
to the destruction, of the Temple. The interest in chronology testifies to a powerful historical consciousness, a concern to construct a
coherent account of what had happened to Israel. But, as we see,
the destruction of the Temple marks the end of that coherent historical pattern that was sought. From that point forward, we have slight
information: no equally detailed picture of things that happened, no
corresponding interest in differentiating historical periods and their
significance. The same passage cited leads to the statement that the
world is to exist for six thousand years; two are void, two are the
"period of Torah," and the last two thousand are the period of the
Messiah—"Through our many sins, a number of these [years of the

period of the Messiah] have already passed [but the Messiah has not yet come]" (B. A.Z. 9a). Accordingly, the interest in periodization and schematization of history formed an integral part of reflection on the question of the end: when the Messiah would come, and what would happen then.

Focus upon the destruction of the Temple as the high point of Israel's history meant that historical narrative, so far as people created it, would have to deal extensively with the important event. In fact, the Babylonian Talmud presents the largest and most ambitious account of the destruction found in all of the rabbinic canon of late antiquity. Only the collection at Lamentations Rabbah, cited above, comes close in scope and narrative power. This enormous compilation of tales of the destruction, found at B. Git. 55b–58a, presents a wide variety of narratives, far more extensive than anything we have seen to date (except for Lamentations Rabbah). To gain perspective on the historical doctrine that emerged in response to the destruction of the Temple, it will suffice to cite one brief passage.

B. GITTIN 56b–57a
(TRANSLATED BY MAURICE SIMON, PP. 260–61)

Onkelos son of Kolonikos was the son of Titus's sister. He had a mind to convert himself to Judaism. He went and raised Titus from the dead by magical arts, and asked him, "Who is most in repute in the [other] world?" He replied, "Israel." "What then," he said, "about joining them?" He said, "Their observances are burdensome and you will not be able to carry them out. Go and attack them in that world and you will be at the top . . . ; whoever harasses Israel becomes head." He asked him, "What is your punishment [in the other world]?" He replied, "What I decreed for myself. Every day my ashes are collected and sentence is passed on me and I am burnt and my ashes are scattered over the seven seas." He then went and raised Balaam by incantations. He asked him, "Who is in repute in the other world?" He replied, "Israel." "What then," he said, "about joining them?" He replied, "*You shall not seek their peace nor their prosperity all your days for ever*' [Deut. 23:7]." He then asked, "What is your punishment?" He replied, "With boiling hot semen." He then went and raised by incantations the sinners of Israel. He asked them, "Who is in repute in the other world?" They replied, "Israel." "What about joining them?" They replied, "Seek their welfare, seek not their harm. Whoever touches them touches the apple of his eye." He said, "What is your punishment?" They replied, "With boiling hot excrement, since a Master has said, 'Whoever mocks at the words of the sages is punished with boiling hot excrement.' Observe the difference between the sinners of Israel and the prophets of the other nations who worship idols."

Clearly, the interest of the narrator is in making didactic points, of which there are two important ones. First is the climax, the contrast between Israelite sinners and pagan prophets, and second is the repeated message that it is hard, but rewarding, to be a Jew, and that outsiders refrain from joining Israel because of the burden of Israelite religion. There in fact is no real historical interest at all; the entire story, though using names of historical figures—Titus's sister and Balaam—is constructed to make polemical and apologetic points. So the uses of narrative for teaching lessons of an essentially historical order can scarcely be said to characterize a passage of this sort.

The notion of historical causation, of course, invokes issues of personalities and accidents. We cannot expect sophisticated conceptions of why the Romans attacked Jerusalem. Given the didactic interest of the document at hand, indeed, we may hardly be surprised that a principal purpose of discussing causation was to make homiletical and polemical points. Jerusalem was destroyed, we find, because of the following:

B. GITTIN 55b–56a
(TRANSLATED BY MAURICE SIMON, P. 254)

The destruction of Jerusalem came through a Kamza and a Bar Kamza in this way. A certain man had a friend Kamza and an enemy Bar Kamza. He once made a party and said to his servant, "Go and bring Kamza." The man went and brought Bar Kamza. When the man [who gave the party] found him there he said, "See, you tell tales about me; what are you doing here? Get out." Said the other: "Since I am here, let me stay, and I will pay you for whatever I eat and drink." He said, "I won't." "Then let me give you half the cost of the party." "No," said the other. "Then let me pay for the whole party." He still said, "No," and he took him by the hand and put him out. Said the other, "Since the rabbis were sitting there and did not stop him, this shows that they agreed with him. I will go and inform against them to the government." He went and said to the Emperor, "The Jews are rebelling against you." He said, "How can I tell?" He said to him, "Send them an offering and see whether they will offer it [on the altar]." So he sent with him a fine calf. While on the way he made a blemish on its upper lip, or as some say on the white of its eye, in a place where we [Jews] count it a blemish but they do not. The rabbis were inclined to offer it in order not to offend the government. Said R. Zechariah b. Abkulas to them, "People will say that blemished animals are offered on the altar." They then proposed to kill Bar Kamza so that he should not go and inform against them, but R. Zechariah b. Abkulas said to them, "Is one who makes a blemish on consecrated animals to be put to death?" R. Yohanan thereupon remarked: "Through the scrupulousness of R. Zechariah b. Abkulas our House has been destroyed, our Temple burnt and we ourselves exiled from our land."

Whatever the polemical purpose of the story, the striking point for us is the way in which the historical event is explained. While from a later perspective it is easy to conclude that the account is trivial, in fact the story answers important questions for the sages who told and preserved it. First, Israelites make the worst trouble for their own group. That claim then reinforces the conception everywhere that Israel governs its own destiny. What Jews do, or fail to do, determines what happens to them. That of course is far from the fact. But it is the most important assertion of a historical character to be found in the sources from beginning to end. Second, the story leaves the impression that the Romans had no long-standing complaint against the Jews. Here too, therefore, Jews caused their own destruction. Third, rabbis were warned not to apply the law too literally when the welfare of the community was at stake. While it is easy to see other dimensions of meaning in the tale, it suffices to notice, once more, the revision of historical events that actually took place into paradigmatic and instructive occasions. The sole fact, of course, was the destruction of A.D. 70 and the radical change in Israel's condition thereafter. In no significant sense do we find an interest in historical narrative. Instead we observe the capacity to make use of tales, some of which allude to events we might regard as historical, for didactic and other homiletical purposes.

One therefore need take only a very short step from fictive tales of an apologetic character to reflection on the causes or meaning of what has happened. For, as I have proposed, the entire historical enterprise, beginning to end, served theological purposes, just as we should expect of the document as a whole. At issue in the Talmud of Babylonia, as in other compositions in the canon of the rabbis, is how to design the life of Israel. What should Jews do? What should they be? How should they cope with their present condition and circumstance? Everything said about the past constituted a statement and judgment upon these issues. But why should that not have been the case, since, as is clear, the entire structure of law, the prescriptions for the communal and individual conduct of everyday life, served precisely the same ultimate purpose. When, therefore, we come to the contrast between the period of the first and second Temples and the reasons for the destruction of each, we find ourselves on entirely familiar ground.

How then did people theorize about historical causation? They turned to events that had been adequately explained, and compared them with events requiring explanation—a reasonable inquiry. This allowed for the elimination of clearly irrelevant matters and the specification of what remained—a quite critical mode of thought. In the present case, therefore, the well-documented conditions for the destruction of the first Temple were examined and were found to have been absent on the occasion of the destruction of the second. As in the Bar Kamza tale, needless dissension was at fault:

B. YOMA 9a–b
(TRANSLATED BY A. MISHCON, PP. 37–40)

R. Yohanan b. Torta said, "Why was Shiloh destroyed? Because of two [evil] things that prevailed there, immorality and contemptuous treatment of sanctified objects. . . . "Why was the first Sanctuary destroyed? Because of three [evil] things which prevailed there: idolatry, immorality, bloodshed. . . ."

. . . Therefore the Holy One, blessed be he, brought them three evil decrees as against the three evils which were their own: *"Therefore shall Zion for your sake be plowed as a field, and Jerusalem shall become heaps and the mountain of the house as the high places of a forest"* [Mic. 3:12].

But why was the second Sanctuary destroyed seeing that in its time they were occupying themselves with Torah, [observance of] precepts, and the practice of charity? Because therein prevailed hatred without cause. That teaches you that groundless hatred is considered as of even gravity with the three sins of idolatry, immorality, and bloodshed together. . . .

199

R. Yohanan said, "The fingernail of the earlier generations is better than the whole body of the later generations." Said Resh Laqish to him, "On the contrary, the latter generations are better, for, although they are oppressed by the governments, they are occupying themselves with the Torah." He [R. Yohanan] replied, "The Sanctuary will prove [my point] for it was restored to the former generations, but not to the latter ones."

The effort to find an inductive explanation for the destruction of the Temple competed with yet another. Social critics among the rabbinical movement simply specified various vices as the reason for the destruction of the Temple. In so doing, obviously, they tried to persuade people to avoid these same vices. Accordingly, we deal with moralistic, and not historical, thinking. Here is a repertoire of such explanations.

B. SHABBAT 119b
(TRANSLATED BY H. FREEDMAN, PP. 589–90)

Abaye said, "Jerusalem was destroyed only because the Sabbath was desecrated therein. . . ."

R. Abbahu said, "Jerusalem was destroyed only because the reading of the *Shema* morning and evening was neglected [therein]. . . ."

R. Hamnuna said, "Jerusalem was destroyed only because they neglected [the education of] school children. . . ."

Ulla said, "Jerusalem was destroyed only because they [its inhabitants] were not ashamed before each other. . . ."

R. Isaac said, "Jerusalem was destroyed only because the small and the great were made equal. . . ."

R. Amram son of R. Simeon b. Abba said in R. Simeon b. Abba's name in R. Hanina's name, "Jerusalem was destroyed only because they did not rebuke each other: for it is said, *'Her princes are become like harts that find no pasture'* [Lam. 1:6]. Just as the hart, the head of one is at the side of the others' tail, so Israel of that generation hid their faces in the earth, and did not rebuke each other."

Rab Judah said, "Jerusalem was destroyed only because scholars were despised therein. . . ."

Raba said, "Jerusalem was destroyed only because men of faith ceased therein. . . ."

Other explanations appealed to Israelite sins of different sorts, e.g., improper leadership. For example, a generation overwhelmed by troubles will find itself subject to the rule of improper Israelite judges (B. Shab. 139a). Again, as we recall, "When the haughty cease to exist in Israel, magi will disappear from among the Iranians; when judges cease in Israel, chiliarchs [rulers of thousands] will cease among the Iranians" (ibid.).

Like the statement, "[If Israel will . . .] the Messiah will come," so too "Jerusalem was destroyed only because . . ." therefore serves as a conventional component of a routine sentence. Here we have the moralistic protasis for whatever apodosis the theologian required. No interest in historical records of actual events characterizes discourse of this second sort. On the contrary, all prophetic passages were made to refer equally to the same event. All applied as much to the one destruction as to the other. For, in the present context of mourning for the calamity of the final destruction, who distinguished which Jerusalem was under discussion? The same redactional context, moreover, contains statements about the importance of disciples of sages and of learning, to which the recurrent symbol of the destruction of Jerusalem is not attached—for instance, "The world endures only for the sake of the breath of school children. . . . Every town in which there are no school children shall be destroyed." Accordingly, the destruction of Jerusalem served here merely as an excuse, a way of emphasizing the importance of what the apologists wished to advance, normally social virtues and learning. Here, too, the specific is treated in a general way, emptied of all concrete meaning. We have seen a similar treatment of the hope for the coming of the Messiah. "The Messiah will not come because . . ." or "until . . ." may then be followed by pretty much anything the speaker favors or opposes, as the case may be. And over and over again, these specific, concrete, and fundamentally historical symbols—destruction of a city or restoration of the fortunes of the nation in historical time or through political means—served moral and theological, hence ahistorical, purposes. Events and fantasies attached to them were thus absorbed into a quite separate ontological structure, involving timeless virtues and eternal sacralities. The ideas are historical-eschatological, but the mode of thought is philosophical and taxonomic—hence mishnaic. Accordingly, the single most important comment on the destruction, made in this document, is that God himself mourns for the destruction of the Temple and the present condition of Israel:

B. BERAKHOT 3a
(TRANSLATED BY MAURICE SIMON, P. 6)

R. Isaac b. Samuel says in the name of Rab, "The night has three watches, and at each watch the Holy One, blessed be he, sits and roars like a lion and says, 'Woe to the children, on account of whose sins I destroyed my house and burnt my temple and exiled them among the nations of the world.'"

Along these same lines, God weeps "for the glory that has been taken from Israel and given to the nations of the world" (B. Hag. 5b).

We now come to that second, and separate, grid of historical interpretation, the one constructed out of the sequence of four animals (lion, bear, leopard, and the horned beast) in the vision of Daniel (Dan. 7:3–8) on the one side, and of four pagan empires, on the other. Here, once again, when we study this Talmud, we enjoy the result of systematic redactional work, particularly at B. A.Z. 2a–b, below. The theme of the four animals/empires is vastly expanded and carefully spelled out in a single, lengthy statement. The Iranians were identified with the bear of Daniel's vision.

B. QIDDUSHIN 72a
(TRANSLATED BY H. FREEDMAN, P. 368)

"And three ribs were in his mouth between his teeth" [Dan. 7:5]. Said R. Yohanan, "This refers to Hulwan, Adiabene and Nesibin, which it [Persia] sometimes swallowed and sometimes spat out."

"And behold another beast, a second, like to a bear" [Dan. 7:5]. R. Joseph recited, "This refers to the Persians, who eat and drink like a bear, are fleshy like a bear, overgrown with hair like a bear, and have no rest like a bear." When R. Ammi saw a Persian riding he would say, "There is a wandering bear!"

Once a theory to encompass not only Rome but also Iran had come into formation, it became necessary to relate Rome to Iran. The Talmud of Babylonia presents the view that Iran would ultimately conquer Rome:

B. YOMA 10a
(TRANSLATED BY LEO JUNG, PP. 43–44)

R. Joshua b. Levi in the name of Rabbi said, "Rome is designed to fall into the hand of Persia, as it was said, *'Therefore hear ye the counsel of the Lord, that he has taken against Edom; and his purposes that he has purposed against the inhabitants of Teman: surely the least of the flock shall drag them away, surely their habitation shall be appalled to them'* [Jer. 49:20]."

Rabbah b. Bar Hana in the name of R. Yohanan, on the authority of R. Judah b. Illai, said, "Rome is designed to fall into the hands of Persia, that may be concluded by inference *a minori ad majus:* If in the case of the first Sanctuary, which the sons of Shem [Solomon] built and the Chaldeans destroyed, the Chaldeans fell into the hands of the Persians, then how much more should this be so with the second Sanctuary, which the Persians built and the Romans destroyed, that the Romans should fall into the hands of the Persians."

Rab said, "Persia will fall into the hands of Rome." Thereupon R. Kahana and R. Assi asked of Rab: "[Shall] the builders fall into the hands of the destroyers?" He said to them, "Yes, it is the decree of the King." Others say he replied to them, "They too are guilty for they destroyed the synagogues."

It has also been taught in accord with the above, Persia will fall into the hands of Rome, first because they destroyed the synagogues, and then because it is the King's decree that the builders fall into the hands of the destroyers.

Rab also said: "The son of David will not come until the wicked kingdom of Rome will have spread [its sway] over the whole world for nine months, as it is said, *'Therefore will he give them up, until the time that she who travails has brought forth; then the residue of his brethren shall return with the children of Israel'* [Mic. 5:2]."

The mélange of opinions proves distinctive to the Babylonian rabbis, who had to include Iran in the larger history of the world and work out a theory of the relationship of Rome to Iran, and of both to Israel. Of special interest is the fact that the relationship between Rome and Iran, the power of the one to subdue the other, depended upon the relationship of both of them to Israel. What each had done to Israel governed the destiny of the two empires. The concluding statement in the construction, Rab's, then makes the most important point: the two empires would come to an end with the coming of the son of David. So, in all, the rabbinic system took within itself the history of the great empires of the day.

The theory of the four empires—Rome and, for Babylonian Jews, Iran, being the principals—was thus taken a further step. Israel is at the center and heart of human history. Whatever the nations do is judged by God for its meaning for Israel's life. God will determine the fate of each nation in accord with that criterion. The following presents a completely articulated statement of that view:

B. ABODAH ZARAH 2a–b
(TRANSLATED BY A. MISHCON, PP. 2–4, PASS.)

R. Hanina b. Papa—some say R. Simlai—expounded thus, "In time to come, the Holy One, blessed be he, will take a scroll of the Law in his embrace and proclaim: 'Let him who has occupied himself herewith, come and take his reward.' Thereupon all the nations will crowd together in confusion. . . . The Holy One, blessed be he, will then say to them: 'Come not before me in confusion, but let each nation come in with its scribes.' . . . Thereupon the Kingdom of Edom [Rome] will enter first before him. . . . The Holy One, blessed be he, will then say to them, 'Wherewith have you occupied yourselves?' They will reply, 'O Lord of the Universe, we have established many marketplaces, we have erected many baths, we have accumulated much gold and silver, and all this we did only for the sake of Israel, that they might [have leisure] for occupying themselves with the study of the Torah.' The Holy One, blessed be he, will say in reply, 'You foolish ones among peoples, all that which you have done, you have only done to satisfy your own desires. You have established marketplaces to place courtesans therein; baths, to revel in them; [as to the distribution of] silver and gold, that is mine. . . .' They will then depart crushed in spirit. On the departure of the Kingdom of Rome, Persia will step forth. (Why Persia next? Because they are next in importance. And how do we know this? Because it is written, 'And behold another beast, a second like to a bear' [Dan. 7:5], and R. Joseph learned that this refers to the Persians, who eat and drink greedily like the bear, are fleshly like the bear, have shaggy hair like the bear, and are restless like the bear.) The Holy One, blessed be he, will ask of them, "Wherewith have you occupied yourselves?' And they will reply, 'Sovereign of the Universe, we have built many bridges, we have captured many cities, we have waged many wars, and all this for the sake of Israel, that they might engage in the study of the Torah.' Then the Holy One, blessed be he, will say to them, 'You foolish ones among peoples, you have built bridges in order to extract toll, you have subdued cities, so as to impose forced labor. . . .' They, too, will then depart crushed in spirit. (But why should the Persians, having seen that the Romans achieved nought, step forward at all? They will say to themselves: 'The Romans have destroyed the Temple, whereas we have built it.') And so will every nation fare in turn. (But why should the other nations come forth, seeing that those who preceded them had achieved nought? They will say to themselves: The others have oppressed Israel, but we have not. And why are these [two] nations singled out as important, and not the others? Because their reign will last till the coming of the Messiah.)"

Alongside the doctrine of the four kingdoms comes the affirmation that, through them all, God remains loyal to his covenant with Israel:

B. MEGILLAH 11a
(TRANSLATED BY MAURICE SIMON, PP. 61–62)

Samuel quoted, "'I did not reject them, neither did I abhor them to destroy them utterly' [Lev. 26:44]. 'I did not reject them' in the days of the Greeks; 'neither did I abhor them' in the days of Nebuchadnezzar; 'to destroy them utterly'—in days of Haman; 'and to break my covenant with them'—in the days of the Persians; 'for I am the Lord their God'—in the days of Gog and Magog."

In a Baraitha it was taught: "I have not rejected them" in the days of the Chaldeans, when I raised up for them Daniel, Hananiah, Mishael and Azariah: "neither did I abhor them" in the days of the Greeks, when I raised up for them Simeon the Righteous and Hasmonai and his sons, and Mattathias the High Priest; "to destroy them utterly"—in the days of Haman, when I raised up for them Mordecai and Esther; "to break my covenant with them"—in the days of the Persians, when I raised up for them the members of the house of Rabbi and the Sages of the various generations. "For I am the Lord their God" in the time to come, when no nation or people will be able to subject them.

The periodization of Israel's history, in line with biblical apocalypse, thus reaches its climax with the end of the two empires and the coming of the Messiah. No "history" in the ordinary sense would follow the demise of Rome and Iran as they then were known. Both nations would come to an end, moreover, because of their failure to study and carry out the Torah, on the one side, and of their disgraceful treatment of Israel, on the other. Here too, the operative power in history remains the same: Israel's condition, measured by the criterion of God's revelation. History then is yet another expression and testimony to the Torah. Since Israel bears responsibility for studying and carrying out the Torah, once more it is claimed that Israel governs its own history and shapes its own destiny through its own deeds. To this essentially supernatural interpretation of events, actualities of power and realities of civil and political conduct bear no relationship whatsoever.

Representing the nations as pleading before God on the basis of the good that they have done for Israel (in particular for rabbinic Israel) articulates the main point. The Talmud's philosophy of world history flows from the conviction that, first, Israel sits at the center of history, and, second, the rabbis' particular point of distinction and emphasis, the study of Torah, governs what happens in Israel. Whatever apocalyptic doctrine has led to the identification of the bear with Iran and to the notion of Rome at the center and end of time plays only a slight role here. Rather, the facts of apocalypse serve the dynamic doctrine of the scribal emphasis on learning. History in the end is made by people who study Torah. But in reality the one thing you do not do when you study Torah is make history. For learning, in the rabbinical framework, provided an essentially passive experience, which involved simply memorizing what had been said earlier and carefully handing on to disciples what had been memorized. The process of learning therefore worked against change, denied consequence to one-time events (the concrete insight of a named individual), and, in all, presented a deeply ahistorical and antihistorical experience. So, once more, we observe that, when the Talmud on the surface explores historical issues, at the foundation the modes of thought remain those of the Mishnah, and the ultimate result, therefore, proves deeply mishnaic. In a word, the Mishnah's insistence upon a life of Israel lived above and beyond time, on eternal waves of nature and supernature, absorbed the established messianic symbolism, with its interest in eschatology framed around the Messiah. The Mishnah's mode reshaped that symbolic system of the eschatological teleology within the pattern of the Mishnah's own mode of existence. If, therefore, we say that the Mishnah's system has been messianized, we have also to recognize that the Messiah myth for its part is radically revised too.

In line with earlier documents in the rabbinical canon, the Talmud of Babylonia took up the problem of the history of the pagan kingdoms in relationship to that of Israel. Once more it was asserted that Israel controlled the history of the world. When Israel sinned, its enemies prospered. So Rome's ascendancy was explicitly alleged to correspond to Israel's decline. To begin with, Rome came into being precisely when state idolatry began in Israel:

B. SHABBAT 56b
(TRANSLATED BY H. FREEDMAN, P. 264)

Rab Judah said in Samuel's name, "When Solomon married Pharaoh's daughter, Gabriel descended and planted a reed in the sea, and it gathered a bank around it, on which the great city of Rome was built."

In a Baraitha it was taught: On the day that Jeroboam brought the two golden calves, one into Bethel and the other into Dan, a hut was built, and this developed into Greek Italy.

That is why when Rome prospers, Israel must be suffering, and vice versa. Accordingly, we find the following:

B. MEGILLAH 6a
(TRANSLATED BY MAURICE SIMON, P. 29)

Caesarea and Jerusalem [are rivals]. If one says to you that both are destroyed, do not believe him; if he says that both are flourishing, do not believe him; if he says that Caesarea is waste and Jerusalem is flourishing, or that Jerusalem is waste and Caesarea is flourishing, you may believe him, as it says, "I shall be filled, she is laid waste" [Ezek. 26:2]; if this one is filled, that one is laid waste, and if that one is filled, this one is laid waste.

The primacy of Rome in the sequence of pagan kingdoms was taken for granted even in the Talmud of Babylonia. The wealth of the world moved from empire to empire in sequence, ending, for the moment, in Rome. In the account that follows, we see how a linear and sequential view could accommodate a whole list of kingdoms, without in any way changing the fundamental judgment that the world now lay in the hands of Rome. The insistence, then, that in the time to come Israel would become the final kingdom under the Messiah's rule, could generate a pattern capable of finding room for any number of stages or periods of history.

B. PESAHIM 119a
(TRANSLATED BY H. FREEDMAN, P. 614)

Rab Judah said in Samuel's name, "All the gold and silver in the world Joseph gathered in and brought to Egypt, for it is said, 'And Joseph gathered up all the money that was found [in the land of Egypt, and in the land of Canaan]' [Gen. 47:14]. Now I know it only about that of Egypt and Canaan; whence do we know it about that of other countries? Because it is stated, 'And all the countries came unto Egypt [to Joseph to buy corn]' [Gen. 41:57]. And when the Israelites migrated from Egypt they carried it away with them, for it is said, 'and they despoiled the Egyptians' [Exod. 12:36]. . . . Thus it [the treasure] lay until Rehoboam, when Shishak king of Egypt came and seized it from Rehoboam, for it is said, 'And it came to pass in the fifth year of king Rehoboam, that Shishak king of Egypt came up against Jerusalem; and he took away the treasures of the house of the Lord, and the treasures of the king's house' [1 Kings 14:25–26]. Then Zerah, king of Ethiopia, came and seized it from Shishak; then Assa came and seized it from Zerah king of Ethiopia and sent it to Hadrimon the son of Tabrimon. The Ammonites came and seized it from Hadrimon the son of Tabrimon. Jehoshaphat came and seized it from the Ammonites, and it remained so until Ahaz, when Sennacherib came and took it from Ahaz. Then Hezekiah came and took it from Sennacherib, and it remained thus until Zedekiah, when the Babylonians [Chaldeans] came and seized it from Zedekiah. The Persians came and took it from the Chaldeans; the Greeks came and took it from the Persians; the Romans came and took it from the Greeks, and it is still lying in Rome."

When the document at hand came to closure, Rome, understood in the East to mean Byzantium, ruled the whole West, and even threatened the existence of the Iranian empire. The assertion that the prosperity of Rome was weighed in the balance against the prosperity of Israel bore no relationship whatever to the facts of the age. The theory of Israelite history, spun out in every possible setting, accounted for the views expressed here as well. That theory in the end absorbed history into the framework of theology, in no way permitting actual events to govern the formation of the theory to explain what had happened.

The final problem in the theory of Israel's history and destiny addressed the matter of the exile, that is, the experience of Israel in Babylonia. No one doubted that the condition of exile resulted from Israel's sin. But we find a second, and quite fresh, conception, that

Israel in exile had a task of cosmic importance, to bring proselytes to God's service.

B. PESAHIM 87b
(TRANSLATED BY H. FREEDMAN, P. 463)

R. Eleazar also said, "The Holy One, blessed be he, did not exile Israel among the nations save in order that proselytes might join them, for it is said, '*And I will sow her unto me in the land*' [Hos. 2:25]; surely a man sows a *seah* in order to harvest many *kor!*" While R. Yohanan deduced it from this: "*And I will have compassion upon her that has not obtained compassion*' [Hos. 2:25].

Assigning a positive value to the exile formed part of the larger historical apologetic constructed by the Babylonian Talmud. Even in Babylonia Israel had its appropriate task. Historical meaning therefore informed the suffering of exile.

At the same time, Israelites in the exile knew full well that they bore the hatred of Gentiles. That permanent fact of their condition required explanation, and, within the rabbinic system, the character of the explanation is readily predictable. It would have something to do with a life subject to Torah which constituted the principal concern of the system as a whole. In fact, it is the Torah which causes idolaters to hate Israelites.

B. SHABBAT 89a
(TRANSLATED BY H. FREEDMAN, PP. 424–25)

R. Hisda and Rabbah the son of R. Huna both said, "What is [the meaning of] Mount Sinai? The mountain whereon there descended hostility [*sinah*] toward idolaters."

We may hardly be surprised, in light of these views, to find the key to the Jews' security in their adherence to the Torah. Whether in the land or in exile, the Jews should find protection in their religious duties: "The congregation of Israel is compared to a dove. . . . Just as a dove is protected by its wings, so Israel is protected by religious duties" (B. Shab. 49b). Again, Israel will prevail when it accepts the Torah:

B. ABODAH ZARAH 5a
(TRANSLATED BY A. MISHCON, PP. 20–21)

The effect of Israel's acceptance of the Torah would be that no nation or tongue could prevail against them, as it is said, *"That it might be well with them and their children after them"* [Deut. 5:26].

The principal result of Israel's loyal adherence to the Torah and its religious duties will be Israel's humble acceptance of God's rule. That humility, under all conditions, makes God love Israel.

B. HULLIN 89a
(TRANSLATED BY ELI CASHDAN, P. 497)

"It was not because you were greater than any people that the Lord set his love upon you and chose you" [Deut. 7:7]. The Holy One, blessed be he, said to Israel, "I love you because even when I bestow greatness upon you, you humble yourselves before me. I bestowed greatness upon Abraham, yet he said to me, *'I am but dust and ashes'* [Gen. 18:27]; upon Moses and Aaron, yet they said, *'And we are nothing'* [Exod. 16:8]; upon David, yet he said, *'But I am a worm and no man'* [Ps. 22:7]. But with the heathens it is not so. I bestowed greatness upon Nimrod, and he said, *'Come, let us build us a city'* [Gen. 11:4]; upon Pharaoh, and he said, *'Who is the Lord?'* [Exod. 5:2]; upon Sennacherib, and he said, *'Who are they among all the gods of the countries?'* [2 Kings 18:35]; upon Nebuchadnezzar, and he said, *'I will ascend above the heights of the clouds'* [Isa. 14:14]; upon Hiram, king of Tyre, and he said, *'I sit in the seat of God, in the heart of the seas'* [Ezek. 28:2]."

So the system emerges complete, each of its parts stating precisely the same message as is revealed in the whole. The issue of the Messiah and the meaning of Israel's history framed through the Messiah myth convey in their terms precisely the same position that we find everywhere else in all other symbolic components of the rabbinic system and canon. The heart of the matter then is Israel's subservience to God's will, as expressed in the Torah and embodied in the teachings and lives of the great sages. When Israel fully accepts God's rule, then the Messiah will come. Until Israel subjects itself to God's rule, the Jews will be subjugated to pagan domination. Since the condition of Israel governs, Israel itself holds the key to its own redemption. But this it can achieve only by throwing away the key!

The paradox must be crystal clear: Israel acts to redeem itself through the opposite of self-determination, namely, by subjugating itself to God. Israel's power lies in its negation of power. Its destiny lies in giving up all pretense at deciding its own destiny. So weakness is the ultimate strength, forbearance the final act of self-assertion, passive resignation the sure step toward liberation. (The parallel is the crucified Christ.) Israel's freedom is engraved on the tablets of the commandments of God: to be free is freely to obey. That is not the meaning associated with these words in the minds of others who, like the sages of the rabbinical canon, declared their view of what Israel must do to secure the coming of the Messiah.

In reviewing the Babylonian Talmud's repertoire of ideas about the Messiah and about Israel's history and destiny, we may easily miss the single most obvious trait of the entire set of materials. It is this: We have not found one source focused upon the individual Israelite, nor does anyone link the coming of the Messiah to the eschatological forgiveness of sins. The Messiah myth speaks about Israel, the nation, not about the individual Jew. The theory of Israel, the nation, focuses upon the spiritual condition of the people as a whole. True, the rabbinical system takes full account of the moral condition of the individual. It provides ample means for recognizing and confessing sin, on the one side, and securing penitence and forgiveness, on the other. But the system does not make use of the Messiah myth in this connection. Nor does the sinful condition of Israel as a whole form the principal focus and message. On the contrary, the Messiah myth turns out to center upon one particular consideration, a single sort of public sin, arrogance, and its remedy, humility.

The concluding passage, praising Israel for its humility, completes the circle begun with the description of Bar Kokhba as arrogant and boastful. Gentile kings are boastful; Israelite kings are humble. So, in all, the Messiah myth deals with a very concrete and limited consideration of the national life and character. The theory of Israel's history and destiny as it was expressed within that myth interprets matters in terms of a single criterion. What others within the Israelite world had done or in the future would do with the conviction that, at the end of time, God would send a (or the) Messiah to "save" Israel, it was a single idea for the sages of the Mishnah and the Talmuds and collections of scriptural exegesis. And that conception stands at the center of their system; it shapes and is shaped by their system. In context, the Messiah expresses the system's meaning and so makes it work.

THE CANONICAL CONTEXT

This protracted survey reveals two significant facts. First, conceptions of the Messiah and doctrines of Israel's history and destiny take shape through a substantial range of specific symbols and myths. They certainly are not scattered at random across the entire corpus of canonical rabbinic writings. They fall into clear-cut groups. Documents that contain one distinct set of facts stand apart from those that contain another.

Second, many, though not all, of the symbols and myths a document does utilize turn out to play a significant part in expressing the fundamental viewpoint of the document in which they occur. The principle of selection is not random. On the contrary, we discern clear configurations of meaning that emerge from a given set of messianic symbols and myths revealed in a given document.

This is assuredly the case with the Mishnah. What its philosophers say about the Messiah turns out to be fully congruent with what they say about a great many other subjects. In a curiously convoluted way, the same is true also for the Talmud of Babylonia. But the purpose is different. We can scarcely point to a significant idea from some other, probably earlier, document that we do not find in the Babylonian Talmud. If the compilers of that immense work had left an editors' manifesto, stating their intention to provide a compendium of opinions, a *summa* of Judaism, we should not be surprised. For that is precisely what they have given us.

Yet, even here, among the masses of data they assemble, some facts play a substantial part, while others do not. The former serve larger doctrinal purposes, contribute to a more considerable argument, and make commonly invoked propositions in their own particular terms. Other facts are preserved but hardly touched. They appear normally (though not invariably) in the names of isolated individuals, not as the consensus of sages. The ideas expressed scarcely undergo development. No effort goes into relating those ideas to any others, even for the purpose of harmonization.

So, in all, the Mishnah stands at one side, the Talmud of Babylonia at the other, both in date of formation and closure—ca. A.D.

200 and 600, respectively—and in character. The one expresses a single system. The other contains and encompasses a well-composed worldview, while it does not make an effort to present only one set of ideas.

The intermediate documents tend to group themselves around one or the other of the poles, as the following summary tables indicate. The Tosefta, Sifra, and the other so-called tannaitic midrashim (compositions of scriptural exegesis serving the Pentateuch and containing the names only of authorities who also appear in the Mishnah) and the Rabbah compilations may be grouped around the Mishnah's pole. The Talmud of the Land of Israel and Pesiqta deR. Kahana tend to take a position around the Babylonian Talmud's pole (to speak anachronistically).

The two charts that follow list the principal facts—viewpoints, convictions, and allusions to mythic conceptions—which have been surveyed up to now. The rough provenience of these facts, the documents in which they occur, is indicated (covering only materials cited in this book). The important result is, as I just said, to show us that the Mishnah and its associated documents of amplification and exegesis present a small number of selected facts. The other half of the canon, the Talmud's half, presents nearly all of the facts at hand. What this result, as illustrated in the tables, means may be stated both negatively and positively.

First, it does not mean that the authors of the Mishnah portion of the canon did not know, or did not accept the validity of, the facts they did not use. Second, it certainly does not mean that the messianic eschatology entered the rabbinic system and served as its teleology only when the amplification of the Mishnah had run its course late in the formation of Judaism. Third, it further does not mean that opinion among the rabbis who were responsible for these documents (let alone among Jews not within the rabbinical framework) shifted radically from the second century to the fourth or fifth. We cannot demonstrate any of these three (attractive) propositions.

What, then, do we know? On the positive side, we may reach the following simple conclusions. First, when constructing a systematic account of Judaism—that is, the worldview and way of life for Israel presented in the Mishnah—the philosophers of the Mishnah did not make use of the Messiah myth in the construction of a teleology for their system. They found it possible to present a statement of goals for their projected life of Israel which was entirely separate from appeals to history and eschatology. Since they certainly knew, and even alluded to, long-standing and widely held convictions on eschatological subjects, beginning with those in Scripture, the framers thereby testified that, knowing the larger repertoire, they made choices different from others before and after them. Their document accurately and ubiquitously expresses these choices, both affirmative and negative.

Second, the appearance of a messianic eschatology fully consonant with the larger characteristic of the rabbinic system—with its stress on the viewpoints and prooftexts of Scripture, its interest in what was happening to Israel, its focus upon the national-historical dimension of the life of the group—indicates that the encompassing rabbinic system stands essentially autonomous of the prior, mishnaic system. True, what had gone before was absorbed and fully assimilated. But the rabbinic system, expressed in part in each of the non-mishnaic segments of the canon, and fully spelled out in all of them, is different in the aggregate from the mishnaic system. It represents more, however, than a negative response to its predecessor. As I shall argue, the rabbinic system took over the fundamental convictions of the Mishnaic worldview about the importance of Israel's constructing for itself a life beyond time. The rabbinic system then transformed the Messiah myth in its totality into an essentially ahistorical force. If people wanted to reach the end of time, they had to rise above time, that is, history, and stand off at the side of great movements of political and military character. That is the message of the Messiah myth as it reaches full exposure in the rabbinic system of the two Talmuds. At its foundation it is *precisely* the message of teleology without eschatology expressed by the Mishnah and its associated documents. Accordingly, we cannot claim that the rabbinic system in this regard constitutes a reaction against the mishnaic one. We must conclude, quite to the contrary, that in the Talmuds and their associated documents we see the restatement in classical-mythic form of the ontological convictions that had informed the minds of the second-century philosophers. The new medium contained the old and enduring message: Israel must turn away from time and change, submit to whatever happens, so as to win for itself the only government worth having, that is, God's rule, accomplished through God's anointed agent, the Messiah.

To state matters in unrefined terms, salvation depended upon sanctification, which therefore took precedence as the governing principle of the worldview and way of life commanded by the rabbis' Torah. It follows, of course, that the rabbis who stand behind the principles of messianic eschatology, worked out in the Talmuds, in fact continued on an absolutely straight line the fundamental convictions of the Mishnah. That document they claimed to continue and complete. Superficially, that claim is without justification. But at a deeper level it is quite proper.

We now turn to the summary tables, which, as I indicated, show us the provenance of diverse assertions concerning the Messiah on the one side (see pp. 216–218) and concerning Israel's history and destiny on the other (see pp. 218–219) that add up to the canonical corpus on Judaism's teleology. I list the topics in order of their appearance in the pages of this book. Then I indicate where they occur in the documents according to the sequence in which we have reviewed them. The important point, however, is not documentary sequence. We must not confuse an evident precedence of one compilation over another with the historical pattern in which a given fact appeared before some other. That claim has not been made in this book; it is indemonstrable and, further, it is quite beside the point I wish to make.

Tracing the principal expressions of the Messiah myth across the canon of rabbinical writings tells us more about the canon than about the history of the Messiah myth. We see which documents tend to group themselves around a given set of ideas, and which stand essentially distinct from others. As I suggested above, the Mishnah and its close associates, Abot, the Tosefta, and Abot deR. Nathan, fall together on the one end of the spectrum, while the Talmud of the Land of Israel and the Talmud of Babylonia fall on the other. Closer to the former pole are the exegetical compilations serving the Pentateuch, specifically, Mekhilta, Sifra, Sifré Numbers, and Sifré Deuteronomy (and some Targums). The Rabbah collections of the pre-Islamic period (Genesis Rabbah, Leviticus Rabbah, Lamentations, Song of Solomon, Ruth, and Esther Rabbah I) fit somewhere closer to the pentateuchal-exegetical compilations than they do to either of the two Talmuds; Pesiqta deR. Kahana adjoins the Talmud of Babylonia. The synagogue-based writings, both Siddur and Targum, form a group by themselves, and treat the Messiah

The Messiah	Mishnah	Tosefta, Abot, and Abot deR. Nathan	Talmud of the Land of Israel	Mekhilta, Sifra Sifré Num., Sifré Dt.	Gen. Rabbah and Lev. Rabbah	Lam. R., Esther R., Song R., Ruth R.	Pesiqta de R. Kahana	Talmud of Babylonia	Siddur	Targum Onqelos to the Pentateuch	Targum Pseudo-Jonathan to Pent.	Fragmentary Targum to the Pentateuch
1. Messiah: anointed priest	*	*	*	*	*							
2. Messiah: son of David (Ruth, Boaz)	*				*	*	*	*	*	*	*	*
3. This age vs. age of the Messiah	*	*		*	*			*				
4. Tribulations before Messiah	*			*		*	*	*				
5. Sages suffer before the end	*					*		*				
6. David's dominion is eternal			*					*	*			
7. David's son restores horn of Israel			*					*	*			
8. Messiah's coming and resurrection of dead			*					*	*			
9. David as a rabbi			*					*				
10. Messiah's name: Menahem			*									
11. Messiah from Bethlehem			*									
12. Messiah born when Temple destroyed			*									
13. Aqiba said Bar Kokhba was a messiah			*									
14. When Israel repents, they will be saved (no messianic reference).			*					*				
15. Israel must be humble to bring Messiah. Bar Kokhba was arrogant and no messiah, so he lost			*					*				
16. Israel punished for neglect of Torah			*									
17. If Israel would do . . . , the Messiah would come			*	*				*				
18. Because Israel does . . . , the Messiah has not come								*				
19. Messiah: David-Hillel					*							
20. Messiah will gather exiles					*			*	*			
21. Israel will not require the Messiah as teacher					*							

The Messiah	Mishnah	Tosefta, Abot, and Abot deR. Nathan	Talmud of the Land of Israel	Mekhilta, Sifra Sifré Num., Sifré Dt.	Gen. Rabbah and Lev. Rabbah	Lam. R., Esther R., Song R., Ruth R.	Pesiqta de R. Kahana	Talmud of Babylonia	Siddur	Targum Onqelos to the Pentateuch	Targum Pseudo-Jonathan to Pent.	Fragmentary Targum to the Pentateuch
22. Messiah records peoples' good deeds					*			*				
23. Unusual incidents prior to Mishnah						*		*				
24. Messiah comes to worst generation						*	*	*				
25. Messiah will come when God chooses, do nothing in advance						*		*				
26. Reckoning the end						*		*			*	*
27. Gentiles convert when Messiah comes							*					
28. Gentile rule ends							*	*				
29. God clothes Messiah							*					
30. Description of person of the Messiah							*	*				
31. God restores Jerusalem, Zion, Temple cult, through the Messiah								*		*	*	*
32. 6000 years: Messiah's age the middle 2000								*	*			
33. Messiah came in Hezekiah's time. (Denied)								*				
34. Messiah's name was Shiloh, etc.								*				
35. Length of Messiah's rule								*				
36. Messiah in Nisan							*	*				
37. Messiah in 7th year								*				
38. Messiah not coming on a Sabbath								*				
39. Prayer may bring the Messiah								*	*			
40. Messiah comes in 468								*				
41. Messiah will only replace pagan rulers								*				

The Messiah

	Mishnah	Tosefta, Abot, and Abot deR. Nathan	Talmud of the Land of Israel	Mekhilta, Sifra Sifré Num., Sifré Dt.	Gen. Rabbah and Lev. Rabbah	Lam. R., Esther R., Song R., Ruth R.	Pesiqta de R. Kahana	Talmud of Babylonia	Siddur	Targum Onqelos to the Pentateuch	Targum Pseudo-Jonathan to Pent.	Fragmentary Targum to the Pentateuch
42. Sinners punished by Messiah								*				
43. Israel will be served by Gentiles, Messiah will rule Gentiles								*	*	*		
44. Messiah comes when souls are all born								*				
45. Messiah comes when patriarch and exilarch so deserve								*				
46. Messiah of house of Joseph killed								*				
47. Messiah called "Holy One"								*				
48. Messiah created before creation								*				
49. Messiah comes only after Rome rules the whole world								*				
50. King-Messiah is a captive in Rome, etc.												*

Israel's History and Destiny

	Mishnah	Tosefta, Abot, and Abot deR. Nathan	Talmud of the Land of Israel	Mekhilta, Sifra Sifré Num., Sifré Dt.	Gen. Rabbah and Lev. Rabbah	Lam. R., Esther R., Song R., Ruth R.	Pesiqta de R. Kahana	Talmud of Babylonia
1. Destruction in 70 marked decline in supernatural world and in life of the sages	*	*						*
2. Legal changes after 70	*	*						*
3. Periods of history marked by location of cult	*	*	*					
4. This world/the world to come, life/death		*						*
5. Why was Jerusalem destroyed	*	*						*
6. Tales about sages	*	*						*
7. Tales about priests, cult and supernatural events in cult		*						*

Israel's History and Destiny	Mishnah	Tosefta, Abot, and Abot deR. Nathan	Talmud of the Land of Israel	Mekhilta, Sifra Sifré Num., Sifré Dt.	Gen. Rabbah and Lev. Rabbah	Lam. R., Esther R., Song R., Ruth R.	Pesiqta de R. Kahana	Talmud of Babylonia
8. Rome's history is the counterpart to Israel's			*					*
9. Rome's deeds explicable in terms of Israel's logic			*					*
10. Age of idolatry vs. God's reign			*					*
11. Days distinguished by secular events, not only by natural ones			*					*
12. When Israel learns lessons of its history, it commands its destiny			*					*
13. Israel saved by submission to God, not arrogance of its own deeds			*					*
14. Four kingdoms, four periods (four animals)					*	*		*
15. Just as punishment has come, so redemption will surely follow						*	*	*
16. Israel must accept pagan rule, pagans must not oppress Israel too much. Israel must not act on its own.					*			*
17. Iran (Persia) parallel to Rome								*
18. Various empires' histories governed by their relationship to Israel								*
19. Nations wise to treat Israel well								*
20. Israelites are own worst enemy but control own destiny								*
21. Decline in merit of generations								*
22. God shares Israel's fate								*
23. Empires' histories governed by study of Torah								*
24. Exile of Israel is so that proselytes might join them								*
25. Nations hate Israel because of the Torah								*
26. God loves Israel because it is humble (cf. #13)								*

myth in an entirely different way. Concretely, they evoke the theme in all its mythic manifestations—David, Jerusalem, Temple, cult, and the restoration of all of these—but scarcely follow up with discussion of a single one of the propositions important in the scholastic compositions, e.g., factual statements and systemically consequential doctrines.

Overall, we may group the rabbinical canon in two parts and the entire corpus of Judaic writing from late antiquity into three: the Mishnah and its circle, on one side; the two Talmuds and their associates, in the center; and outside of the circle of schools, the synagogal compositions. Of these three, there can be no doubt about the principal and single most comprehensive document: the Talmud of Babylonia covers everything found in all the other writings. It is the great vacuum cleaner of ancient Judaism, sucking up the entire antecedent corpus. The achievement of its compilers, as is now clear, was to create encyclopedic summaries of all the data at their disposal, then to attempt, with only limited success to be sure, to harmonize the mass of contradiction and conflict which resulted.

Let us once and for all close off narrow, historical questions. This account of how things look at the end provides no insight into the history of the Messiah myth, how each of its components took shape, or about the state of the myth at the several stages in the history of the Jews in their dispersion. We do not know when the Messiah myth became important, or which elements of the myth proved compelling under diverse circumstances, or how the myth's components related to the social condition of the Jews at any specific point. We cannot explain where the myth proved significant, or under what circumstances it would be ignored. None of the principal issues of interest to historians generally, or to historians of religion in particular, can be addressed on the basis of the survey now completed. The data I have assembled and the ways I have analyzed them provide information on a different set of questions, nonhistorical questions. We asked questions about the canon. We found answers about the canon.

Specifically, what we now see clearly is how the Mishnah and its associated compositions relate to the Talmuds and their literary fellows. As I said at the outset, the two components of the great rabbinical canon stand essentially separate from one another, though they are related in important ways. They are separate in that the Mishnah's circle covers a very limited number of topics and does so in a quite distinctive way. The Talmuds' circle covers the Mishnaic material but encompasses a very much larger territory of its own as well. The Mishnah's circle exhibits its own traits of mind and method, presenting a system unto itself. The two Talmuds fully cover the Mishnah's range in their own way, absorbing the Mishnah's entire repertoire of ideas, one by one, but making those ideas, taken up discretely, into something quite other than what they had been when they were viewed as a whole.

The principal result of this survey has been to uncover, for the subject at hand, two concentric circles. These contain two "Judaisms" so to speak—one small, the other huge, one quite compact and internally coherent, the other, while not totally formless, not entirely self-consistent. The Mishnah presents us with a complete system. The Talmuds offer us a huge repertoire of facts, a fair number of which serve as major elements in the system, while others remain unintegrated and discrete. As we have seen time and again, the Mishnah integrates everything that comes its way or that it selects. The Talmud uses to its own advantage some of the components of the larger Messiah myth while preserving, but essentially neglecting, others.

If I had to specify the *systemically* characteristic, even definitive, elements of the larger factual catalogues at hand, I should have no difficulty in pointing to what the Mishnah finds critical, namely, the few topics appearing in the Mishnah column of the catalogue (Nos. 1–5 on the Messiah list, fewer still on the other list). Indeed, what the Mishnah does not utilize is more interesting than what it does. The Mishnah's framers chose for their system five facts, three of them commonplaces and (once the subject comes up) unavoidable. These are, first, that the Messiah comes from the house of David; second, that there is a difference between the present age and the age of the Messiah; and, third, that there will be tribulations before the coming of the Messiah for people in general, but especially for sages.

These commonplaces, deriving from Scripture and well known to virtually every writer on the subject of the Messiah, are joined by two others. First, there is no such thing as *the* Messiah; there is only the classification *messiah*. Into that classification fall two kinds of messiahs: priests anointed for office as specified in Mosaic law, and another kind. The former appear extensively and play a significant part in specified tractates. *The* Messiah in the other guise, the one familiar to everyone else, appears only as part of the undifferentiated background of accepted, but systemically neutral, facts. The Messiah receives no close attention; no problems take shape around the laws affecting him or his age. That is, no generative problematic emerges out of the topic of the Messiah around which a tractate, an intermediate unit of discourse, or even a single pericope (even M. Sot. 9:15) might take shape. Obviously, the Mishnah's framers wished to reshape the issue into terms they found interesting, hence their special concern for the classification "Messiah-priest" and their special pleading about the special suffering of sages in the awful times prior to the Messiah's coming. These facts about the use and neglect of the Messiah myth point to a single conclusion. The philosophers of the Mishnah chose to talk about other things. Hence they were addressing people other than those eager to learn about the Messiah, about when he would come, and what he would do.

The same pattern repeats itself when we turn to the issue of the meaning of the history of Israel, the message of Israel's destiny. What the Mishnah's framers said about history parallels what they reported about the Messiah—as little as they possibly could. And what they did say expressed, in this detail, the larger polemic of their whole system. They regarded the critical issue of Israelite reality as sanctification and the operative dimension as timeless ontology. They therefore had no difficulty in singling out a particular historical event, namely, the destruction of the Temple in 70. But that event proved critical for the Mishnah's framers because of its twofold impact, upon the supernatural world, on the one side, and the moral life of Israel as lived by sages, on the other. That affirmation runs parallel to (indeed, appears in the same pericope with) the conviction that sages, in particular, would suffer when the messianic age drew near. The event of 70 marked changes in the condition of the cult and produced legal revisions to compensate for this change. Naturally, periods of Israelite history—bisected first by the destruction of the Temple—would find further differentiation based on places where the cult had been located. To be sure, the Tosefta's repertoire of historical points of interest is somewhat longer, but its additions—tales about sages and priests, about the cult and super-natural events affecting them, and explanations for Jerusalem's destruction—prove entirely congruent to the Mishnah's lines of in-quiry. Just as the Messiah myth turns out to have been shaped by, and cut down to fit the interests of, the larger system of which it would form a part, so the issues of Israel's historical life were de-fined by the encompassing system of the Mishnah. The topics dis-cussed and the ways in which they were worked out constitute mere expressions of that larger, uniform, mishnaic construction of which they formed a relatively inconsequential part.

We need hardly belabor the fact that the rest of the rabbinical canon saw matters otherwise. Our tables require no substantial am-plification. What we do not find in the Mishnah, we find every-where else. The points of literary and canonical classification, emerging from the distribution of facts among two or more collec-tions, yield no important insight. The development of the rabbinical theory of history and the theology of Israel's history within a mythic framework is not before us.

What we do find are answers to two questions. First, which facts specifically serve the larger system and which ones simply occur at random in the documents? The answer to that question emerges from a larger theory about the character of the rabbinical system. Second, what was rabbinic in particular? That theory, to begin with, has to explain the relationship between what was distinctive to the schools and what was part of the general heritage of the Jewish na-tion. Let us begin with this matter, since the answer to our question is right on the surface.

When our documents treat the structure of the liturgy, they take for granted that rabbis bore responsibility for the organization of the prayers and arranged them in accordance with their standard mode of thought (exegesis of pertinent verses of Scripture). Hence, we need not doubt that the liturgy speaks for the rabbinical estate. The use of the liturgy in synagogues beyond rabbinical influence cannot be demonstrated. But we need claim no more than that the liturgy served people in synagogues—whether or not in *all* syna-gogues—and so spoke out of a common national-religious heritage. When viewed this way, the prayers tell us what formed part of a generally accepted heritage of conviction about the Messiah and about Israel's history. That heritage, then, presents commonplaces about the Messiah's bringing God's rule and his restoring Israel's Land, its holy city, and holy place.

Distinctive to rabbis, then, are two views about the Messiah. First, they expressed in their particular way what were in fact generally held convictions. Second, some of their formulations constitute doctrines which were distinctive to their own estate. In the present context, we may point to the notion that Israel can hope for just government only when God rules. That belief, though stated in a way peculiar to rabbis, in fact expresses what must have been a widespread yearning. But the doctrines that to prove worthy of God's rule Israel must accept the dominion of Gentiles and must demonstrate its humility in order to make itself worthy, and that rabbis must provide the model for the way in which Israel at large must live, derive from and express the larger system of the rabbinical canon. They do not stand upon a single continuum with the generally held beliefs of the nation at large. They mark the rabbinical canon as distinctive, different from the literary-theological heritage of the people in general (if, beyond Scripture, such a thing can be said to have existed at all). So they express part of what made the rabbi rabbinical.

Bearing in mind this distinction between what was part of the antecedent, universal heritage of Israel, and what emerged from the distinctive system of the rabbis, we may rapidly review our catalogue of topics. Those that I regard as falling into the two categories just defined are as follows:

Generally held elements of the Messiah myth (including biblically supplied information)			Facts particular to the rabbinical canon and expressing its distinctive conceptions		
1	11	33 (?)	5	19	40
2	20	34	9	21 (?)	43 (?)
3	23	35	12 (?)	22 (?)	44
4	24 (?)	38	13	25	48 (?)
5	26 (?)	41 (?)	14	31 (?)	49 (?)
6	27	42	15	32	
7	28 (?)	45	16	36 (?)	
8	29	46	17	37 (?)	
10 (?)	30	47 (?)	18	39 (?)	

Obviously, the range of uncertainty spreads over the whole. Were we able to consult sources beyond those at hand, moreover, we should find reason to treat as generally known (if not demonstrably believed) facts the broader and perhaps different range of conceptions from those listed here. But all we have beyond the writings of the schools are the writings of the synagogue.

When we ask about the canonical context of the Messiah that emerges from the formative centuries of Judaism as we know it, we nonetheless can point with some certainty to elements congruent with broader national convictions and also can point out some elements which are distinctive to the rabbinical system. Indeed, we may claim to distinguish, among the latter, two systems—the mishnaic and the talmudic. We may point to that rather small set of facts deemed by the former to be systemically important, as distinct from the much larger set of facts (including the small set) utilized by the latter. Why can we not specify that all facts found in the Talmuds play some clear part in the articulation of the rabbinical system exposed therein? The reason is that the Talmuds make no attempt to frame a complete and exhaustive statement of their viewpoint but include everything relevant, while excluding the irrelevant and, finally, systematize the whole.

We must point out that this set of questions may not apply to our catalogue of components in the canon's picture of Israel's history and destiny. My impression is that virtually the entire corpus may prove distinctive to rabbinical circles. But the prayer book provides no control. So we have no way of knowing what ideas proved congenial to elements of the nation at large and which ones served to express viewpoints particular to rabbis. Concepts deriving from the apocalyptic tradition—e.g., the four kingdoms as represented by four animals—clearly come from people who lived prior to the formation of the rabbinical movement. How these symbols were revised to serve the rabbinical system, I cannot now suggest.

Let me now summarize these somewhat complex results. We see two clearly differentiated sections within the rabbinical canon. One is well defined in its interests. We can offer a plausible explanation of the way in which, along with those larger systemic points of insistence, the Messiah myth makes its modest contribution. The other, more encompassing section of the canon also yields a coherent viewpoint. In accordance with that larger viewpoint, we can discern the systemic usefulness of parts of the larger representation of facts about the Messiah. But a number of facts referred to in the second sector of the canon do not clearly relate to the systemic interests of that sector as a whole. If, then, we take seriously the differentiation of the larger canon of formative Judaism into two separate, though related, sectors, we may tell the story of the Messiah in the present context in just a few words.

First, the Mishnah's framers formulated a worldview and a way of life for the Jewish nation in which historical events played little part. They insisted on uncovering the continuing patterns of life and the external laws of nature and supernature. To these points, the concept of the Messiah and of the meaning and destiny of Israel among the nations proved irrelevant. The framers of the Mishnah spoke of other things. We do not know to whom they wished to address their vision.

Second, the talmudic continuators of the Mishnah constructed their exegetical essays both *through,* but also *around,* the Mishnah. They explained and expanded upon the Mishnah's points. But they also made provision for expressing their own views, as distinct from those stated in the Mishnah. Do these other, extra-mishnaic, views come later in time? Obviously the answer is partly yes, partly no.

On the one hand, the facts, in the main, can be shown to have circulated before, during, and after the time of the Mishnah's formulation. The first and second centuries, after all, encompassed the greatest messianic explosion in the history of Judaism. Coming at the end, the Mishnah expressed its implacable judgment upon that age of messianic expression. Its authors cannot have failed to know what everyone else in Israel knew full well. So what the Talmud knows about the Messiah, generally, derives from a heritage of facts which had earlier circulated in Israel.

On the other hand, much that the Talmuds' authorities wish to say about these ancient facts and to express through them speaks to a range of conceptions peculiar to the talmudic rabbis themselves. In its particular form and point of insistence, what is distinctive also comes later in the formation of the canon.

So some ideas are general and early and some are particular and late. The governing criterion is special to the canon. What is distinctive to the Mishnah, namely its unfriendly neglect of the Messiah myth, reaches expression early in this canon. What expresses the rabbinical perception of the Messiah reaches its present condition later in the formation of the canon, even though the facts that are reshaped are of ancient origin. So the question is, what in fact happened to the Messiah myth in the canon of rabbinical Judaism in its formative centuries? We turn, now, to this final question.

THE MESSIANIC IDEA IN JUDAISM

Bibliography

Joseph Klausner. *The Messianic Idea in Israel: From Its Beginning to the Completion of the Mishnah.* Translated from the 3d Hebrew ed. by W. F. Stinespring. New York: Macmillan Co., 1955.
Gershom Scholem. *The Messianic Idea in Judaism And Other Essays on Jewish Spirituality.* New York: Schocken Books, 1971. In particular, "Toward an Understanding of the Messianic Idea in Judaism," pp. 1–36.

We find in the rabbinic canon no such thing as *the messianic idea*. The sources we have surveyed reveal no such harmonious, encompassing construct. Once we differentiate among stages of a given canon of sources or among types of canonical writings, we discover distinctions among assertions about the Messiah. More important, we discern diverse ways in which the Messiah myth serves these several compositions. It follows that the conception of a single prevailing construct, to which all assertions about the Messiah by definition testify, does not exist. When we look at the origins of statements about *the* Messiah (as about any other topic), we turn out to "de-construct" what has been invented whole and complete in our own time. Klausner and Scholem provide portraits of a composite that, in fact, never existed in any one book, time, or place, or in the imagination of any one social group, except an imagined "Israel" or a made-up "Judaism."

Once we distinguish one type or system of Judaism or one group of Israelites from another, recognizing commonalities and underscoring points of difference, we no longer find it possible to describe and analyze *the* messianic idea at all. Indeed, in the present context, we can no longer even comprehend the parallel categories, *the . . . idea,* and *in Judaism.* The upshot is that a new classification is re-

227

quired and new categories must be defined. These appear, I have shown, in two ways. First, they emerge from the differences between one book and another related book. Second, they arise from the recognition that categories of books reflect different life situations. Both of these types of categories form commonplaces in contemporary learning.

The figure of the Messiah serves diverse purposes, which are defined by the framers of the larger systems in which the Messiah myth finds a place. We know that the authors of the Mishnah assigned an insubstantial role to the Messiah. But did the framers of the ultimate rabbinical system, in particular the great encyclopedists of the Talmud of Babylonia, simply open the gate to admit "the Messiah" at large? I think not. What we find in the talmudic sector of the formative canon of Judaism is not merely an established, general conception of the Messiah, which now was invited to serve (as it had so well elsewhere) as the principal teleological justification of the rabbinical system. True, the Messiah enters. But he does so only on the rabbis' terms. So he is incorporated into the rabbinical realm through a process of assimilation and (from the viewpoint I think dominant among the Mishnah's philosophers) also of neutralization.

Under the circumstances, it is difficult to see that the rabbis had much choice. The vivid expectation of the imminent advent of the Messiah could hardly continue indefinitely. For instance, decades after Paul's declarations on that matter, people were still dying and the assembled people of God was still suffering, just as the Gospels' authors realized. So the Messiah had to find secondary, long-term embodiment in some form: rabbi, priest, master, and divine model on earth—God with us, the Word made flesh, Son of Man in the image of God—and in heaven, yet other tasks. So the ahistorical Christ of Paul, lacking all biography, then became the Jesus of Q, Matthew, Mark, and Luke, ended up as the Jesus Christ of John and of everyone beyond. He was no longer merely the celebrant of the end of time, but the center and pivot of all time, all being, all history. Shall we then conclude that the established, inherited conception of the Messiah as termination of life and time defined for the heirs and continuators of Christ in the Church what they would see in him and say about him? Quite to the contrary. They inherited but also reshaped the inheritance. Whatever happened in the beginning, Christ as Messiah continued to serve, long after the moment that

THE TALMUD OF BABYLONIA AND OTHER EXTANT WRITINGS

should have marked the end of time. Now as the ever-stable focus and pivot of Christian existence, the Messiah became something other and far more useful. Insofar as the apocalyptic expectations were not realized—indeed, could not have been realized—the Messiah had to become something other than what people originally expected. True, he will still be called Christ. But he will be what the Church needs him to be: anything but the terminus of a world history that—up to now—refuses to come to an end.

So too was the case of the Messiah in the formative canon. That is, if we take for granted that people originally imagined the Messiah according to the promises of old, we must assume that at the outset they saw the Messiah as an apocalyptic figure, coming at the end of time. A dominant and definitive pattern, that version of the Messiah myth then passed from the center of the stage. Other patterns—attempts to explain the same unclassifiable figure—came into use. As to the Mishnah's part of the canon, at the beginning the authors wished so far as possible to avoid all reliance upon the Messiah as an apocalyptic figure. Even the language was given a meaning not primary in the prior writings: "messiah" as (mere) high priest, "messiah" as something other than eschatological savior, whether priest or general, whether from David's line or from the house of Joseph. But then in the Talmuds' sector of the canon the figure of the Messiah, and the concerns addressed through discourse about that figure, came to the fore in powerful expression.

So, to state the argument briefly, just as established conventions of the Messiah myth served the Church merely to classify Jesus at the outset while other taxa later came into play, so the Messiah myth found no consequential place in the rabbinical canon at the outset, that is, in the Mishnah, but later on became the moving force, the principal mode of teleological thought in the talmudic sector.

If I had to guess why the Talmuds gave prominence to a concept ignored in the Mishnah, I should have to appeal to the evidence of what the nation, Israel at large, had long had in mind. It seems to me self-evident that a Judaism lacking an eschatological dimension must have contradicted two established facts. First, the people read Scripture, which told them about the end of days. Second, the condition of the people, deteriorating as it was, called into question the credibility of the ahistorical construction of the Mishnah. So, I should imagine, for the Mishnah to be of any practical use, it required not only application to diverse circumstances (which the rabbis gave it), but also required expansion, not only by augmenting what was there, but also by exploring dimensions not contained therein at all. By reshaping the teleology of the mishnaic system into an eschatological idiom—indeed, by restating the eschatology in the established messianic myth—the rabbis of the Talmud made over the Mishnah's system.

But if the Mishnah was thus forced into that very grid of history and eschatology that it had been formulated to reject, the Mishnah's mode of being in turn drastically modified the Messiah myth. For the latter was recast into the philosophical mode of thought and stated as teleology of an eternally present sanctification which was attained by obedience to patterns of holiness laid out in the Torah. This grid is precisely the one that the framers of the Mishnah had defined. By no means may we conclude that what changed, in the end, was the Mishnah's system. Its modes of thought intact, its fundamental points of insistence about Israel's social policy reaffirmed, the Mishnah's system ended up wholly definitive for Judaism as it emerged in the canon at the end of its formative centuries, the "one whole Torah of Moses, our rabbi."

How so? The version of the Messiah myth incorporated into the rabbinic system through the Talmuds simply restates the obvious: Israel's sanctification is what governs. So if Israel will keep a single Sabbath (or two in succession), the Messiah will come. If Israel stops violating the Torah, the Messiah will come. If Israel acts with arrogance in rejecting its divinely assigned condition, the Messiah will not come. Everything depends, then, upon the here-and-now of everyday life. The operative category is not salvation through what Israel *does* but sanctification of what Israel *is*. The fundamental convictions of the Mishnah's framers, flowing from the reaction against the apocalyptic and messianic wars of the late first and early second centuries, here absorbed and redirected precisely those explosive energies that, to begin with, had made Israel's salvation through history the critical concern. So while the Talmuds introduced a formerly neglected myth, their version of the Messiah became precisely what the sages of the Mishnah and their continuators in the Talmud most needed: a rabbi-Messiah, who would save an Israel sanctified through Torah. Salvation then depends upon sanctification, and is subordinated to it.

The Mishnah, then, proposed to build an Israelite worldview and way of life that ignored the immediate apocalyptic and historical terrors of the age. The Mishnah's heirs and continuators, who produced the other sector of the formative canon, did two things. They preserved that original policy for Israelite society. But they also accommodated an ongoing social and psychological reality: the presence of terror, the foreboding of doom, and Israel's ironclad faith in the God who saves. Israel remained the old Israel of history, suffering, and hope. The Mishnah's fantasy of an Israel beyond time, an Israel living in nature and supernature, faded away. It was implausible. The facts of history contradicted it.

Yet Israel's condition, moral and social, must govern Israel's destiny—in accordance with the Torah's rules, but also precisely as biblical prophecy and mishnaic doctrine had claimed. What then could Israel do about its own condition? How could Israel confront the unending apocalypse of its own history? Israel could do absolutely nothing. But Israel could be—become—holy. That is why history was relegated to insignificance. Humble acceptance of the harsh rule of Gentiles would render Israel worthy of God's sudden intervention, the institution of God's rule through King-Messiah.

Under the circumstances from that day almost down to our own time, that counsel proved not only good theology but also astute social policy. Until nearly our own time the nations did not oppress Israel "too much," Israel did not rebel "too soon." What the rabbinic canon set forth at the end, in its rich eschatological-messianic myth and symbolism, states precisely what the Mishnah at the outset had defined as its teleology, but in the idiom of life and death, nature and supernature. The rabbinical canon in its ultimate form delivered the message of sanctification, garbed in the language of salvation— but not garbled by that expression.

To end where we began, Judaism in its formative canon does not fall into the classification of a messianic religion. It makes use of messianic materials to make its own statement. That statement, never intact but always unimpaired, speaks for the Mishnah. If the hands are the hands of the inherited eschatological faith of prophecy and apocalypse, the voice remains the true voice of Jacob.

APPENDIX

The Messiah
Outside the Rabbis' Canon

A BRIEF OVERVIEW

Bibliography

Yehudah Ibn Shemuel. *Midreshé ge'ullah*. *Pirqé ha'apoqalipṣah hayyehudit meḥatimat hattalmud habbabli ve'ad re'shit ha'elep hashshishi*. Jerusalem and Tel Aviv, 1954. 2d ed. [English: Exegeses concerning redemption. Chapters of Jewish apocalypse from the closure of the Babylonian Talmud to the beginning of the sixth millennium.]

The other extant literary testimonies to Jews' imaginative life in the centuries in which the rabbinic canon came to closure present one fundamental problem. We do not know the relationship between these other documents and the compositions distinctive to the rabbis and created out of their exegesis of the Mishnah and Scripture. We know only that, at some unknown point and under indeterminable circumstances, the rabbinic system and structure received into itself, and made its own, writings deriving from a life situation different from that of the schools. Exhibiting a quite different character from the collective and anonymous canonical literature which was distinctive to master-disciple circles and written down in the Talmuds and exegetical collections, these other writings must now briefly come under consideration. The reason is not that, by bringing all the documents together, we gain a picture of a single "Judaism." Still less can we imagine that every document from late antiquity provides a glimpse into *"the* mind" of the rabbinical schools and circles, let alone of the entire Jewish nation of the Land of Israel and Babylonia. Neither of these useless propositions bears any pertinence whatsoever to our problem. For if we ask about the unfolding of the Messiah myth in the rabbinical canon of late antiquity ("formative Judaism"), we cannot introduce into our account the picture emerging from documents that at that age did not clearly form part of that canon. At the same time, we are not free entirely to ignore them. A very rapid survey suffices.

233

Two social-institutional settings produced the extant writings of ancient Judaism: the school and the synagogue. As is clear, the rabbinical canon of exegetical works, except for the Pesiqta, derives from the school. Out of the synagogue come three additional types of writings: first, a liturgy of prayers, found in the collective, anonymous *Siddur* and *Maḥzor* for ordinary days and Days of Awe respectively; second, poetry written (and sometimes signed) by individuals and known as *piyyut*; and, third, translations of Scripture into Aramaic for popular utilization in the synagogue, called *Targumim*.

There is yet a fourth kind of writing, collected under the title "exegeses on themes of redemption," and dating likewise to the last century before the rise of Islam and the first centuries afterward. Here we have no clear idea at all of the institutional life-setting which we are dealing with. Since, in *Midreshé ge'ullah* (p. 55 of the Introduction), Ibn Shemuel maintains that the compositions about redemption speak out of the age of the cataclysmic changes of the seventh century and the period thereafter, we shall not take account of those writings. It suffices to say that the fall of Iran, the near-defeat of Rome (Byzantium), and the rise of Islam marked, for Israel, a time of intense apocalyptic speculation and messianic expectation. But for our purposes, subsequent compositions fall beyond the chronological limits of the formative rabbinic canon and therefore must be set aside.

THE MESSIAH IN SYNAGOGUE LITURGY

Bibliography

Joseph Heinemann. *Prayer in the Talmud: Forms and Patterns.* Translated from the Hebrew by Richard S. Sarason. Berlin and New York: Walter de Gruyter, 1977.

Lawrence A. Hoffman. *The Canonization of the Synagogue Service.* Notre Dame and London: University of Notre Dame Press, 1979.

Our problem with these types of writings is that we do not know who originally produced the works (except for the Piyyut poems that are signed). We do not know the role of the rabbinical estate in defining the ideas of these compositions. We are therefore unable either to include within the framework of formative Judaism or definitively to exclude from it a rather sizable and important body of literature. My survey will be very brief and touch only on the main traits pertinent to our question. For liturgy and Targum, I summarize the current and definitive scholarly works.

In the talmudic writings rabbis refer to the synagogue and its liturgy, in which they participate, and the beliefs and petitions of which they wholly share. But they tend to speak of prayer, in general, as something belonging to "them," that is, ordinary Jews, and regarding the activities of the schools—Torah learning, discipleship—as an alternative, and superior, form of divine service. Accordingly, when we turn to the synagogue liturgy, the *Siddur*, we stand, if close to the rabbinical estate, essentially at the margins of that protean social entity. We cannot doubt that rabbis legislated the conduct of the prayer service. Both the Mishnah's laws and the Talmud's exegesis and expansion of them prove it, as we have now seen. But we do not know who organized and arranged the prayers in the form which has come to us. References to the service take for granted an established order of prayer, with which, in some minor details, rabbis too may tinker. But the givenness of the basic order of service, even in the references in the Mishnah at the beginning of the rabbinic canon, suggest that the established mode of synagogue worship comes prior to rabbis' engagement with it. That is to say, the formation of the social group and literary document out of which Judaism as we know it took shape intersects with other facts of an encompassing system, a Judaism in large measure concentric, but not totally symmetrical, with the rabbis' system. When, therefore, we find in the *Siddur* references to the coming of the Messiah, which express a larger construct of how history will come to an end and when Israel's destiny will reach fulfillment, we cannot be certain that rabbis framed and stood behind that construct. We know for certain only that all rabbis, in the centuries under study, affirmed and shared in that same set of convictions.

The *Siddur*, the order of the Judaic service, very simply is a messianic liturgy. Saturated through and through with the raw hope of the Jewish nation for the long-delayed Messiah, for a resolution of the this-worldly history of Israel, and for fulfillment of the redemption promised long ago, the *Siddur* fully expresses the Messiah myth as part of the larger, conventional eschatology. Wherever we look, at daily, Sabbath, festival or holy day prayers, we find that same simple and compelling petition. There is no type of prayer, no occasion within the larger order of service, in which the Messiah in particular, or, at the very least, eschatological redemption in general, does not appear. True, at some points, the Messiah myth may be bypassed in its definitive symbols, as in the *Qaddish*, and repeated through the service. In contemporary wording:

> Magnified and sanctified be his great name in the world which he hath created according to his will. May he establish his kingdom during your life and during your days, and during the life of all the house of Israel, even speedily and at a near time, and say ye, Amen. [*The Authorised Daily Prayer Book*, trans. S. Singer (London, 1953), p. 37 and passim]

235

But the rather general reference to "God's kingdom" does not end the matter. On the contrary, the Prayer, or so-called Eighteen Benedictions, does not speak only of gathering in the exiles and restoring Israel's own judges and counselors. There are two explicit components, among the definitive number of nineteen, that make explicit reference to the coming of the Messiah. These deal, first, with the restoration of Jerusalem, then, with the advent of the Davidic monarchy, and, finally, with the rekindling of the fires on the altar of the Temple in Jerusalem (Singer, pp. 49, 50):

And to Jerusalem, thy city, return in mercy, and dwell therein as thou hast spoken; rebuild it soon in our days as an everlasting building, and speedily set up therein the throne of David. Blessed art thou, O Lord, who rebuildest Jerusalem.

Speedily cause the offspring of David, thy servant, to flourish, and let his horn be exalted by thy salvation, because we wait for thy salvation all the day. Blessed art thou, O Lord, who causest the horn of salvation to flourish.

Accept, O Lord our God, thy people Israel and their prayer; restore the service to the oracle of thy house; receive in love and favor both the fire offerings of Israel and their prayer; and may the service of thy people Israel be ever acceptable unto thee.

And let our eyes behold thy return in mercy to Zion. Blessed art thou, O Lord, who restorest thy divine presence unto Zion.

To give further instances, at the beginning of the new month, on the appearance of the New Moon, on the intermediate days of Passover and Tabernacles, in the Grace after Meals said on those days, we find further explicit references of the same character:

Our God and God of our fathers! May our remembrance rise, come and be accepted before thee, with the remembrance of our fathers, of Messiah, the son of David thy servant, of Jerusalem thy holy city, and of all thy people the house of Israel, bringing deliverance and well-being, grace, lovingkindness and mercy, life and peace on this day. . . .

The equivalent Prayer for the New Year liturgy follows along these same lines (Singer, p. 239a):

Give then glory, O Lord, unto thy people, praise to them that fear thee, hope to them that seek thee, and free speech to them that wait for thee, joy to thy land, gladness to thy city, a flourishing horn unto

David thy servant, and a clear shining light unto the son of Jesse, thine anointed, speedily in our days.

True, the theme of the Messiah's coming tends to serve in a subordinate position as part of the larger expression of hope for God's own rule. Nearly every explicit reference to the Messiah's coming occurs in a setting in which God's sole rule over the whole world forms the paramount petition. But the picture is clear and unambiguous. The cited passages form a small but representative corpus of evidence to show that, as I said, the liturgy of the synagogue constitutes a protracted plea for the coming of the Messiah, the end of history as Israel now endures it, and God's sole government begins upon earth.

To be sure, the wording in the formulations of the liturgy just reviewed derives from the liturgical canon framed long after the period under discussion. But the basic organization and arrangement of the prayers are generally regarded as the work of authorities prior to the formation of the rabbinical movement. Heinemann states the consensus: "The basic structures and content of the [statutory] prayers, determined at that time [in the generation following the destruction of the Temple], have never since been altered, and to this very day constitute the essential components of the Jewish liturgy" (p. 13). He maintains that communal prayer received its fixed order of topics toward the end of the period before 70. "It seems reasonable to conclude that the Eighteen Benedictions antedate the destruction of the Temple by a considerable period of time" (p. 22). What testifies to the liturgy of the period is not the exact wording, but the fundamental themes of the Prayer. Hence we may assume with some confidence an early provenance for the explicit references to, and petitions for, the coming of the Messiah. It follows that the basic characterization of synagogue liturgy stands firm. We deal with eschatological prayers framed mainly, though not solely, within the familiar messianic myth and symbols.

But the figure of the Messiah, the casting of the experience of worship around the coming redemption, and the framing of prayers to confront Israel's collective experience in history and politics do not speak in particular for the rabbinical group. In no way do they constitute a statement distinctive to the rabbis' viewpoint. What is far more likely is that that group took for granted and made its own—as it found useful and relevant—an established viewpoint, which, of course, it shared anyway. The larger issue before us is whether or not the liturgy contains marks of the rabbis' intervention. Did the rabbis reframe to their own measure the messianic symbol or the larger eschatological motif? The answer is that we discern not a trace of evidence of such a process. Whatever the wording, the fundamental topics remained fixed: restoration of Israel, Jerusalem, Zion, the Messiah; God's return to Zion; and reconstitution of the sacrificial cult. None of these were introduced by the rabbis. These powerful motives recur in daily and Sabbath worship, on festivals and holy days, in the synagogue and in the Grace after Meals, and on virtually every other occasion for public prayers that one can imagine. The state of affairs taken for granted in the liturgy—the destruction of Jerusalem and the end of the cult—of course indicates that the liturgy in its final form reflects conditions after 70. But if the frame of mind of the survivors prevails, it is a persistent viewpoint, an ongoing and (alas) permanently appropriate petition.

POETRY

Bibliography

Ezra Fleischer. "Piyyut." *Encyclopaedia Judaica* 13:573–602. Jerusalem, 1971.

———. *Shirat-haqqodesh ha'ibrit bimé habbenayyim.* Jerusalem, 1975.

———. "Simeon ben Megas Ha-Kohen." *Encyclopaedia Judaica* 14:1561. Jerusalem, 1971.

"Kallir, Eleazar." *Encyclopaedia Judaica* 10:713–16. Jerusalem, 1971.

Aaron Mirsky. *Reshit happiyyut.* Jerusalem, 1965.

Jakob J. Petuchowski. *Theology and Poetry. Studies in the Medieval Piyyut.* London: Routledge & Kegan Paul, 1978.

Zvi Meir Rabinowitz. *Halakha and Aggada in the Liturgical Poetry of Yannai. The Sources, Language and Period of the Payyetan.* In Hebrew. Tel Aviv, 1965.

J. H. Schirmann. "Yannai." *Encyclopaedia Judaica* 16:712–14. Jerusalem, 1971.

———. "Yose ben Yose." *Encyclopaedia Judaica* 16:856–57. Jerusalem, 1971.

Menahem Zulay. "Haduta ben Abraham." *Encyclopaedia Judaica* 7:1056. Jerusalem, 1971.

———. *Piyyuté Yannai. Liturgical Poems of Yannai. Collected from Geniza-Manuscripts and Other Sources.* In Hebrew. Berlin: Schocken/Jewish Publishing Co., 1938.

During the last three centuries before the Muslim conquest, synagogue liturgy expanded to encompass poetry by individual authors, the three best known of whom were Yose b. Yose, Yannai, and Kallir. Their liturgical compositions for Sabbaths, fast days, and the like, served to ornament the rites. Fleischer places the earliest poetry in the fifth century. The bulk of these poems has yet to be translated in such a way that the Hebrew governs the English (Petuchowski, p. 7). Mirsky argues plausibly that the *piyyutim* provide a glimpse into the life of the people. The life-setting—synagogue liturgy—governed which poems would find a place, and which would not. Accordingly, he maintains, from the synagogue poetry we gain insight into the life and mind of the people at hand. While the poets therefore may well present us important evidence on the state of mind of worshipers in the synagogue, the available monographic studies tend to deal with the poetry in literary terms only. Matters of religious, theological, and historical interest are not yet amplified in a systematic way. Rabinowitz does propose to demonstrate that between Yannai and the various components of the rabbinic canon we may find close and intimate relationships. In my view, therefore, we have one systematic effort to prove that one poet finds a place within the rabbinic framework. But the consequences for doctrine and myth remain to be explored. How Yannai uses and revises what he receives is not worked out with regard to principal ideas, only with respect to language and formulation of images. Accordingly, to utilize the poetry for the purpose at hand—to survey the Messiah myth and the theory of Israel's history and destiny—is not possible. It would scarcely suffice to present a few lines of this and that. What is needed is a full and systematic picture of what available ideas proved useful to the poets, and how various poets shaped these ideas for their own purposes. We thus should welcome a reasoned account of the larger worldview expressed in the respective poems of several representative and important figures. None of this is yet available. Not qualified to provide it, I am left simply to point in a direction in which we should some day proceed.

THE MESSIAH IN THE TARGUMS
OF THE PENTATEUCH (WITH PAUL FLESHER)

Bibliography

Michael L. Klein. *The Fragment Targums of the Pentateuch According to their Extant Sources. Analecta Biblica,* 76. Rome: Biblical Institute Press, 1980.

Samson H. Levey. *The Messiah: An Aramaic Interpretation. The Messianic Exegesis of the Targum.* Cincinnati, New York, Los Angeles, and Jerusalem: Hebrew Union College and the Jewish Institute of Religion, 1974.

Alexandro Diez Macho. *Neophyti 1.* 6 vols. Madrid and Barcelona, 1968–1977.

It is clearly a mistake to treat as a corpus so varied a set of writings as the Targums—the Aramaic translations of Scripture generally assumed to have been read in the synagogue for the benefit of Jews who did not understand Hebrew. One Targum, that bearing the name of Onqelos, cites passages from the Mishnah. So Targum Onqelos may be assumed to have been completed after ca. A.D. 200 and to fall within the rabbinic framework. But we do not know that that Targum—or any other—constitutes a unitary document, accomplished at essentially a single moment and not the result of a process of collection and agglutination of ad hoc translations over a long period of time. We have no firm evidence about the dates of any of the other Targumim, or who may have done the translating, or why and for what particular audience or circumstance the work was undertaken.

True, we can show that certain facts (e.g., tales or details added to the Hebrew text by the Aramaic versions and taken for granted by translators of Scripture) were known early on. These details, then, must have circulated among some Jews at a fairly early time relative to the point at which a given Targum is first independently attested. It follows that Targums contain ideas from a time prior to their own closure and redaction. But how those ideas took shape and came to expression in any given Targum is hardly clear. More important, the appearance of an idea otherwise attested at an early date does not constitute sufficient evidence that everything else in the Targum containing that early idea is equally early. All we know is that the translators, whenever they did their work, drew upon facts—ideas, myths, motifs—that circulated before their time. That by itself settles few questions.

When we reach this problem, we ask about the place of the Messiah in the various Targums. We briefly review the panoply of symbols and images in which the Messiah myth is expressed, and look at the larger theory of Israel's history and destiny contained within that expression. In the extant evidence, however, the answers to our questions become difficult to evaluate. This is because we do not know whether rabbis in particular speak through any or all of the Targumim (apart from Onqelos) or whether rabbis stand behind the translations. Since we cannot say when and where the documents came into being, we cannot know whose viewpoint they express or of which system they form a part. Still, Levey's collection does make possible a rapid survey and does permit some preliminary observations. However, we have to supplement our survey with two further editions of Targum texts, those of Diez Macho and M. Klein.

The first observation is that, for the Pentateuch, the several Targumim make little effort to introduce the theme of the Messiah at points where the text itself does not demand, or at least invite, it. We are reminded of the similar policy of Sifra and the two Sifrés. Indeed, there are points without any allusion to the Messiah, where we might have expected the Messiah myth to make an appearance within the translators' exegesis of the Hebrew text. This includes, for instance, the prophecies, blessings, and curses of Leviticus 26—27 and Deuteronomy 28 and 32.

If we rapidly survey the several Targumim to the Pentateuch, what do we find? Let us begin with Onqelos, the most important for our purpose, and contrast what we find with the other Targumim. Onqelos's translation into Aramaic speaks of the Messiah in the following passages only (Levey, pp. 7, 21):

Gen. 49:10
> *The scepter shall not depart from Judah, nor the staff of law from between his feet until Shiloh comes. And unto him shall be the obedience of the peoples.*

Onqelos
> The transmission of dominion shall not cease from the house of Judah, nor the scribe from his children's children, forever, until the Messiah comes, to whom the Kingdom belongs, and whom nations shall obey.

Gen. 49:11
> *He binds his foal to the vine, his colt to the choice vine; he washes his garment in wine, and his robe in the blood of grapes.*

Onqelos
> He shall enclose Israel in his city, the people shall build his Temple, the righteous shall surround him, and those who serve the Torah by teaching shall be with him. His raiment shall be of goodly purple, and his garment of the finest brightly dyed wool.

Num. 24:17
> *I see him, but not now, I behold him but not near; a star shall step forth out of Jacob, and a scepter shall arise out of Israel, and shall crush the corners of Moab, and break down all the sons of Seth.*

Onqelos
> I see him, but not now; I behold him, but he is not near; when a king shall arise out of Jacob and be anointed the Messiah out of Israel. He shall slay the princes of Moab and reign over all mankind.

Num. 24:18
> *And Edom shall be an inheritance, and an inheritance, too, Seir, his enemies; but Israel shall do valiantly.*

241

Onqelos
   Edom shall become an inheritance and Seir shall become a possession of its enemies, but Israel shall prosper in wealth.

   Since Targum Onqelos stands well within the rabbinic system, as I said,
we are hardly surprised by the reference, along with the Messiah, to "those
who serve the Torah by teaching." In the light of our survey of rabbinic
compositions, Onqelos' references prove sparing, indeed, nearly perfunctory. It is difficult to imagine how Gen. 49:10 can have been read as other
than a messianic prediction. But then the substance is routine. The Messiah will rule and restore the Temple. Num. 24:17, with its reference to the
"star out of Jacob," presents no surprises. The rest of the passage, which I
have not cited, has Israel enjoying victory over its enemies, all of whom
bear biblical names. So the repertoire of references is both limited and
conventional. In this regard, Levey comments, "The main emphasis . . . is
[on] the destruction of Rome, its utter annihilation down to the last man.
The Messiah is a military figure performing relatively moderate deeds of
valor, who becomes the ruler of the entire world" (p. 22).
   The so-called "Palestinian" translations of the Pentateuch present a larger
set of facts about the Messiah, but none of them can be shown to tell us
what the rabbis, in particular, had in mind. Levey's collection of Pseudo-
Jonathan and the Fragmentary Targum (hereinafter PsJ and F) permits a
rapid survey. We shall use Levey's translation of PsJ, the translation of
Targum Neofiti (hereinafter, TN) found in Diez Macho, and, following
Klein's edition of the Fragmentary Targumim, we shall note the presence
of Messiah references in both ms. P and ms. V, but we shall quote only one
text.
   In the days of the King-Messiah, the enmity between the serpent and
woman will come to an end (Gen. 3:15, PsJ, TN, P, V). The King-Messiah
will reveal himself at the tower of Eder (Gen. 35:21, PsJ). Gen. 49:1 is of
special interest:

Gen. 49:1
   *And Jacob called to his sons and said, "Gather together, and I will
   relate to you what will happen to you at the end of days"* (Levey, p.
   5).

PsJ
   Then Jacob called his sons and said to them: "Purify yourselves of
   uncleanness, and I will tell you the hidden secrets, the concealed
   date of the End, the reward of the righteous and the punishment of
   the wicked, and what the pleasure of Paradise will be." The twelve

sons of Israel gathered together around the golden bed on which he lay. As soon as the date of the End when the King-Messiah would arrive was revealed to him, it was immediately concealed from him; and therefore, instead (of revealing the date) he said: "Come, and I will relate to you what will happen to you at the end of days" (Levey, p. 5).

F (ms. P) (also ms. V)

And Jacob called his sons and he said to them: "Gather together and I shall tell you what will befall you; the giving of reward to the righteous and the punishment that is destined to come upon the wicked, when they are all gathered together in the end of days." They thought that he would reveal to them everything that is destined to come about in the final messianic period. However, after it was revealed unto him, it was concealed from him; and Jacob arose and blessed them, each according to his measure of [deserving] blessing did he bless them (Klein, 2:30).

TN

And Jacob called his sons and said to them: "Gather together and I will tell you the concealed secrets, the hidden ends, the giving of rewards of the just and the punishment of the wicked and what the happiness of Eden is." The twelve tribes gathered together and surrounded the bed of gold on which our father Jacob was lying after the end was revealed to him that the determined end of the blessing and the consolation be communicated to them. When the end was revealed to him the mystery was hidden from him. They hoped that he would relate to them the determined end of the redemption and the consolation. [But] when the mystery was revealed to him, it was hidden from him and when the door was open to him, it was closed from him. Our father Jacob answered and blessed them: each according to his good works he blessed them (Diez Macho, 1:633).

The conception that the time of the coming of the Messiah had been revealed and then forthwith concealed is familiar. The translators represented by PsJ expand on the description of the King-Messiah at Gen. 49:10. But they add no striking facts. The Fragmentary Targum combines the details of both Onqelos and PsJ to the same passage, while TN elaborates upon the circumstances of the vision.

On the other hand, the Fragmentary Targums to Exod. 12:42 are truly formidable and original:

Exod. 12:42

It was a night of watching for the Lord, to bring them out of the land of Egypt. This same night for the Lord is one of watching for all the children of Israel throughout their generations (Levey, p. 12).

F (ms. V) (ms. P. at Exod. 15:18)

It is a night that is preserved and prepared for salvation before the Lord, when the Israelites went forth redeemed from the land of Egypt. For four nights are written in the Book of Memories: The first night: when the *memra* of the Lord was revealed upon the world in order to create it; the world was unformed and void, and darkness was spread over the surface of the deep; and the *memra* of the Lord was light and illumination; and he called it the first night. The second night: when the *memra* of the Lord was revealed upon Abram between the pieces; Abram was one hundred years old, and Sarah was ninety years old; to fulfill that which Scripture says; "Behold, it is possible for Abram, at one hundred years, to beget [a child], and it is possible for Sarah at ninety years to give birth." Was not Isaac our father thirty-seven years old at the time that he was offered up upon the altar; the heavens bent low and descended; and Isaac saw their perfection, and his eyes were dimmed from [what he had beheld of] the heights; and he called it the second night. The third night: when the *memra* of the Lord was revealed upon the Egyptians in the middle of the night; his left hand was slaying the firstborn of the Egyptians; and his right hand was rescuing the firstborn of Israel; to fulfil that which Scripture says: "Israel is my firstborn son"; and he called it the third night. The fourth night: when the world will reach its fixed time to be redeemed; the evil-doers will be destroyed, and the iron yokes will be broken; and Moses will go forth from the midst of the wilderness and the King-Messiah, from the midst of Rome: this one will lead at the head of the flock, and that one will lead at the head of the flock; and the *memra* of the Lord will be between both of them; and I and they will proceed together. This is the Passover night before the Lord; it is preserved and prepared for all the Israelites, through their generations (Klein, 2:126).

The substance of this passage, with its invocation of Moses as part of the eschatological drama, carries us far away from the ideas we have seen up to this point. Why thought about the Messiah should have taken this turn is not difficult to suggest, given the New Testament Gospel's identification of Jesus and Moses (see Levey, p. 13). So far as we know, the rabbinic canon does not resort to this same comparison. Hence the detail testifies to a theory of the Messiah of a system other than the rabbinic one. Accordingly, it serves a purpose to be investigated in a quite separate context from the present one.

Reference to anointing oil, Exod. 40:9–11, leads PsJ to refer to the consecration of "the tabernacle and all that is in it for the crown of the kingdom of the house of Judah and the King-Messiah, who is destined to redeem Israel at the end of days." Both fragmentary Targums add the actual prophecy of Eldad and Medad, Num. 11:26, which addresses Gog and Magog and their defeat by the King-Messiah (Ezek. 39:9–10). When PsJ reaches the prophecy of Balaam, Num. 24—17, the translation, unlike that of Onqelos, makes explicit reference to contemporary times, e.g., the Messiah's destruction of "the sinful city of Caesarea, the mighty city of the Gentiles." Here we recall the view that when Caesarea prospers, Jerusalem pines, and the contrary. But I see no direct connection. An example of the way in which PsJ treats the matter is as follows, at Num. 24:24:

> Troops ready for battle, with great armed might, shall go forth from Italy in Liburnian ships, joining the legions which shall go forth from Rome and Constantinople. They shall afflict the Assyrians and subjugate all the sons of Eber. However, the end of both these and those shall be to fall by the hand of the King-Messiah and be destroyed forever.

Such an explicit reference to the Messiah's engagement in specific contemporary events is rare in the rabbinic canon. Levey comments (p. 24), "The Messianism is more drastic than that of O[nqelos]."

References to the Messiah in translations of Deuteronomy prove unexceptional. Deut. 25:19, "You must not forget," is expanded by PsJ, "Even unto the days of the King-Messiah, you shall not forget." Deut. 30:4, on gathering in the exiles, is referred to the messianic time: "He shall bring you back by the hand of the King-Messiah." That does not seem a farfetched expectation, within the established framework. But Elijah is included in context. So while the Messiah stands for the critical figure in eschatological time, he does not work alone. There is no detailed account of his person and origin.

What conclusions are we to draw? On the one side, it is clear that Onqelos, the translation within the setting of the rabbinic system, proves reticent to introduce the Messiah at all. What Targum Onqelos does say falls entirely within the range of familiar details. The different Palestinian Targums cover a wider variety of details. But the basic tendency of reticence on messianic themes observed at the outset characterizes these Targums as much as the other. Where the text of Scripture does not absolutely demand a messianic exegesis, e.g., by referring to the end of days or some other eschatological notion, the authorities behind the various Palestinian

Targums are not much more likely to introduce the figure of the Messiah than are those behind Onqelos. The contrast to the exegesis of the Pentateuch revealed in writings of the Church fathers, with their persistent interest in the messianic dimension in every detail, hardly requires extensive illustration.

That fact tells us two things, neither of which is surprising. First, the Christian exegetes find the exegetical fulcrum of all scriptural statements at the verses' relevance to the figure of Christ, the Messiah. What else should we have expected? Then, second, the rabbinic and other Jewish exegetes have something else on their mind, at many points, than the figure of the Messiah in particular. What is that other point of insistence? For both the more and the less rabbinic of the translations, it is the history of Israel the Jewish people, and the labor of the Messiah in behalf of Israel in the eschatological conclusion to history. The larger systemic framework, in which both the Targum of Onqelos and the other Targumim find their appropriate location, is Israel's history and destiny. But how the specific assertions about the Messiah, and references to Israel's history and destiny encompassed within those assertions, serve the larger interests of a particular and distinctive system—a kind of "Judaism"—I cannot say. As we see in Levey's summary, the main emphases of both Targumim, the Onqelos and the Pseudo-Jonathan, prove entirely consistent with the main outlines of messianic doctrine revealed in the rabbinic canon surveyed up to this point. Having relied so heavily on Levey, let us let his summary conclude our discussion (pp. 31–32, parenthesis mine):

> Targum Onqelos is most sparing in its messianic exegesis, and has messianic references only to Gen. 49:10–12 and Num. 24:17–20, 23–24.
>
> The Messiah is portrayed as a symbol of security, culture and refinement in Genesis, and in Numbers as a leader who will restore the political and military strength of Israel by gaining dominion over the entire world after he utterly destroys Rome. Jerusalem and its inhabitants will enjoy divine protection, represented by a rebuilt sanctuary. The social order will be undergirded by peace, prosperity, and righteousness, all under the influence of Torah which will become the universal law, and by the ideal of education, which will become a universal reality. Since O is composite, differing views are to be expected, here and there.
>
> Targum Pseudo-Jonathan has messianic references in its interpretations to Gen. 3:15; 35:21; 49:1, 10–12; Exod. 17:16; 40:9–11; Num. 23:21; 24:17–20, 23–24; Deut. 25:19; 30:4–9.
>
> The messianism in PsJ is not at all consistent. For example, in

Num. 24:17 it is the Messiah who will vanquish Gog; in Exod. 40:11 this is to be achieved by the Ephraimite Messiah. In Deut. 30:4 the ingathering of the exiles is to be effected both by Elijah and by the Messiah. PsJ dips into the messianic much more readily and freely than O, and he interprets as his fancy strikes him. Yet, considering the vast amount of Scriptural resources, he does not have an overabundance of messianic references.

The picture of the Messiah as portrayed by PsJ embraces all the features found in O, and a number of others besides. The Messiah son of Ephraim is introduced, something which is not found in the messianism of the official Targumim, whether to the Pentateuch or to the Prophets. The vindication of Israel and the destruction of its enemies will be accomplished by a blood-bath, performed by the Messiah, who as the aggressive war-lord of the future, will himself be covered with the blood of the slain foe. Notwithstanding this, the era which he inaugurates will mark the end of war, the establishment of peace, justice and righteousness. The dispersed Jews will be gathered in, established once again on their own land, and will be purified by the elimination of the evil impulse and thereby will attain eternal life. This idea is tied with the Torah and ethic, and hinges on the performance of the commandments. PsJ also discourages speculation as to the date of the advent of the Messiah.

The Fragmentary Targum (mss. P&V) contains messianic interpretation in Gen. 3:15; 49:1 (ms. P only), 10–12 (ms. P v. 10 only, ms. V vv. 10–12); Exod. 12:42; Num. 11:26; 24:7, 17–20, 23–24.

The messianism of F is essentially the same as that both of O and PsJ, with several added features. F draws a comparison between Moses and the Messiah. He has the Messiah coming from Rome, not Palestine. He interprets the prophecy of Eldad and Medad as messianic prophecy.

Targum Neofiti follows that other Palestinian Targum when it mentions the Messiah, but it refers to the Messiah in only one passage not found in TO, Gen. 3:15. The other passages are Gen. 49:10–12; Num. 24:17–20 and 23–24. The messianic exegesis found in Genesis is similar to that of PsJ, whereas that in Numbers resembles the passages in the Fragmentary Targums.

The obvious question raised by this survey is this: What is distinctive to the canon of formative Judaism as against that which is shared in common with the antecedent heritage of Israel, in general, and with nonrabbinic Jews of contemporary times?

Bibliography

All titles listed here appear in abbreviated form in the text.

Appointed Times: Jacob Neusner. *A History of the Mishnaic Law of Appointed Times*. 5 vols. Leiden: E. J. Brill, 1981–.

Damages: Jacob Neusner. *A History of the Mishnaic Law of Damages*. 5 vols. Leiden: E. J. Brill, 1984.

EJ: Encylopaedia Judaica. Jerusalem, 1971. i–xvi.

Heer, *Mekh.*: M. D. Heer. "Mekhilta of R. Ishmael." *EJ* 11:126, 7–1270.

Heer, *Midrash*: M. D. Heer. "Midrash." *EJ* 11:1507–14.

Heer, *Sifra*: M. D. Heer. "Sifra." *EJ* 14:1517–19.

Heer, *Sifrei*: M. D. Heer. "Sifrei." *EJ* 14:1519–21.

Holy Things: Jacob Neusner. *A History of the Mishnaic Law of Holy Things*. 6 vols. Leiden: E. J. Brill, 1978–79.

Jastrow: Marcus Jastrow. *A Dictionary of the Targumim, the Talmud Babli and Yerushalmi, and the Midrashic Literature*. 2 vols. Reprint. New York: Pardes Publishing House, 1950.

Klein: Michael L. Klein. *The Fragment Targums of the Pentateuch*. 2 vols. Rome: Biblical Institute Press, 1980.

Purities: Jacob Neusner. *A History of the Mishnaic Law of Purities*. 22 vols. Leiden: E. J. Brill, 1974–77.

Saldarini: Anthony J. Saldarini. *Scholastic Rabbinism*. Chico, Calif.: Scholars Press for Brown Judaic Studies, 1982.

Women: Jacob Neusner. *A History of the Mishnaic Law of Women*. 5 vols. Leiden: E. J. Brill, 1979–80.

Index of Passages

RABBINICAL LITERATURE

Index of Subjects

Abaye, 150, 169–70, 173, 200
Abba b. Kahana, 149, 151, 156
Abbahu, 174, 178, 200
Abot, genealogy of Torah, 53, 75–76
Abtalion, 46, 48
Aha, 95, 97, 122, 128
Alexandri, 172, 188
Ammi, 202
Amram, 200
Antigonos of Sohko, 45, 47–48
Aqiba, 27, 60, 62–63, 134, 146–47; and
    Bar Kokhba, 93–95, 108, 115–17,
    126, 145, 171; exile of Ten Tribes,
    136; last judgment, 51–52; martyr-
    dom, 141; Temple cult, 72–73
Ashi, 170
Assi, 203
Azariah, 154–55

Ba, 114
Ba Bar Binah, 128
Babba b. Buta, 66
Bar Kokhba, messianic hope, 7, 10, 15,
    19, 24, 27, 31, 60, 74, 93–95, 108,
    115–17, 126, 145, 152–53, 189–90,
    211
Bar Qappara, 89
Ben Azzi, 27
Ben Zoma, 27
Braude, William and Israel J. Kapstein,
    154–59
Bun, 94

Cashdan, Eli, 210
Christianity, shaping of, 2
Cohen, A., 145–47

Davidic dynasty: and messianism, 153–
    56, 169–79, 182–83, 186–91, 203–4;
    messianic hope of, 88–95, 98, 103,
    130
Diez Macho, Alexandro, 238–39, 241–
    42

Diocletian and rabbis, 106–7
Donaldson, James, 159
Dosa, 174

Eighteen Benedictions, 182–83, 235–36
Eleazar, 127, 173, 193, 209
Eleazar b. Azariah, 27, 146, 174
Eleazar b. Damah, 62
Eleazar b. R. Menahem, 92
Eleazar of Modiin, 116, 134
Eleazar b. R. Simeon, 172
Eliezer, 50, 62–63, 96, 134, 172, 174
Eliezer the Great, 28
Eliezer b. Jacob, 64
Elijah, 30, 73, 74, 170, 179, 185, 246;
    and resurrection of the dead, 30, 74
End of time, calculation of, 59–60
Essenes. See Qumran sect

Finkelstein, Louis, 137
Fleischer, Ezra, 237
Freedman, H., 138–39, 169, 180–81,
    190–91, 200, 207, 209

Gamaliel, 146; genealogy of Torah, 46–
    48, 50
Gamaliel the Elder, 27–28
Giddal, 173
Goldin, Judah, 123

Hama b. Hanina, 172
Hamnuma, 200
Hanan, 128
Hanan b. Tahlifa, 171
Hanin, 139
Hanina, 172, 179, 200
Hanina of Bet Hauran, 128
Hanina b. Dosa, 27
Hanina b. Papa, 204
Haninah, 174
Heer, M.D., 132–33, 145–46
Heinemann, Joseph, 233, 236
Helbo, 152

257

3 5282 00096 8571